THE ABDUCTION OF BETTY AND BARNEY HILL

THE ABDUCTION OF
BETTY AND BARNEY HILL

Alien Encounters, Civil Rights,
and the New Age in America

Matthew Bowman

Yale
UNIVERSITY PRESS
NEW HAVEN & LONDON

Published with assistance from the foundation established in memory of Philip Hamilton McMillan of the Class of 1894, Yale College.

Yale University Press books may be purchased in quantity for educational, business, or promotional use. For information, please e-mail sales.press@yale.edu (U.S. office) or sales@yaleup.co.uk (U.K. office).

Set in Yale and Alternate Gothic type by IDS Infotech, Ltd.
Printed in the United States of America.

Library of Congress Control Number: 2023930240
ISBN 978-0-300-25138-8 (hardcover : alk. paper)

A catalogue record for this book is available from the British Library.

This paper meets the requirements of ANSI/NISO Z39.48-1992 (Permanence of Paper).

10 9 8 7 6 5 4 3 2 1

CONTENTS

THE ABDUCTION OF BETTY AND BARNEY HILL

INTRODUCTION

Tic Tacs

Late in the night of September 19, 1961, Betty and Barney Hill were driving home on a lonely state road in central New Hampshire when they saw a flying saucer. What follows is a largely narrative account of their lives before their encounter and for the decade or so afterward. The Hill case is one of the best known and most written about of American cases of strange things seen in the sky and is regarded as the first case in the United States of what has come to be called "alien abduction," in which human beings are captured by beings from a craft in the sky.

I became interested in the Hill case because I was exploring American culture in the mid-twentieth century. The Hills' story seemed to me to encapsulate much of what was happening to the United States in those years. Betty and Barney Hill were a Black man and a white woman, in early middle age in 1961, supporters of the Democratic Party dominant in American politics in those days. They were active in the civil rights branch of the Black freedom movement that pushed for racial integration. Betty was a college graduate, Barney was not. They belonged to a politically and theologically progressive, yet entirely respectable and conventional Unitarian congregation in their home in Portsmouth, New Hampshire. They embodied both the middle and the peripheries of American culture in those years.

They were also, like many Americans at the time, aware of and a bit ambivalent about the concept of flying saucers. Betty was more interested in the idea than her husband. After the Hills saw the craft, Betty Hill remembered asking Barney, "Do you believe in flying saucers now?" He replied, "Of course not."[1]

Betty Hill called it a "flying saucer" because that was the language of the time. The term had grown popular over the past fifteen years to categorize strange things Americans were seeing in the sky. A wave of such sightings had been widely reported in 1947, and new such "flaps" (as they are called) occurred in 1952 and again in 1957. Americans had grown accustomed to the term "flying saucers," and many unquestioningly embraced the assumptions it carried. The first was that these objects were technology, something built by intelligent beings (rather than things supernatural or living). The second assumption was that technology in the sky was the province of the American military. In 1948, the Air Force — wary of rockets, jets, and bombers — mounted a study of flying saucers because of concerns that these things were hostile technology, perhaps developed by a foreign power. Perhaps the Soviet Union. The Air Force redubbed them "unidentified flying objects" to indicate their seriousness. The Hills, like most Americans in the early 1960s, believed that the state could be trusted to handle whatever challenge these sightings might pose.

In 1958, the American National Election Study found that 73 percent of Americans said they trusted the federal government to do the right thing; by 1964, that number had reached 76 percent. The Hills were among this number. They were part of what has sometimes been called the "New Deal coalition," a collection of American voters who, for at least a generation after Franklin Roosevelt's death in 1945, would make the Democratic Party dominant in national politics. They liked the Democrats' support for a host of government programs, from Social Security and unemployment insurance to a strong standing military and an active foreign policy. This coalition began to fray in the late 1960s, and by the 1980s it unwound entirely, made to appear naïve by a host of government scandals and challenged by a rising conservative movement, on the one hand, and liberation movements driven by young radicals and people of color, on the other. Amidst the fracturing, trust in government began to plummet, and so did trust in its various appendages. Some Americans invoked the alliance between the state's national security agencies and the corporations that provided them with research and equipment, ominously labeled the "military-industrial complex" by President Dwight Eisenhower in a speech in January 1961. In September of that year, the Hills still presumed the good intentions of their government and considered it their obligation to notify the Air Force of their strange sighting. But by the end of the decade, they would not be so sure.[2]

In part, then, this is the story of how, in an environment of growing cynicism about the state and the science that the state sponsored, a strange encounter propelled Betty and Barney Hill toward suspicion of traditional sources of authority and a consequent exploration of more esoteric possibilities. It was a path many other Americans traveled in the 1960s.

But if the Hills' trajectory was familiar, they followed it for reasons that were their own. They held to a vision of "science" that involved public discussion, deliberation, and debate.[3] They believed this in part because they were New Deal liberals who believed in responsive government. But they also believed it because they were Unitarians, a denomination that in the mid-twentieth century insisted that science policy as a way of generating national knowledge should not be restricted to cloistered experts, but open to democratic discussion.

The Hills expected that the government agencies they contacted would take their story seriously. But they were disappointed. By the time they reached out to the Air Force, the US government's interest in UFOs had shifted away from the hard sciences of engineering and physics. In a series of reports, panels, and investigations over the twenty years from the late 1940s to the late 1960s, the state turned the problem from a potential technological threat into a mental aberration internal to those who saw UFOs. Sightings were a threat to the psychology of the United States, not to its military power. The Hills found both the Air Force and their own psychiatrists treating their experience as a problem in their heads rather than in the skies.

The experience disillusioned the Hills. But rather than surrender their belief about what they had seen, they changed the communities that they looked to for support. They joined the loose network of esoteric practitioners affiliated with what is often called the "New Age," and they increasingly embraced conspiracy theory. By the last decade of her life, Betty Hill was writing that "governments separate and divide us," describing strange black helicopters she often saw over

---

New Hampshire, and warning that "I learned to distrust anyone who offers to analyze anything I find."[4]

I am interested in the story of the Hills as an account of the shifting winds in American politics and culture in the second half of the twentieth century and, particularly, how one family – typical in some ways, quite atypical in others – followed them. I am less interested in exploring why Americans see strange things in the sky than in how the Hills in particular, some of the first Americans to have such a strange encounter, came to interpret what they had seen as something they called first "a flying saucer" and then "a UFO"; how they moved from believing merely that they had seen something strange to believing that they had been abducted by aliens, and how this process went hand in hand with their growing skepticism about mainstream authority in American life.

This is not an entirely novel approach. Many scholars, beginning with the famed psychologist Carl Jung, have explored and nuanced the Air Force's conclusion that UFOs were, to use a term popular among UFO researchers, "psychosocial," which is to say they were an expression of human feelings about modern life thrown into technological form. Jung's short 1959 book, *Flying Saucers: A Modern Myth of Things Seen in the Sky*, suggested that whatever the actual "external stimulus" for a UFO sighting was, Americans were perceiving them as "flying saucers," with all the connotations that term implied. The shape was significant. Jung identified the saucer as a mandala, a universal symbol of wholeness and completion that Jung believed people particularly longed for in the unruly world of the Cold War.[5]

For Jung, a UFO might ultimately be strangely comforting, a symbol of longing and desire. Many other more recent scholars agree that it is a symbol but are inclined to see the UFO as projection of anxiety and unease. Bridget Brown, Jodi Dean, and Susan Lepselter have connected belief in UFOs to disempowerment and imprisonment; the sense that Americans – and especially those who believe in UFOs – are not fully in control of their own lives. According to these authors UFO believers stand outside relentless narratives of national pride, progress, and growth that the American establishment promulgated throughout the twentieth century. Modern mass media has connected us – but also has obliterated any possible assumption that Americans might share common presumptions about credibility and truth. Modern science has made possible great advances, but it has also rendered citizens passive subjects of machines and technology they do not understand and cannot control, particularly in such intimate regions as their own bodies. Modern America celebrates freedom—but many people find themselves captive to financial, racial, and historic oppressions. The story of the UFO, told as a story of strange invasion, abduction, and captivity, finds resonance as it explores and touches on these truths. The seeming outlandishness of alien abduction might seem less unfamiliar—and indeed, even more plausible—when set against the aggravating and sometimes terrifying realities of, for instance, modern medical bureaucracy. To some Americans today, the pessimism that has crept into UFO narratives since the Hills told their story of frightening abduction might seem prescient.[6]

In American popular culture alien abduction is told in stories designed to frighten or unnerve. That was, at times, how Betty and Barney Hill told their own story. And yet we should not conclude that UFOs are simply signs of fear and unease. Rather, even if they are the product of no more than creative misinterpretation, they have also served as grounds for a new sort of world-building, the rewriting of disempowerment into a strange new power. In 1994, the Harvard psychologist John Mack argued in his controversial *Abduction: Human Encounters with Aliens* that UFO encounters sometimes left those he interviewed with what he called "a new and altered sense of their place in the cosmic design" that left them at peace, with new knowledge and beliefs that revived their sense of efficacy in the world around them.[7]

That was Betty and Barney Hill's story as well. Their reshaping of the reality they believed in grew from the frightening and disempowering aspects of their experience and from the promise of renewed and different potential realities as well. One benefit of a close examination of the lives of two particular "abductees," to use a term the Hills adopted to describe themselves, is to trace the evolution of their stories and beliefs about their experience alongside and through their experience in the United States in the 1960s and 1970s. By closely examining the shifting patterns of the Hills' story, how they told and retold the story as their contexts and experiences and even memories changed, I track how their beliefs about their world and the power they had in it changed as well.

5

When they began their journey down New Hampshire's Route 3, the Hills' world made sense to them. They had clear ideas about what science was, about the relationship between Americans and their state, about the meaning of race and what good, appropriate religion should be. One way of thinking about what happened to them is not to explore what the light that they saw actually was (an ultimately fruitless quest, I think), but to see the reality of its power in their lives. It upset and blurred the boundaries they had laid down. The Hills grew less certain about what was science and what wasn't as they sought to reconcile what they believed they had seen with what scientific authorities told them was possible. Because the state did not respond to their experience as they hoped it would, they grew increasingly frustrated about the role it should have in their lives. That, in turn, cast doubt upon those scientific authorities, and more, upon whether or not legally enforced desegregation would bring about the sort of integrated society they hoped for. They had thought that religion was one thing — the congregational, respectable, rational Unitarianism they had adopted — and now they came to wonder if it could be something else. The weirdness of what they encountered that fall night was not only a puzzle of itself. It destroyed the presumptions they had about the world. The social and cultural lines that delineated reality in American society faded in the harsh light of high strangeness.[8]

That was why Barney Hill said "of course not" when his wife asked, after seeing a strange light in the sky, whether he now believed in "flying saucers." Barney believed then in racial uplift. He hoped that respectability would bring equality, and the light in the sky seemed to threaten that goal. By 1961, "flying saucers" were the stuff of disreputable fanatics and the uneducated. It was aggravating on multiple levels when Barney found himself not believed, and he and his wife reshaped the boundaries of authority, legitimacy, and respectability in their worlds in recompense.

By the 1980s, the Hill story was famous. In 1966 a journalist named John Fuller published *The Interrupted Journey,* a book that told Betty and Barney's story between September of 1961, when the two saw that strange light in the sky, to the spring of 1964, when they concluded hypnosis and emerged reporting newly recovered memories of their own close encounter. They now remembered small, humanlike beings who kidnapped them, took them aboard that light (which turned out to be a craft), and subjected them to medical experimentation. They told this story repeatedly to Fuller, to the news media, on television.[9]

In the decades that followed, investigators (or "ufologists") like Mack and the New York artist Budd Hopkins formulated a template for a certain subset of encounters, like the one Barney and Betty Hill described, and termed them "abductions." Both assumed that such experiences were encounters with extraterrestrial life that had reached Earth via spacecraft. Both interviewed dozens of abductees and wrote books trying to systematize the phenomenon and determine what these other beings were trying to accomplish. Hopkins acknowledged the Hill case to be a central archetype, a "classic illustration," the model from which many other abduction stories took their frame.[10]

Unlike later abductees, the Hills did not have the benefit of a template for their narrative. Their story was told and retold many times, and it grew in the telling—but this should not be merely a signal of its unreliability. Rather, their retellings reflected the various authorities they turned to. The military did not seem interested in the Hills' story. Psychiatrists pathologized it. White supremacists used it as evidence of the Hills' unreliability. As the Hills moved from meaning to meaning, not only did their confidence in these authorities begin to wane, but so did their perception of knowledge itself. And finally, they embraced conspiracy theory. By the end of the 1960s, they, like so many others, had lost much faith in the American state. The scandals of the Vietnam War and the Nixon administration opened pathways the Hills and many others were willing to venture down. Their story can help us understand why it was that they—and so many others—found the possibility of extraterrestrial intelligences visiting Earth plausible just as Americans' trust in each other was beginning to dwindle.[11]

As UFO researcher Stanton Friedman put it, linking together demonstrated deceptions in American society to those he and other UFO believers merely suspected, the United States faced a "cosmic Watergate." By the end of the decade, Albuquerque businessman Paul Bennewitz was marshaling evidence that the United States government was operating a secret base under the New Mexico town of Dulce for the purposes of joint human-alien military maneuvers.[12] Betty Hill was writing about black helicopters surveilling her friends and faceless government bureaucrats rifling through her mail. The scholar Michael Barkun has identified conspiratorial thinking as its own strain of politics that flourished in the cracks of the New Deal order: a strain of politics that downplayed belief in common identity, in good faith debate, and in pragmatic policies. Instead, conspiracy theory emphasized the helplessness of individuals and cast suspicion on the efficacy of democracy, locating power in a shadowy and sometimes interchangeable elite. Conspiracy theory grew among those who either rejected conventional politics, like many white advocates of the New Age, or those whom it failed, like Black Americans. And many UFO believers, as they felt rejected by the American establishment like the Hills did, embraced this alternative.[13]

The issues that strained the Hills as they sought to come to terms with their experience remain unsettled in the early twenty-first century, and of course, UFOs remain as well.

On November 14, 2004, Kevin Day was serving as a radar operator on the USS *Princeton*, a small missile cruiser traveling with the USS *Nimitz*, one of the largest aircraft carriers in the world, a nuclear-powered warship the size of a football field engaged in exercises off the coast of San Diego. As the *Princeton* cruised in the Pacific, Day sat in front of his radar screen staring at strange clusters of five to ten blips. They were moving too slowly to be regular aircraft, around 130 miles an hour. They were too high up to be birds—around 28,000 feet, nearly the height of Mount Everest. They rose and plummeted and vanished out of radar range, over and over. Finally, Day asked David Fravor, commander of the *Nimitz* fighter plane squadron, to investigate.

Fravor was on a training mission with another pilot when Day contacted him. They had taken two Super Hornet aircraft to a point around miles off the coast. He said when he arrived at the spot to which Day directed him at first, he saw nothing, but then he looked down. The ocean's surface was frothy and roiling. Darting back and forth above the churn was a dull white cylinder that Fravor pegged at forty feet long. He said it looked like a Tic Tac. Suddenly it darted away. "It accelerated like nothing I've ever seen," he told the *New York Times*. An hour later, another pilot found the object—or one similar—and filmed it. The camera footage captures a whitish, oblong shape that suddenly darts from the frame.[14]

Fravor's story was part of a cascade of revelations that began with a 2017 story in the *New York Times* that described the *Nimitz* encounter and culminated in a host of summer 2020 disclosures from the Pentagon, including the declassification of several very similar videos. The *Times* story claimed that in 2007, Senator Harry Reid had commissioned the Advanced Aerospace Threat Identification Program (AATIP), a small operation in the Pentagon that appeared designed to evaluate UFO sightings. Twenty-two million dollars was poured into AATIP, much of it used to pay contracting fees to an associate of Reid, a billionaire and UFO investigator named Robert Bigelow who ran an aerospace research firm. Over the few years that followed, other sightings occurred and other investigators claimed that AATIP was only a portion of a much larger investigation that Reid had initiated years earlier. Reid suggested that though he did believe something strange was happening, observers should not assume that the money was put up to investigate aliens. After all, he pointed out, "UFOs" simply refers to unidentified flying objects, not necessarily extraterrestrial craft, and such a study might be valuable for military reasons unrelated to alien life. Reid noted that many government officials had begun using the acronym UAP (for unidentified aerial phenomena) rather than UFO, hoping to avoid the weird associations the latter term conjured. But he continued to use UFO himself, and in this book I will do the same. It was the term the Hills used.[15]

Claiming that national security validated the study of strange things in the sky and insisting they might be no more than advanced earthly technology put Reid in the same camp as some Air Force officials who first took the story on. But it was evident that other figures in the story believed in other stories UFOs might tell. One, Luis Elizondo, is a former staffer in the Office of the Undersecretary of Defense for Intelligence who claims to have run AATIP. He treats the Navy videos as a warning of sinister government conspiracy. "I took my mission of exploring unexplained aerial phenomena quite seriously," Elizondo told the *Washington Post*. He claimed he resigned because the Department of Defense would not give his investigation "the resources that the mounting evidence deserved." He darkly assured journalists that he knew the Department of Defense would hide his involvement in the program. "When you dis-establish an organization, there's a paper trail," he said. "You won't find one for this program."[16]

It is easy to forget that behind the dizzying spiral of names, bureaucracies, revelations, and denials is the simple strangeness of those videos — just as the Hills' experience began with a strange light in the sky that Betty Hill fumbled to describe. Media commentators, UFO investigators, and scientists labeled the odd objects in the *Nimitz* and other videos everything from genuine evidence of extraterrestrial intelligence to equipment artefacts to drones to odd weather events. Each of these acts of interpretation drew the primal strangeness of the Tic Tacs into differing networks of meaning and ways of understanding the world. For Reid, the fact of strange flying objects in the sky validated his concerns for the interests of American national security. But if flying saucers were alien craft the government was covering up, Luis Elizondo's broad network of conspiracy might be genuine. It should be of little surprise that the Mutual UFO Network (MUFON), a nationwide organization investigating UFOs in the United States since its founding in 1969, began in the mid-2010s to struggle with growing numbers of members attracted to political extremism and the conspiracy theories stoked by President Donald Trump. Doug Wilson, MUFON's director of investigations, told the *Washington Post* that he had once believed that UFO believers were "sympathetic to marginalized communities because they themselves had once felt dismissed" — but he was increasingly worried about "strains of extremism" in the organization.[17]

Of course, as Wilson acknowledges, there may never have been a time in American history when UFO belief has not been bound up with marginalization, suspicion, and fear of conspiracy.

The Hills' story is, then, more than a story about the couple themselves and their strange experiences, whatever they might have been. It is a story about two Americans, a white woman and a Black man, and what they believed it was to be an American in the middle decades of the twentieth century. It is the story of how those beliefs were tested and how the Hills, like so many other Americans, came to believe something different about the world than they once had.

What the Hills said they saw in the sky does not appear to be the Tic Tac that David Fravor and the other Navy men would report half a century later. But it was equally inexplicable, and like Fravor and the other military men, the Hills interpreted it with the tools they had to hand. What it actually was may never be known. The Hills' psychiatrist, Benjamin Simon, insisted on that: "What was sighted I don't know; nor do the Hills know," he said, with all the brusque confidence of the expert establishment the Hills came to resent.[18]

But I think he was right. I don't know what the Hills saw in the sky that night, but I do think they saw something they could not identify. I explore some of the possibilities in the conclusion to this book. I do not believe that the Hills were abducted, though. As some other commentators on the Hill case have noted, the story of medical evaluation and star maps that emerged from their hypnosis with may, oddly, be too simple. I interpret their abduction as Simon did. The strange thing in the sky was a mirror that Simon, the Hills, and everyone else they drew into the story would project themselves upon. Whatever actually happened remains unknown to us and probably uninterpretable. For Betty and Barney Hill, the task of coming to understand the UFO was coming to understand who they were.

CHAPTER 1

BETTY

When Betty and Barney Hill awoke in their home at three in the afternoon on September 20, 1961, all that lingered in their memories' earliest draft was a strange light in the sky that chased them down New Hampshire's Route 3 through the mountainous Franconia Notch into the early morning of the night before. After they roused themselves, Betty wandered over to the closet and shoved everything she had worn the previous night deep into the back. The reasons why were not quite clear to her. Barney meanwhile examined his shoes with confusion. He did not remember them being scuffed on the top. Later, Betty went to the kitchen to call her sister Janet.[1]

The Hills lived in Portsmouth, New Hampshire, an old town of roughly 25,000 people that sits on the south bank of the Piscataqua River just where it pours into the Atlantic Ocean on the state's eastern coast. Indigenous peoples of the Algonquin-language nations have lived there for centuries, but the first Europeans arrived in 1630 and the town became a booming port for lumber, furs, and fish. It flourished economically, relying on shipping and the first federal naval shipyard, built on an island in the mouth of the Piscataqua in 1800. What industry emerged apart from the shipyard sat farther inland, and in part because of that, downtown Portsmouth, near the water, remains densely packed with small, winding streets, colonial-era homes, shops, and historic public buildings. Betty and Barney lived at 953 State Street, in an 1880s white clap-board house Betty had purchased before their marriage. It sits in a residential neighborhood a mile or so inland from Market Square, the hub of the town's commerce close to the old harbor.[2]

Betty's sister Janet Miller lived near their parents in Kingston, New Hampshire, twenty miles farther inland, one of many smaller towns scattered around Portsmouth in the woods of Rockingham County. Betty was close to her sister. The two were descended from an old New England family that in Betty's childhood during the Great Depression moved decisively toward the politics of the Democratic Party. Under the leadership of Franklin Roosevelt, who won the presidency in 1932 on a promise to fight the Great Depression, the Democratic Party assembled a coalition of white southern voters, workers in northern cities, and increasing numbers of Black voters (who to that point had overwhelmingly been loyal to the Republican Party) that made the party dominant in national American politics for the next forty years. Roosevelt also bent the party in new directions, committing it to an agenda born of his struggle with the Great Depression and World War II that he and his followers called the New Deal. While some in his administration pled for more ambitious plans, and even some form of democratic socialism like that becoming popular in Europe, by the time of Roosevelt's death in 1945 the Democratic Party was committed to what Roosevelt and his supporters called "liberalism." Liberals believed in capitalism, but they also believed that it was the government's responsibility to protect in-dividual rights from the damage that unrestrained business could wreak. Under the host of federal regulations included in the New Deal, Roosevelt secured un-employment insurance, workplace safety laws, and Social Security, all efforts to guarantee individual economic safety.[3]

On the ground, in American factories and shops, the New Deal worked a transformation in Americans' lives and expectations for politics, including Betty's family, the Barretts. As corporations and private organizations suffered under the weight of economic collapse, working Americans turned to the gov-ernment for help and began to organize to demand it. More than anything else their vehicle was the union movement. Over the course of the 1930s, the Barretts, like millions of other workers, came to believe that unions and other groups could achieve reforms, grew confident that the federal government was a tool for meeting the needs of working-class Americans, and cultivated a sense of cross-ethnic solidarity.[4] Betty's parents, Raymond and Florence Rollins Barrett, grew increasingly committed to this sort of liberalism while Betty was growing up, and well into her adulthood Betty would be a loyal New Deal liberal.

The seeds of activism were planted deep in her parents' family history. Both the Rollinses and the Barretts were old New England clans, and Betty prized their legacy of tough-minded independence and care for the marginalized. She remembered a family tale about her mother's people, the Rollinses. They arrived in Hampton, New Hampshire, "a few years after the Mayflower," only to discover two Quaker women "stripped to the waist and being dragged behind horses through town" by Puritan residents scandalized by their unorthodoxy. "In anger and disgust my family did not stop," Betty remembered, but moved right through the port town, settling further inland, away from the Puritans. Before long, they were Quakers themselves.[5]

Her father's family — the Barretts — were Irish Catholics that had abandoned the faith in her grandfather's generation. John Barrett was an atheist but of a genteel ecumenical sort. He quit attending Mass when he became an adult, but he also built a small chapel on his property in Kingston at the request of his wife Lizzie Trafton soon after they married in 1887. Lizzie wanted to be married by a Methodist minister, and Barrett was accommodating.[6] He ensured, though, that the ministers who preached on his property taught the sort of ethical and ecumenical religion he agreed with — "service to the community, an upright life, and do unto others as you would like others to do to you," as his granddaughter Betty remembered it. He always carried a bag of candy in his pocket, which he distributed to his grandchildren as a surprise. During hard economic times, when transients looking for work reached the Barrett home, John would offer them "a bath, shave, clean clothing, a room to sleep in during the night, and dinner."[7]

John Barrett was a farmer and shoemaker and his children, including Betty's father Raymond, followed him into the latter profession. Raymond was particularly known for his talent in crafting men's slippers. He also adopted his father's version of what good religion should be. By the time Eunice Barrett (who would go by Betty) was born on June 28, 1919, in Rockingham, New Hampshire, the family was largely unchurched. After her grandfather died her father took over the chapel he built. He entrusted the pulpit to a small group of local women who recruited ministers to fill it. "Once in a while we might get some minister who was always praying or something like that and we'd have to tolerate it," Betty sighed to a journalist. They wanted preachers who would promise their "only emphasis would be on community service and being ethical." The Barretts had little interest in otherworldly religion.[8]

Betty wrote about her life ceaselessly as she grew older, leaving one published semi-autobiography and many unpublished memories and scraps of memoir. The memories she recorded not only recount the events she recalled but also why they were important to her. In Betty's earliest memory she was about four years old. She stood in her family's kitchen and marveled as her mother for the first time pressed a switch and lit the room with a newly installed electric light. "Off and on, off and on," Betty remembered. The light was followed by radio, then automobiles and paved roads through Kingston. When she was a teenager she noticed a tickle in her throat that eventually intensified into great pain, and she was laid into her bed with what was then called "quincey." Her family worried her life was in danger. Her doctor struggled with his conscience before suggesting an experiment with a new sulfa drug, and Betty recovered from what later came to be known simply as strep throat. "I consider my life as having been lived during a time of miracles," wrote Betty late in her life, and an essential optimism about human ingenuity, progress, and social reform never left her. Betty Hill believed the world could be a better place, and for much of her life she thought that accomplishment would come through liberal reform.[9]

As she wrote her own life history Betty emphasized that she was raised by activists. Her family's heterodoxy in religious faith was joined with a streak of utopianism, an interest in reform, and a dash of confidence. From her youth she was surrounded with people who encouraged her to trust her own abilities to contribute to the betterment of the world. The doctor who treated her throughout her youth reminded her, on every visit, "I was to go to college, and maybe some day I might become a medical doctor." A few years later, she asked her mother if fairies really existed, and rather than simply giving Betty an answer, her parents told her to study the situation herself. "For several mornings I ran out to the garden and I carefully examined every dew-laden flower," she remembered, until "I made my great decision—there were no fairies."[10] That Betty remembered these stories as significant later in her life was as important as whether they happened precisely as she recalled; they signaled her ambition and her confidence.

She grew to adulthood during the Great Depression. While Betty was a child in the 1920s her father's shoe and leather business did well. She recalled that her father was one of the few men in town with a car, noting one long trip when the family hauled gasoline in jugs because there were few service stations in New Hampshire. Raymond was elected as one of three town selectmen in Kingston and spent much of the 1920s helping to administer the town, and as Betty remembered he was an advocate for helping the town's poor, pushing aid for disabled people and for orphans, and sometimes giving outright from the Barretts' own resources if the town could not pull through. At one point in 1925, Raymond Barrett, while serving as a selectman, covered part of the property taxes of a man named George Bailey, who presumably could not afford them himself.[11]

Occasionally Raymond would pick up odd jobs for the town, as did many other men: painting a bridge, for instance, or helping to lay a road. But by the mid-1930s, he, like many men in Kingston suffering under the weight of the Great Depression, was receiving far more such work. By 1935 although he was no longer a selectman, he earned more money from the city than he had in previous years, doing labor for the town fire department. But by the following year, he no longer appeared in the town's annual financial reports.[12] Raymond Barrett grew seriously ill in the mid-1930s, and the Depression smothered such small-scale relief efforts as part-time work. The Barretts, like so many others, were left floundering.

Betty's mother, Florence, found a manufacturing job, one she intended to be temporary and part time. She was not alone in seeking work during the period. Alice Kessler-Harris notes that after an initial sharp decline early in the decade, women's proportion of the workforce "inched up" during the 1930s. Seventy-five percent of "new" workers, those who had not sought employment before the Depression, were women, and most of them were over twenty-five years of age and married. And while Depression-era government codes in many cases institutionalized inequities in pay and allowed for the firing of married women by virtue of their gender, they at least standardized pay rates and provided white women in particular with greater stability in employment than they had enjoyed before the Depression.[13]

———

Florence enjoyed her work. And then, Betty remembered, "the labor organizers came and my mother was enthralled." Bolstered by the growth of women in industry and new government protections, unions saw women as a source of new votes, and many were recruited. Florence ended up serving on the union board, led a number of strikes, and marched on picket lines. Betty remembered that she feared for her mother's safety, of "attacks by the hecklers and arrest by the police." But at the same time, she could not help but being "very proud."[14] Soon, teenage Betty was drawn into the effort. "Our home was filled with union organizing activities, which I loved," she wrote. One of her uncles was organizing in General Electric plants in Massachusetts, not far south of Kingston, and a family friend named Fred had begun working for the Congress of Industrial Organizations (CIO) soon after its organization in 1935. Betty's mother was affiliated with the rival American Federation of Labor (AFL), and Betty recalled spirited disputes around their family's kitchen table that went late into the night. In 1937 Betty graduated from high school, took a job at a shoe factory, and promptly got herself fired because she told officials from the government that the factory's posted working hours were "all wrong, in that we all worked many more hours than those listed." Betty's employers sent her home on the spot, and she found that her mother was "delighted with my firing." For the rest of the summer Betty worked for Fred, to Florence's mind a far better boss than the supervisors at the shoe factory, keeping the books for the local CIO in Lawrence, Massachusetts.[15]

Unions were growing stronger and stronger in Portsmouth in the New Deal years because industry in the city was expanding rapidly. The population of Portsmouth exploded from the low thousands in the 1930s to nearly 27,000 in 1960. The factory that fired Betty was probably the Continental Shoe Factory, one of a number of light manufactories operating in Portsmouth's western reaches along the railroad. And there were a number of connections between Portsmouth's industries and those surrounding Boston, only sixty miles or so south.[16]

One of the lessons that Betty learned from her mother's union activity, and one the Congress of Industrial Organizations particularly embraced in the 1930s, was that the federal government was a close ally of common people and a defender of economic and political liberty. John L. Lewis, the CIO's charismatic leader, cannily saw that the union movement's greatest hopes for success lay with the Democratic Party of Franklin Roosevelt. Other more radical or more utopian union movements were suspicious of binding their movement too closely to the power of the federal government. Some, like the long-faded Knights of Labor, had hoped for a reformulation of capitalism itself. Others, like the American Federation of Labor that Betty's mother was sympathetic to, feared that a powerful federal government deciding what was fair in any given workplace would drain the union's power and autonomy. But it was Lewis's strategy of alliance that carried the day in the late 1930s. "The president wants you to join a union," he would bellow at organizing meetings. Between 1933 and 1937, when a CIO strike at General Motors forced a remarkable settlement with the company, unions signed up five million Americans. "You voted New Deal at the polls and defeated the Auto Barons," organizers told automobile workers in midwestern plants. "Now get a New Deal in the shop." As historian Meg Jacobs describes it, for working people like the Barretts, union organizing provided active, democratic middle ground between rule by corporations and laissez-faire economics, on the one hand, and statist totalitarianism of the sort rising in Germany and the Soviet Union, on the other.[17]

Later in her life Betty recalled the sort of politics she had believed in on the brink of World War II. "We began looking to the future, happy, successful, healthy," she wrote. "Social security benefits" and "medicine and health would give us long lives." There would be effective policies to stop "causes of depressions, from which we were recovering."[18] Eighteen-year-old Betty went to the University of New Hampshire and promptly began drawing bad grades, which she blamed on her activism. She seemed to spend more time sitting on committees than in classrooms. She served as "chairman of the Inter-Race Commission and was offered the New England Chairmanship of the Student Christian Movement. I was an officer in the International Relationship Club." She recalled that it felt as though "I had the weight of the world upon my shoulders."[19]

Betty worked as though it was her personal responsibility to bring about that happy future she hoped for. As an officer of the student club on international relations, she agitated against New Hampshire's isolationism and for Franklin Roosevelt's strong desire to aid the Allies against Hitler's expansionism in 1939 and 1940. She recalled later being called a traitor for it.[20] It was, however, the sort of work the Student Christian Movement could support. The Movement was a liberal Protestant organization vociferously dedicated to the New Deal. Betty recognized this version of Christianity as that which she grew up with, and she threw herself into the work. The October of Betty's first year at the university, the Movement organized intercollegiate "peace panels" and discussion groups targeted at "current problems." In the years Betty was at UNH, the Movement sponsored radio programs, brought speakers to campus, and arranged weekend and weekly retreats with ministers and activists from around the world. The Movement titled its events "The Church and the Social Battle," and "Democracy and Education," calling for economic and social policies of the sort that the *New Hampshire,* the University of New Hampshire college newspaper, worriedly dubbed "communistic."[21]

Such fears were typical. New Hampshire was a rock-ribbed Republican state throughout most of the twentieth century — the myth that the Republican Party was founded in New Hampshire instead of Ripon, Wisconsin, where most historians locate it, was popular while Betty grew up — and Franklin Roosevelt had lost the state to Republican Herbert Hoover in 1932. Although Roosevelt would win the state in his next three presidential campaigns, the vote was always close, and Republicans began winning again after his death in 1945. The work must have seemed tremendous for young liberal activists.[22]

Betty was overwhelmed. In 1939 the local newspaper reported that she had a "nervous breakdown," but it was more than that. She suffered an intense fever and infection of her ovaries that left it unlikely she could have children of her own. The medical bills piled up; her parents were having a "difficult time" financially, so she took some time off from school and took a job as a waitress at a restaurant called Ruby's Farm Kitchen.[23] There Betty met a divorced chef named Robert Stewart (whom she called Bob), and they married in June 1941. Robert had three young children, and Betty adopted them. She left the workforce and her education for homemaking and childrearing.[24]

On the face of it, Betty's journey might seem typical, perhaps even a foreshadowing of what was soon to come for American families. Despite her mother's experience, many young women in the Depression felt pressure to exit the workforce upon marriage, as writers and politicians alike worried they were taking jobs from men with families. As of 1940, for instance, only a quarter of school districts in the county would employ single women. And though millions of women joined the workforce during the war, by 1947 at least three million of them no longer held those jobs. Many returned to the home. When Betty married in 1941 only one in four of women in her age group – eighteen to twenty-four – were married. But by 1950, nearly two-thirds of women in that group were married, and most were homemakers. The statistics tilted even further for white women like Betty, who were generally married at higher rates than women of color, and whose husbands were more likely to earn enough to enable them to support a family on a single income. Forty percent of Black women worked outside the home in the 1940s and 1950s, but more and more white women lived lives like Betty.[25]

The vast expansion of federal funding on national defense in the decade made it possible for white men like Robert Stewart to pursue stable and even prosperous lives for their families. Soon after they met, Robert secured a good position at the Portsmouth Naval Shipyard, and the pair began to buy property: furniture, then an apartment, then the entire apartment building, which they began renting. For Betty, having seen the impact of financial strain upon her parents, the government largesse that made such progress possible in the world seemed a blessing. The close connections between federal funding and her own economic security were not lost on Betty. By the 1940s, Portsmouth was booming, fueled by military manufacturing at the shipyard and the demands of Pease Air Force Base, originally a small municipal airport transformed by the military through the 1940s and formally opened in 1951. Betty, watching this, insisted that it was federal funding that saved her community from the Great Depression and continued to sustain it. "No balanced budget to destroy our economy," she demanded in a local newspaper. New Hampshire had seen "no major depressions since that time" when the government began spending.[26]

Betty's expectations of her marriage mirrored those of many women who would marry in the next twenty years. "Bob Stewart seemed the best thing on the horizon, so I grabbed him," she later remembered to her niece. "Most people didn't even have jobs. We were coming out of the depression. He was hard-working, and anything that I wanted he got for me." She was "intrigued at the idea of being a step-mother and considered him an uncut diamond who could be polished."[27] The division of labor Betty expected, with her husband as provider and herself as caretaker both of the children and her husband, who would require her to provide a firm moral grounding for him and the family, was increasingly typical of the time. Such arrangements and expectations were built out of the economic prosperity of the 1940s and 1950s, the worry for the preservation of democracy that World War II and the Cold War fostered, and the increasingly popular disciplines of psychology and psychiatry. In these marriages, women were not simply to be nannies and homemakers. Rather, husbands and wives learned that their marriages were between equals as understood in a complementarian fashion: men and women were psychologically equipped for different duties and thus could build an equal marriage once each understood their responsibilities toward the other.[28] In a 1956 cover story, *Life* magazine warned of what might happen when men and women failed at fulfilling their roles. The magazine complained of "that common urban phenomenon known as the career woman. And that fatal error that feminism propagated sank deeply into the national consciousness." Citing five male psychiatrists, *Life* explained that a society with high female employment was in danger of succumbing to a divorce epidemic, rampant juvenile delinquency, alcoholism, and apathy about progress and consequent failed self-government.[29]

And yet, few marriages in the United States were as idyllic as *Life* magazine promised they might be. Many women, even middle-class white women like Betty, found it necessary to work outside the home (though "career women" were a less common phenomenon). Similarly, though divorce rates declined throughout the 1950s, it was also clear that unhappy marriages were as common as ever. Marriage counselors in the period often blamed such struggles on a couple's failure to negotiate their expected roles and acknowledged that the rapid social and economic change of the period could make such efforts difficult.[30] The Stewart marriage was an example. Robert Stewart's behavior became erratic, and in Betty's mind he betrayed their implicit contract. "He became more demanding, refused to give me any money, and insisted I go to work," she complained. And then he became abusive. He once broke down the door to their home after a terrified Betty locked him out. She suspected infidelity, and then became certain of it. She secured a restraining order and decided she would stay until the youngest child, Connie, turned sixteen. The divorce was finalized on Connie's sixteenth birthday in 1955. That year Betty turned thirty-six.[31]

Her experience set her on a path different than what she had expected upon her marriage, in two ways. First, Betty had indeed gone to work as a saleswoman at the local W. T. Grant, a chain of variety stores that thrived in the 1940s and 1950s. She later remembered that she "enjoyed the work" and realized that she wanted a career. Second, through the marriage, Betty insisted on remaining committed to her activism. Like many liberal women in the 1940s and 1950s, Betty channeled her work through a church. The connections between liberal politics and religion she had seen in her university's Student Christian Movement led her, and many other white activists, into churches that were committed to activism. She persuaded Robert to join her at the local Methodist church, where she signed up for a community service committee – a way that women could participate in politics while still upholding the postwar marital ideal.[32]

By the time her marriage ended, her experience with the children focused her idealism upon a particular social problem she wanted to solve. Her liberalism guided her to the state as a site for solving it. In 1956 she returned to the University of New Hampshire, intent on a degree in social work and a job working for the state in child welfare. "This time I did my homework," she laughed.[33] She was notably frustrated with the college campus she returned to. The University of New Hampshire in the late 1950s was, like many American universities, flush with money from generous government contracts, the federal commitment to fund the education of veterans, and the steadily growing baby boom generation. Even its president, Harold Stoke, while acknowledging the benefits to the university, worried about the moral impact of such funding: the growing expectation that university education should serve national economic expansion and the research needs of the American military. Betty, for her part, was not impressed. "Before it was planning for a new utopia for the world, a better life for all," she remembered about her earlier experience in college. "Now it was – how many bucks can I make and how fast? . . . Concern for man's progress had been replaced by Playboy." And so, she said, "I became a social worker." Upon graduating in 1958, she took a job with the New Hampshire Division of Welfare, tending to neglected and abandoned children. She bought a home on State Street in Portsmouth with her divorce settlement.[34]

And then Barney Hill, whom she had briefly met while working a summer job several months earlier, reentered her life.

Barney was Black. Under America's persistent Jim Crow regime, laws enforcing racial segregation and restricting African American voting rights flourished in the South and structural inequity and bigotry hampered their lives in the North. Franklin Roosevelt was reluctant to tackle the problem, since the votes of white southerners kept Democrats in power through the 1930s and 1940s. He ordered government contractors and agencies to avoid segregation but avoided confrontation when those orders were ignored, and he never tried to pass a federal civil rights bill. The naval shipyard in Portsmouth where Robert Stewart worked, for instance, employed African Americans but restricted the jobs they could hold. There were protests and demonstrations there well into the 1960s.[35]

When Betty was young, she lived across the street from an interracial couple. Whenever she and her friends walked home from school, they would point at the house and describe the couple in what seemed to Betty derogatory terms. One day when Betty came home her parents were not there, and afraid of being alone she fled across the street and knocked on the door. But when her neighbor answered, young Betty's tongue was tied, and she simply stared at the Black woman, unable to talk. The woman took Betty in and fed her, and Betty remained for a long time. When she finally went home her father threatened her with punishment if she vanished again. "I wondered if he were angry about my lateness, or the fact that I had visited the colored woman," Betty remembered. But her mother took her aside and told her "that some people do not like colored people, but this was not right for they were people just like everyone else, and if we heard anyone talking against them we should speak up." Betty never forgot the lesson. It drew her attention to the great contradiction that lay at the heart of the New Deal politics she came to believe in, and to a certain sort of solution.[36]

Many liberals who hoped for racial reconciliation in the 1940s and 1950s turned to the ideas of the Swedish sociologist Gunnar Myrdal, whose monumental 1944 book, *An American Dilemma: The Negro Problem and Modern Democracy,* offered an optimistic solution to the problem. Invoking principles of government intervention and human reasonableness Myrdal argued that Jim Crow's institutionalized racism would fade as the government enabled Black Americans to rise to more respectable social conditions. "A great majority of white people in America would be prepared to give the Negro a substantially

Betty and Barney Hill pose for *Look* magazine in a field near their home in the late spring of 1966.
Look Magazine Collection, Prints and Photographs Division, Library of Congress, LC 66–2889–2800–02817u.

better deal if they knew the facts," Myrdal wrote. He called for desegregation of schools, the federal bureaucracy, and other American institutions. As integration proceeded, he believed white Americans' irrational prejudices would fade into recognition of human equality.[37]

Betty Hill and her college friends certainly believed Myrdal. By the 1940s many members of the Student Christian Movement were joining liberal organizations fighting for racial equality. Among the most popular was the Congress of Racial Equality (CORE), an interracial organization dedicated to nonviolent forms of direct action. In 1947 the New England Student Christian Movement, of which Betty was a member, endorsed CORE.[38] The leaders of CORE believed that appeals to conscience would produce laws that combatted segregation. Two of its leaders, George Houser and Bayard Rustin, organized the Journey of

Reconciliation, personally leading eight white men and eight Black men on a two-week-long bus tour of the South. They intended to force southern bus lines to acknowledge that the Supreme Court had recently declared segregation in interstate travel unconstitutional. After two weeks of arrests, confrontations with bus drivers, and the occasional flash of violence, Rustin wrote that the Journey caused "confusion" and a "psychological struggle" in southerners. That convinced him that "The great majority of people in the upper South are prepared . . . to ride on buses and trains with Negroes." One white woman who boarded a bus paused for a moment when she saw the CORE activists, and then plopped into a seat next to a Black man, saying simply, "I'm tired."[39] The Unitarian minister Homer Jack, another of CORE's founders and a member of the Journey of Reconciliation concluded that "if any number of whites in America spent no more than thirty seconds as a Negro or as a member of some other minority group under overt discrimination, the terrible inertia responsible for our flourishing racism would be broken." Fortunately, Jack explained, American "institutions are helping Negroes and whites to know each other." Sounding uncannily like Myrdal, Rustin and Jack articulated confidence that racism in America would vanish as soon as laws promoted integration. Betty Hill believed it too. In college, she had made a point of befriending a Black girl who was ostracized by the other white woman in their dorm building, and Betty believed that she herself gained a great deal from the friendship. Falling in love with Barney was, for her, a blessing derived from the open-mindedness her mother had taught her.[40]

CHAPTER 2

BARNEY

Robert Bagnall, rector of the African Episcopal Church of St. Thomas in West Philadelphia, died suddenly of a heart attack in August 1943 at age fifty-nine. He was one of the towering figures of Black America, having melded his ministry with racial activism for most of his career. After initially pursuing a career in the ministry, by his early thirties he was dividing his time between his flock in a Detroit church and civil rights work as one of the founders and leaders of the city's National Association for the Advancement of Colored People (NAACP), then the nation's leading civil rights organization. By 1921 he was working for the NAACP full time. But in 1933, the group was feeling the pains of the Depression as thoroughly as any other organization, and Bagnall had to leave. He returned to the pulpit in Philadelphia, at St. Thomas.[1]

It was an appropriate church for him. St. Thomas was a historic congregation, founded by the eighteenth-century Black leader Absalom Jones, who along with his colleague Richard Allen had walked out of the city's St. George's Methodist Episcopal Church, when they were told they could not join the white congregation on the main floor of the church. After the separation, Allen founded the African Methodist Episcopal Church. Jones became the first African American ordained a priest in the American Episcopal Church and founded St. Thomas in 1794. He had a congregation of five hundred within months.

Throughout its long history, St. Thomas was the home for movements for Black liberation, sponsoring mutual aid and migrant societies and, by the time Bagnall took its pulpit, preaching the NAACP's brand of civil rights liberalism.[2] And Bagnall had few more fervent devotees than a young parishioner whose 1941 marriage he had performed: a postal worker named Barney Hill Jr.

Born in Virginia in 1922, Barney Hill Jr. grew up in the Black communities of Depression-era Philadelphia. The city was home to among the oldest, most populous, and prosperous Black populations in the American North, dominated by the "Old Philadelphians," Black families who had been in Philadelphia for generations. By the early twentieth century Old Philadelphians embraced twin philosophies historians have called, respectively, racial uplift and civil rights liberalism. Many were associated with the National Association for the Advancement of Colored People, an organization that in Philadelphia, at least, adopted its own version of New Deal liberalism. Over the first few decades after its creation in 1909, the NAACP formulated a set of aims and a strategy. The aim was civil rights: the protection of equal rights for Black Americans, targeted at integration of Black people into everyday American life. The strategy was legislative and legal. The NAACP began almost immediately to press for new laws protecting equal rights, and it sued when those laws were broken. It fought disenfranchisement, segregation, and discrimination. Through the 1930s, it pressed the Roosevelt administration to support an anti-lynching law. And though it often mobilized demonstrations and protests and boycotts, the tip of the NAACP's spear was laws passed and upheld. Like many other New Deal liberals, members of the NAACP believed that the government could improve the lives of Black Americans, if it was properly mobilized.[3]

At the same time, the NAACP was, in Philadelphia and nationwide, a largely middle-class organization. Many of its leaders, and particularly those in Philadelphia, believed in what was sometimes called "racial uplift." W. E. B. Du Bois, the Black intellectual who was the driving force behind the founding of the NAACP, argued that the "talented tenth," his term for the educated Black middle class, bore the responsibility to carve a path for other Black people, eventually creating a situation in which all Black Americans could enjoy the economic and educational advantages that would let them join the middle class. This was the aim of the Old Philadelphians. Throughout the 1920s and 1930s, they fought a particularly bitter battle in the city's school boards and courts to ensure equal access to education for Black children and hence — in the troubled world of the 1930s — demonstrate that American democracy was truly inclusive. As the activist, educator, and Philadelphia NAACP member Sadie Alexander put it, "Equal opportunity for everyone would . . . be the best possible answer to demagogues of the left and right who exploit discrimination and segregation in the United States and mock our democratic ideals."[4] Like Gunnar Myrdal later, they hoped that equal rights under law would gradually eliminate institutionalized racism and encourage integration. In turn, more and more Black people would achieve the respectability of the Old Philadelphians themselves.

These were the messages Barney Hill heard from Robert Bagnall at St. Thomas, which he attended in the 1940s, and through his youth in Philadelphia he became a committed civil rights activist and a practitioner of racial uplift on his own.

Barney Hill Jr. was the son of Barney Hill Sr. and Grace Sills, who married in southern Virginia. Like many African Americans in the 1910s and 1920s, Barney Sr. and Grace were the children of southern sharecroppers, and they joined the wave of roughly a million and a half African Americans who moved north in the years between the two world wars. Through the 1940s and 1950s those numbers only increased. In such northern cities as Philadelphia, Detroit, New York City, Chicago, and Cleveland, the population of African Americans spiked dramatically; the Black population in northern states rose by 40 percent. This wave, called the Great Migration, was driven by people seeking economic opportunity in the North and fleeing Jim Crow laws in the South. World War I primed the nation's economic pump, as most wars do, and political and social disenfranchisement for Black people in the South reached what one historian called its "nadir" at the same time.[5] It was an auspicious time to move north.

In the late 1910s and early 1920s, African Americans were arriving in Philadelphia at a rate of 150 per week, drawn by work in the city's railroad, steel, and manufacturing industries. In 1910 there were roughly 84,000 African Americans living in Philadelphia; twenty years later, when the Hills arrived, there were nearly 220,000, in three distinct neighborhoods — one in South Philadelphia, below the city's center at Independence Hall; one farther north; and one around a neighborhood called Haddington in West Philadelphia, near the University of Pennsylvania.[6] As was common in the Great Migration, these migrants often followed paths hewn out by their peers. Many Black Virginians found their way to Haddington, and by 1930 the Hills were living there, in a rented house on Spring Street.[7] In his magisterial book *The Philadelphia Negro,* published two decades before the Hills' arrival in the city, W. E. B. Du Bois observed that many Black people were fleeing the cramped, and infamous, Seventh Ward just south of the city center (where St. Thomas was located at the time) for areas like Haddington, but that throughout the city Black people were crowded into small and sometimes insufficient housing, without running water and at times electricity. The situation had improved by 1930, but poverty remained.[8]

As several observers noted, in Philadelphia as in other cities, the more Black Americans arrived in the city the rawer the animus of white Americans grew, and the more committed the latter became to keeping African Americans out of sight and out of mind. According to the sociologist Emmett Scott, an observer of the Great Migration, hostility was higher in Philadelphia than in other northern cities because of the city's proximity to the Jim Crow states of Maryland and Virginia. In 1917, a mob lynched a Black employee at the naval shipyards. The next year, more mobs attacked Black families seeking to move into neighborhoods around the shipyards. The Black population of the city continued to grow. Tensions remained high.[9]

And yet, when the Hills moved into Spring Street they joined one of the better established Black communities in the American North. The Old Philadelphians who ran the NAACP included the attorney E. Washington Rhodes, editor of the city's Black paper of record, the *Philadelphia Tribune,* the activists and scholars Raymond and Sadie Mossell Alexander, the wealthy real estate broker Isadore Martin, and others. These people had built a strong community infrastructure to serve Black people: hospitals, two newspapers, and a wide range of clubs and social service organizations. And they pressed for laws enforcing integration and equality, confident in the power of government to change American society and the possibilities of racial uplift.

In the early 1920s, despite an 1881 law banning segregation in education, the Philadelphia school board announced its intention to open several new schools in Black neighborhoods that would de facto serve only Black students. The

---

NAACP bristled—despite an organization of Black teachers which argued that such schools would provide them with jobs and protect Black children from discrimination. Robert Bagnall, then working for the NAACP, announced that the organization remained committed to integration. In the pages of the *Tribune,* E. Washington Rhodes wrote that "segregation is taking a death hold on the Negroes of Philadelphia." He argued that if Black people accepted separate schools, they would always and forever remain an economic and political underclass.[10]

The NAACP lost that battle; the schools opened. But, as with the unions of New Hampshire, in the 1930s the NAACP's fortune changed. In that decade, Philadelphia's Black leaders increasingly managed to make common cause with the Democratic Party. Black people had been solid supporters of the Republican Party—Lincoln's party—for decades, but in the 1930s, in reaction to the New Deal, some Black people began to build an alliance with the Democratic Party. The NAACP led rallies, protests, and even school boycotts in the city and its suburbs for fifteen years, and by the time America entered World War II it had successfully gained the appointment of Black members to the city's school board, the hiring of Black teachers, and integration in some schools. A tenement collapse in 1936 led to widespread Black protest and New Deal funding for more and better housing for the city's poor, and especially African Americans. And, invigorated by the New Deal, the city's NAACP worked with the Fair Employment Practices Commission, which Franklin Roosevelt had established in 1941 to eradicate discrimination among federal contractors, to target the city's shipyards and other agencies. In 1944, the NAACP and its allies managed to force the Philadelphia Transit Company to integrate its hiring practices despite a wildcat strike by its white employees.[11]

More than simply politics, the NAACP also pursued a strategy of uplift and respectability. The Old Philadelphians tried to prove through their own tidy, middle-class lives that integration would not disrupt the society and economy of postwar America; rather, that Black Americans could participate in and contribute to a prosperous nation. They cooperated with a number of white activists, particularly among the city's Quakers, and they built organizations that worked to uplift the poverty-stricken. Through the 1920s these groups organized efforts to uplift poverty-stricken recent migrants from the South, providing clothing, homes, and jobs. In 1931, these groups founded the Young People's Interracial Fellowship and a Fellowship Church, an interracial, interdenominational congregation that sponsored job training programs and an integrated summer school. "The America which says and means, 'All men are created equal, [and] possess certain inalienable rights,' that America is in the process of becoming," the Fellowship's mission declared. By the mid-twentieth century, more and more Black people were moving to middle-class Philadelphia neighborhoods. The *Philadelphia Tribune*, by the 1930s, among the most respected Black newspapers in the country, repeatedly invoked the concept of respectability to push for equal rights, arguing, for instance, that interracial marriage promoted a "civilized state" among Americans of all races because "laws against intermarriage endanger [the] structure of respectable society." The paper denounced police raids as especially heinous because there were "cops raiding respectable homes."[12]

The politics of respectability were well known among Black Americans. The Black sociologist C. Eric Lincoln pointed out that Martin Luther King Jr. was keenly aware of "the importance of achieving respectability — even modishness — if racial equality is ever to be achieved." Rosa Parks carefully presented her act of defiance against segregation on the buses in Montgomery, Alabama, as the act of a tired, hard-working, Christian middle-class woman, obscuring her long immersion in the radical activist world of the 1950s for the same reason.[13] For both King and Parks, institutional change required working within the system, and both trusted that such change was possible. The Philadelphia NAACP believed the same.

When the Hills arrived in Philadelphia, they embraced the paired impulses of integration and respectability, and they found that they were able to climb society's rungs in pursuit of both. The Great Migration disrupted the structures of Philadelphia (and Chicago, New York, and all the other cities that absorbed tidal waves of migrants). It changed the city's economic life, its religious worship, its social networks, and its political hierarchies. In so doing, it opened up new possibilities for the newcomers and the Old Philadelphians alike. Upon his family's arrival, Barney Hill Sr. took a job as a custodian, first in a clothing store, later in a post office — but by the end of his life, he had worked his way up in the post office from floor sweeping to postal officer. Barney made enough to pay the rent on a small house, and quickly the Hills became involved in the Black community of western Philadelphia.[14]

—

As did many migrant families, the Hills relied on community organizations of the sort the Old Philadelphians had founded. Specifically, Barney Hill Sr. joined a whist club. Whist is a team card game, and it was widespread among African Americans in the urban North in the early twentieth century; the jazz musician Duke Ellington was a prominent fan. The game served both a private and public function. It was popular at parties but was also a vehicle for social empowerment; many churches and neighborhood associations hosted tournaments as a way to raise money for community causes. For the older Black elite of northern cities, whist was a symbol of their cultured, middle-class status. The Black sociologist E. Franklin Frazier's study of the Great Migration's impact in Philadelphia argued that whist served as a form of social lubricant and social glue, offering a venue for community building, alliance making, and financial interaction.[15]

For Barney Sr. and his friends in Haddington, the Invincible Whist Club became a tool for social aspiration and the construction of new communities out of the shards of the old. Their club rotated its monthly meetings among the homes of its dozen or so members (perhaps, as some clubs did, paying the hosts a portion of club dues). At an April 1932 meeting, Barney Sr. gave a speech to the club, declaring that it should do more than merely offer card games; the Invincible Whist Club should come to see itself as a part of a broader community network designed to promote the well-being of African Americans across the city. The Invincible Whist Club became connected to Philadelphia's Charity Social Club, which held regular fundraisers for Philadelphia's poor Black families, and began to publicize work with white groups like the Young People's Interracial Fellowship. The club also pledged to support the *Philadelphia Tribune*, "to be informed as to what Negroes are doing." The activist bent of Barney Sr. got him elected to club office; he served as vice president for the next several years, as the club broadened from card games to social activism.[16]

By the time World War II had ended, Barney Hill's children had entered a social world that he may not have dreamed of when he first moved his family north. Barney Jr. remembered his father as a good provider. They always had food and celebrated Christmas with gifts and a special meal even in the darkest years of the Depression. Barney's sister became a prominent hostess, regularly entertaining various social clubs and organizations at the Hill home. Barney himself remembered that he learned not to simply endure the realities of white supremacy but to assert himself and push back. He told the journalist John Fuller about a junior high teacher who discouraged him from becoming an engineer because of his race. Barney was disheartened, but also angry. "I have always felt that it's right and proper to defend against an aggressor at all times," he told Fuller. Soon after, he learned a gang of boys were plotting to beat him up, so he biked to the ringleader's backyard and left him battered on the ground.[17]

After leaving junior high, Barney enrolled at South Philadelphia High School, an experimental school founded in 1907 with a reputation for educational innovation. The South Philadelphia school was originally designed for European immigrants, but it quickly expanded, opened a boys' and girls' school, and had integrated its student body by 1918, when Marian Anderson, destined to become one of America's most prominent sopranos, enrolled.[18] By the time Barney arrived the school had committed itself to integrationist liberalism. Ruth Wanger, an influential teacher and administrator, urged other faculty to celebrate diversity and promote racial egalitarianism in the classroom, and also to push the government to end segregation. By the 1940s, Wanger was sponsoring what was then called "Negro History Week" in the school, and in 1939 she delivered a speech urging her students to denounce racial segregation and become "a group worthy of democracy." In 1941, six hundred South Philadelphia High students signed a petition protesting racial segregation in Washington, D.C., noting that Black students could not attend the school's senior trip there because they were not allowed to stay in the city's hotels. Wanger sent the petition to Eleanor Roosevelt.[19]

After briefly attending Temple University, in May 1941 Barney Jr. enlisted in the U.S. Army. But he retained much from his time at South Philadelphia High. He was a quick study, his family remembered, with what they called a "retentive memory" and broad interests. The school's commitment to racial activism stuck with him for the rest of his life. But what probably seemed most important to Barney was his encounter with an artistic student named Ruby Horne. In 1942, the year Barney turned twenty and Ruby eighteen, Robert Bagnall married the two at the African Episcopal Church of St. Thomas. Shortly thereafter Barney was grievously wounded while stationed at Aberdeen Proving Ground ninety miles south of Philadelphia. An accidental grenade explosion damaged his mouth and required him to get dentures. He was honorably discharged with a notation of "excellent" character and service. Afterward he followed his father into the postal service, and he and Ruby moved into a home not far from Barney's parents, on Fifty-first Street in West Philadelphia. There the two committed themselves to the respectable integrationism they learned at South Philadelphia High, embracing the markers of a middle-class lifestyle. Ruby's family recalled her as an "elegant" hostess, whose "elaborate dinner parties were legendary and dramatic for their display of grand presentation and culinary acumen." The two were frequently seen at social events.[20]

They also joined Bagnall's congregation. That this was possible signaled Barney's rise. By the time of Bagnall's death, only two years after Barney and Ruby's wedding, the rector had moved the church into a new building, a neo-Gothic home on the corner of Fifty-second Street and Parrish Avenue, only minutes by car from Barney and Ruby's home. They became active members of the congregation. Barney served its Boy Scout troop, and Ruby joined the women's organization. And Bagnall over and over preached the NAACP's message of integration and respectability, arguing that Black Americans had served the nation well and had every right to participate in its politics, society, and economic life. In celebration of the sesquicentennial of the signing of the Constitution in September 1937, Bagnall delivered a lecture to an audience of several hundred African Americans, and his words are a worthwhile illustration of what Barney Hill would have heard in his congregation. "The Negro has every right to participate in this celebration," Bagnall declared. "America would be sadly lacking in many things, if it were not for the participation of the Negro." He listed Black men who fought or died in the American Revolution. "Crispus Attucks, Peter Salem, and countless other men gave of their blood to preserve the freedom of this country."[21]

Bagnall drew here on a school of African American thought prevalent in the 1920s and 1930s. Scholars like Carter Woodson, a Harvard PhD and professor at Howard University who founded Negro History Week and later Black History Month, followed earlier Black writers like George Washington Williams and Pauline Hopkins to insist that Black history was foundational to American history in total, and thus Black Americans should understand they had equal claim on the workings of American government and pride in American democracy.

The NAACP seized upon these narratives.[22] And Bagnall continued to beat the drum. He repeated the common tale that Alexander Hamilton was of African ancestry. He wrote a column in the *Philadelphia Tribune* that reminded Black people "it is most important that Negroes cast a large vote." He joined the movement calling upon Franklin Roosevelt to stop government military contractors from discriminating in employment.[23] Barney and Ruby heard these messages from the pulpit of St. Thomas, and Barney, at least, remembered. Black people had every claim to participate fully in American democracy. It was a lesson he would take to New Hampshire.

Ruby and Barney had two sons, but the marriage eventually failed. They separated in early 1957, and Ruby took the boys. In the cold January of 1959, Barney Hill, alone, toured the sleek new headquarters of the Consolidated Financial Corporation, a loan and investment firm a few blocks from his parents' home. Hundreds of visitors came to see the marvel of modern architecture, but Barney arrived by himself. In some ways, his visit symbolized the transformations the Great Migration had wrought in his life. The new building marked the economic advances neighborhoods like the Fourth Ward had achieved. The city's leaders in the 1950s were committed liberals who charged the city's Fair Employment Practices Commission to ensure equal opportunity for all races in the city's jobs market. In 1951, Philadelphia's new city charter banned racial and religious discrimination in all city services and employment. In postwar Philadelphia, on the books at least, racial equality of the sort Bagnall dreamed of seemed on the rise.[24]

Similarly, Barney was now the sort of man — with a good job, membership in a respectable and historic religious congregation, and interests in the community — who would attend such a gathering as the open house of a new corporate headquarters. He had become an Old Philadelphian, a respectable middle-class liberal. Barney might have been thinking of these things as he wandered through the building, bundled up on that chilly day. But his loneliness might have dulled his optimism. He had lost his wife. His exposure to Robert Bagnall had sharpened his frustration with the city's racial politics. Betty later remembered that Barney said that later in his life Philadelphia seemed "very segregated" to him, but "not when he was a small child." He remembered playing with white children while he was young, but the older he grew so did his awareness of the realities of discrimination. And so did his dissatisfaction.[25]

CHAPTER 3

THE UNITARIANS

In early 1957 Barney Hill reached out to Betty Barrett Stewart. They had met the previous summer, when Barney, Ruby, and their two sons were vacationing at a boardinghouse at Hampton Beach, a resort town south of Portsmouth. Betty, recently divorced, was living there that summer, waiting for her house to be remodeled and working as a cashier to fund her return to college, and she and the Hills had struck up an acquaintanceship. After Barney took the initiative to renew it, the two began taking weekend trips together, meeting in various places up and down the East Coast, and by the time Barney toured the Consolidated Financial headquarters, he was wishing Betty could be there with him. He eventually proposed — and Betty was taken aback. She wrote later she was worried about both their motives; she feared that the racial divide between them would affect their marriage.[1]

By the late 1950s, the American anti-miscegenation regime was beginning to teeter, but it still had strength. Interracial marriage had never been illegal in New Hampshire, and Pennsylvania had lifted its ban in 1780, but some thirty states still had bans when Betty and Barney began courting. And beyond such formal laws, Gunnar Myrdal observed that fear of interracial marriage was deeply ingrained throughout American culture. "Even in the Northern states where, for the most part, intermarriage is not barred by the force of law, the

---

36

social sanctions blocking its way are serious," he noted, pointing to social ostracism and worry that Black people were simply "unassimilable" among white Americans.[2]

But, of course, such marriages were happening all along, and the Hills would have known of them. W. E. B. Du Bois documented thirty-three such marriages in Philadelphia's Seventh Ward alone in the 1890s and argued that there were probably dozens more across the city. While some people argued that these marriages only occurred among "the worst" and "lowest" sorts, in Du Bois's estimation, proximity seemed a more likely cause. People would marry those around them. And, indeed, as the Great Migration drew more and more Black people into urban areas, and particularly after World War II, intermarriage rates began to increase. Between 1945 and 1960, the number of interracial marriages in the United States in total increased only slightly, to just over 1 percent of marriages. But in Washington, D.C., for instance, the rate increased tenfold in the twenty years between 1941 and 1960. Du Bois's theory about proximity seemed justified.[3]

Also influential were examples. Many Black servicemen during World War II brought home European wives. Increasingly popular African American magazines, particularly *Ebony,* celebrated interracial marriage as a method of racial uplift and respectability. They pointed to the rising numbers of famous Black people with white spouses: the singers Lena Horne and Sammy Davis Jr., the actress Dorothy Dandridge. And Barney Hill personally had some familiarity with interracial sex. According to Betty, there was a long history of it in the Hill family — as there was with most Black families in the South. She remembered Barney's parents had in their home a portrait of one of Barney's great-grandmothers, a white woman with "long blond braids." Barney remembered that when he went to family funerals as a small child in Virginia, "the church would be filled with blacks on one side and whites on the other."[4]

And finally, interracial marriage was, by the late 1950s, becoming a central battlefield in the NAACP's war for equal rights. Soon after he won the famous *Brown v. Board of Education* case in 1954, Thurgood Marshall, the NAACP's chief attorney, turned his sights on laws banning interracial marriage. Courts around the country began to strike down anti-miscegenation laws — most famously in *Perez v. Sharp* in California in 1948 — and states began to follow suit, revoking statutes when the courts did not beat them to it. By the late 1960s, only seventeen

---

southern states still stubbornly held on. But they seemed increasingly isolated. The Supreme Court declared such laws unconstitutional in 1967.[5]

All of this meant that both Hills, given their personal histories and their firm belief in liberal politics, were willing to entertain the possibility of a romance. Barney impressed Betty's family as genteel and well-informed — a testament to his sharp mind and the influence, perhaps, of Ruby's elegance and of the ideologies of racial uplift that had informed him his entire life.[6] They married in Camden, New Jersey, in May 1960.

Despite their wedding, the two lived apart for months until the Boston post office offered Barney a position in March of 1961, allowing him to transfer from his post in Philadelphia. Although far closer to New Hampshire than Pennsylvania, Boston still sat sixty miles south of Portsmouth, and Barney worked the night shift, which meant that the couple had time together only in the evening, before Barney drove to work and Betty went to bed. In the mornings they crossed paths when Barney arrived home while Betty was preparing to leave for work. On the weekends they spent a lot of time camping. And eventually, they joined a church. Betty had liked the Methodist church she attended throughout her first marriage because she thought the minister there, named Brewster, "was a real liberal." He had supported her activism and sponsored the various service committees she worked on, but when he moved on she stopped attending. The new minister seemed to her much more conservative, "and I couldn't tolerate him at all." She and Barney were happily unchurched for a while, and then they met John Papandrew.[7]

Papandrew was born in 1921 in Exeter, just southwest of Portsmouth, where he was a star on the high school football team. He attended the University of New Hampshire at the same time as Betty Barrett, though they did not know each other. In 1942 Papandrew joined the military and served until the end of World War II. He was a tail gunner on a B-17 bomber plane in Italy and flew more than four dozen combat missions in the European theater. He served with the 332nd Fighter Group, better known as the Tuskegee Airmen. Since the US military had been segregated since the Civil War, the 332nd was made up entirely of African American pilots, trained at Tuskegee Air Field near Tuskegee Institute, the historically Black college founded by Booker T. Washington. Papandrew's bombers were escorted by the fighter planes of the 332nd on their

John Papandrew, minister of
South Church in Portsmouth
from 1961 to 1964, an activist
and advocate for civil rights
who drew the Hills into his
congregation.
bMS 1446/333 Unitarian
Universalist Minister files,
1825–2010, Harvard Divinity
School Library, Cambridge,
Massachusetts.

missions. The experience left Papandrew indignant (as were many of the
Tuskegee Airmen) about the persistence of white supremacy in the United
States, and he returned to New Hampshire after the war determined to press for
equality. A friend once called him "an intense, sensitive, and deeply conscienced
[*sic*] person with an unusually high energy output . . . hard-bitten in his dedica-
tion to the solution of interracial problems." In the pulpit of the South Church
in Portsmouth, Papandrew would be assertive, activist, controversial, and precisely what Betty and Barney Hill wanted from their minister.[8]

After graduating from the University of New Hampshire, Papandrew
worked for a while as a high school teacher and at an insurance company but
remained restless. He wanted to change the world, and so he went to divinity
school at Harvard. He was ordained a Unitarian minister in 1955 at South

Church in Portsmouth, and in 1957 moved to New York City to serve as assistant minister at the famous Community Church, where the legendary John Haynes Holmes reigned as senior pastor from 1907 to 1949. The venerable Holmes still sat in the pews every Sunday until his death in 1964, and the church bore his stamp. Holmes was a pacifist who opposed American involvement in both world wars and was one of the leading popularizers of the philosophy of Mahatma Gandhi in the United States; he was president of the American Civil Liberties Union from 1940 to 1950, and he was present at the founding meeting of the NAACP.[9] He was the grand old man of liberal activism when John Papandrew arrived in his pulpit in 1957, and the young minister was awed by him. As the African American leader W. E. B. Du Bois said of Holmes's church, "The Community Church welcomed Negroes; discussed the Negro Problem, and evidently did not believe that the white race was the only race on earth worth saving. That was a difficult creed to live up to in early twentieth century New York."[10]

Papandrew wanted desperately to live up to that creed. He would become close to Betty and Barney Hill because of his full-throated embrace of liberal activism. Throughout his ministry he leaned heavily on mid-century theologians like Dietrich Bonhoeffer, Paul Tillich, and Reinhold Niebuhr. They led the neo-orthodox movement that became popular in postwar American Christianity because it reconciled faith with modern science and the global traumas of the Holocaust and world wars. Neo-orthodox Christians argued that the fundamental realities Christianity taught were less about miracles and heaven than the paradoxes of modern life. The story of Adam and Eve in the Garden of Eden might not be true, but the reality that human beings were prone to sin was painfully tangible in a world scarred by the atomic bomb and racial segregation. The resurrection of Jesus might not be historically genuine, but the idea that all human beings possessed divine potential was. As Papandrew preached, religion in the United States must move "from an emphasis on salvation, which has stifled the church too long, to an emphasis on redeeming our time, concern for this world instead of the next."[11] This would not have been shocking to Unitarians. The denomination had long been skeptical of miraculous claims about the divinity of Jesus Christ or the miracles he performed, preferring to emphasize his ethical teachings and charitable example. Such beliefs seemed heretical when

—

the faith emerged at the turn of the nineteenth century, and they kept the denomination small in the United States, but to believers like Papandrew Unitarianism was an ideal fit for the world after the war.

In March 1961 the South Church congregation invited Papandrew back to New Hampshire to interview for the position of minister. He went, both welcoming the opportunity to return home and sensing promise in Portsmouth, a "vision of a strong community oriented and action church," as he remembered. South Church voted fifty-eight to one to extend the call to him. Yet along with his hopes he also had some concerns. New Hampshire, after all, was a Republican state, and Papandrew was a firm New Deal liberal. "This ministry in New York has been an enriching experience," he wrote to a friend, free from "the narrow loyalties, the stifling particularisms, and stupid conformisms which need no further elucidation to one who has worked in N.H." But he went, because more than anything he wanted to make South Church a center of the struggle for civil rights in New England. He told the Unitarian ministerial committee that he valued Unitarianism because it attracted "many diverse elements and groups. Congregations may differ in kind as well as in degree through the whole spectrum of theological, sociological, political and economic belief." He arrived in Portsmouth in June 1961, ready to take up the challenge.[12]

Papandrew's commitment to racial activism and his certain self-consciousness about it were characteristic of mid-century Unitarians. Theirs was overwhelmingly a white, educated, middle- and upper-class northern denomination, and in the mid-twentieth century these demographics carried with them barriers to the sort of diversity liberals hoped for. In September 1956, the Unitarian *Christian Register* surveyed 287 Unitarian congregations and fellowships across the nation; 80 reported that they had Black members. The *Register* wanted these numbers to rise and claimed those congregations did too. A number, however, reported failed recruitment efforts rooted in their unthinking class and racial biases. One congregation in Florida decided to seek out greater diversity and "inquired whether there were any Unitarians among the faculty and students at the local Negro college," to no avail. Many reported, as did the congregation in Park Forest, Illinois, an upscale Chicago suburb that grew rapidly after World War II, that they hoped their children could "meet freely with Negroes — there are none in Park Forest." The *Register* reported that one congregation "confessed it probably had a reputation as being 'too highbrow' among both whites and Negroes." Another minister in New England reported, "Several of our people possess prejudice against Negroes, judging from things they have said."[13] There were barriers of class and bigotry that all Unitarianism's hopes could not alone destroy.

And yet, overwhelmingly, Unitarian leaders like Papandrew believed America in the 1950s and 1960s was fertile ground for their hopes. Many American religious denominations spent those decades in a flush of optimism as the number of Americans who claimed religious belief, the number of people enrolled in church membership, and the number of church buildings appearing on the American landscape all reached historic highs in the fifteen years after World War II. Roughly half the American population was attending church every Sunday in the mid-1950s — the highest recorded in American history.[14]

But the Unitarians believed that there was something special happening to them. In February 1955, the *Christian Register* applauded the "rising tide of Unitarianism," observing that since the end of World War II, American Unitarianism had grown 60 percent, twice as fast as the American population, though it claimed only 150,000 or so members. Nonetheless, William Roger Greeley, the moderator of the American Unitarian Association in the mid-1950s, asked whether "30 million religious liberals" by 1965 would be an unreasonable prediction. In late 1961, in a step that seemed aimed at fulfilling such predictions, the denomination merged with the Universalist Church of America, a denomination perhaps as old as the Unitarians themselves which taught that all humanity was destined for salvation.[15]

In part their optimism about growth and suitedness for the times was because Unitarians had, perhaps more than most white American Christian denominations, embraced the New Deal liberalism which dominated the political spectrum in mid-century America. "The heart of Unitarianism is not essentially different than from the heart of America," said the great Unitarian theologian James Luther Adams shortly after the end of World War II. What he meant by that was that Unitarianism warmly recommended to its followers "an interest in social, economic and political problems, and in domestic and international well-being and unity."[16] None of this was so different from the conventional American liberalism that had come to dominate American politics by 1945. The Unitarians had been activists for social justice for generations, since the great antebellum abolitionists Lydia Maria Child and William Lloyd Garrison through the long career of John Haynes Holmes.

Just so, many prominent Unitarians in the 1950s were active in liberal and Democratic politics. Some, like Stephen Fritchman, the editor of the *Christian Register* who was sympathetic to European democratic socialism, believed Roosevelt should press for even more reform. But other prominent leaders, for example, Homer Jack, a close associate of Martin Luther King Jr., and Donald Harrington, who replaced John Haynes Holmes as senior minister of the Community Church, were staunch Democrats. In 1960 Harrington endorsed John F. Kennedy for president, declaring that the young senator "must be supported by all who cherish a warmer and wiser program." In 1962, the leadership of the newly unified Unitarian Universalist Association issued a report asking whether the denomination had "an obligation as a religious institution to stand for something? Did we not criticize the German churches that failed to stand up to Hitler? Do we not rightly criticize the churches in our own South which fail to oppose segregation?" The report endorsed civil rights laws and condemned communism, though with the caveat that communism "speaks to other values, like economic justice." It urged the American government to take greater care of the nation's poor. "How can our society be ordered to share our abundance more equitably?" the report asked.[17]

These ideas appealed to John Papandrew and to Betty and Barney Hill. Only a few weeks after assuming the pulpit of South Church, Papandrew caused a stir in Portsmouth. A young Kenyan man, James Karagol, had arrived in Portsmouth to attend high school. The student council of Portsmouth High had been moved by Kennedy's establishment of the Peace Corps in March 1961. Confident in the universality of the liberal ideals of education and tolerance, the agency promised to better American relationships with what was then called the "Third World" through personal contact and service. Young Americans began to be shipped overseas that fall. At about the same time the Corps began, a letter from Karagol arrived in Portsmouth. Karagol described a friend who had attended school in New Hampshire and requested admittance to Portsmouth High School. The student council and school administration, flush with Kennedyesque optimism, voted to admit him and provide room and board. The *Portsmouth Herald* and

Nashua Telegraph endorsed the offer, publishing an editorial invoking the Peace Corps and declaring, "By living and studying in American surroundings, the visitor would acquire first-hand knowledge of the qualities that give this nation its pride and greatness."[18]

But at the last moment, a member of the Portsmouth school board, apparently having discovered Karagol's imminent arrival, protested. At an emergency board meeting Louise McGee offered a number of objections. The high school on its own had no authority to waive the necessary tuition. Doing so, particularly for a foreign student, set a worrisome financial precedent. More, McGee said ominously, it could not be guaranteed that the boy was sufficiently "screened." McGee also served as president of the local chapter of the John Birch Society, a far-right group that believed the New Deal was soft on communism and leading the nation toward socialism and the death of individual liberty. Her myriad objections to Karagol ran the gamut of conservative objections to the reigning power of liberalism and showed that even the New Deal political consensus had its limits.[19]

McGee failed. After hearing her out, the school board voted in favor of offering Karagol a place; she was the only dissenter. But regardless, she raised John Papandrew's hackles. He attended the board meeting, and after McGee levied her warnings, Papandrew rose to castigate her. "If we let this kid down, it will not only be a great injustice to him," he declared to the board. "We should be ashamed of ourselves." He then offered to pay the young man's tuition himself and to take Karagol into his home for the school year. Papandrew's gesture was not necessary; the board gave the boy all the funding he needed. But his moral conviction, his willingness to lecture, his staunch devotion to Unitarian idealism were telling nonetheless.[20] They certainly attracted Betty and Barney Hill.

It is unclear precisely what event led Betty and Barney Hill into membership at South Church, though it happened that summer of 1961, and as Betty claimed, as a result of Papandrew's personal invitation. The South Church building was convenient to them. Appropriately for Portsmouth, it was historic; a large, austere granite building with a tower but no steeple, completed in 1826 at the intersection of State Street and Church Street, a half mile directly down the road from the Hill home. The Hills claimed they became Unitarians because the faith's optimistic creed matched the New Deal liberalism they embraced.

The Karagol incident would have certainly made the two proud of their minister. As Betty put it, "I never knew what my religion was until I went to the Unitarian church and found out that they believed the same way I did." Barney, similarly, claimed to be a "confused Christian," who was frustrated with the mysticism of traditional Christian theology and found comfort in Unitarianism's grounded activism and commitment to reason and rationality. The Hills participated in South Church as Barney and Ruby had at St. Thomas. Barney regularly served as an usher at services, and the Hills worked on the church's many fund drives, both as canvassers and as donors, giving as much as two hundred dollars to South Church during one drive.[21]

By September of 1961, then, the Hills' rather tumultuous lives appeared to have calmed. As Betty Hill wrote later in her life, somewhat nostalgically, "For a while, I thought miracles had ended."[22] She and Barney had settled down together. He had his post office job; she her social work. They had found a congregation they enjoyed and a minister they admired. And then, on Friday, September 15, 1961, Barney requested a few days off. He had impulsively decided to take Betty on a trip. After all, they had never had a real honeymoon. When he returned home early Saturday, the two talked and decided to leave the next day for a drive to Niagara Falls and then to Montreal, where Betty had never been. They didn't have much money available—it was Saturday and the banks were closed; Betty later guessed they had less than seventy dollars in their pockets—but if they avoided expensive restaurants and hotels, they could stretch their cash before they had to come home.[23] They left Sunday morning.

CHAPTER 4

THINGS SEEN IN THE SKY

In 1966, the journalist John Fuller published *The Interrupted Journey: Two Lost Hours Aboard a Flying Saucer,* about the Hills' experience on their 1961 trip to Montreal. The book remains the most frequently referenced source for the bizarre events that were the journey's climax. However, readers who rely too much on Fuller will miss important facts about the case. Several primary sources describing the journey were produced between 1961 and the publication of Fuller's book. Only a few days after their return the Hills reported their sighting to an Air Force officer, who filed an official report of his interview with them. It describes their encounter with the UFO but gives scant attention to the trip surrounding it. Several days later, Betty Hill wrote a letter to a UFO organization describing the event: this account includes details not in the Air Force report. In October 1961, the Hills told the story again to the young, energetic Walter Webb, a lecturer at the Hayden Planetarium in Boston and a National Investigations Committee on Aerial Phenomena (NICAP) investigator. He interviewed the pair and produced a short report. In November 1961 Betty wrote a description of several nightmares she had endured in the few weeks after their encounter, dreams revolving around abduction by small, strange creatures, and in November 1963 the two shared the story with the Two-State UFO Study Group at a meeting in Quincy, Massachusetts. An account of that meeting survives.

In August 1965, Webb produced a second, much longer account of the Hills' case. Finally, in October of that year the *Boston Traveller*, a local newspaper, began a series of articles on the case by reporter John Luttrell. The first was titled "UFO Chiller – Did THEY Seize Couple?" Luttrell had secured recordings of the Two-State UFO Study Group meeting and other sources on the case and had published the story against the Hills' wishes. With that, the Hills' story was in the public arena, and Fuller soon heard of it and began work on his book.[1]

The most extensive primary sources for the Hills' experience are transcripts of two sets of interviews. The psychiatrist Benjamin Simon conducted the first set. Over several weeks in the spring of 1964 Simon interviewed Betty and Barney separately. While one lingered in his waiting room, he placed the other under hypnosis in a private session. In this way Simon interrogated each about the events of their trip to Montreal, from their departure through the strange encounter they had reported to their dazed return home. Simon recorded these interviews, and John Fuller had transcripts made of the recordings. A copy of those transcripts, annotated by Betty Hill and her niece Kathleen Marden, rests in the Dimond Library at the University of New Hampshire.

Two years later, Fuller interviewed Simon, Webb, and both Hills in preparation for his book. Like Simon, he recorded the conversations and had a transcript made; copies are in Fuller's papers at Boston University. *The Interrupted Journey* reproduces material from both of these transcripts, though Fuller occasionally altered them in sometimes critical ways, whether by intention or error. Fuller's text should not, then, be relied upon.

Webb wrote his second report after Simon's interviews became public. In that report, he explained that he distinguished between the Hills' "first encounter" and their "second encounter." The first encounter comprised the story the Hills told him that he recounted in his initial fall 1961 report. It was the story that Betty recounted in her letters and that both Hills told to the Air Force officer. In it, the Hills see a strange craft in the sky and flee after being overcome with terror. But under hypnosis, the Hills recalled much more. They said that the craft's occupants captured them and subjected them to a series of medical tests. This story, recalled years after the "first encounter," inspired Webb to interview the Hills again. He called the events the Hills now remembered the "second encounter" and believed that its recall required him to write a new report.

—

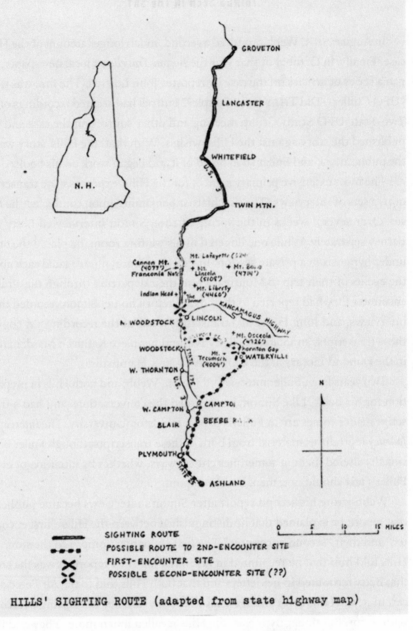

GROVETON

LANCASTER

WHITEFIELD

N.H.

TWIN MTN.

Cannon Mt. (4077')
Franconia Notch

Mt. Lafayette (5249')
Mt. Lincoln (5108')
Mt. Liberty (4460')

Mt. Beach (4719')

Indian Head

KANCAMAGUS HIGHWAY

N. WOODSTOCK   LINCOLN

Mt. Osceola (4326')
Thornton Gap
WATERVILLE

WOODSTOCK

Mt. Tecumseh (4004')

W. THORNTON

W. CAMPTON   CAMPTON

BLAIR   BEEBE R.

PLYMOUTH

ASHLAND

N

0   5   10   15 MILES

—————— SIGHTING ROUTE
• • • • POSSIBLE ROUTE TO 2ND-ENCOUNTER SITE
✕ FIRST-ENCOUNTER SITE
✗ POSSIBLE SECOND-ENCOUNTER SITE (??)

HILLS' SIGHTING ROUTE (adapted from state highway map)

Map of the Hills' route through New Hampshire the night of September 19–20, 1961, printed in the UFO investigator Walter Webb's second report on the Hill's experience, completed in 1965, four years after their sighting of a strange light in the sky and one year after their hypnosis and recovered memories of also being abducted.
From Walter Webb, "A Dramatic UFO Encounter in the White Mountains, New Hampshire, Sept. 19–20, 1961," Box 5, Folder 14, BBHP, University of New Hampshire. Used with permission.

This second report, the Hills' interviews with John Fuller, and all the Hills' later accounts of the case reflect their memories gathered under hypnosis.

The Hills thus told story after story about their encounter, and, naturally, it grew in the telling. But all stories, retellings included, are marked by context. The Hills found that theirs came to mean different things to them as their lives continued and as they lived through the turbulent years of the 1960s. Their beliefs about the world around them changed, and their story changed with those beliefs. Of course they told it again and again. They had to.

A Trip to Montreal

The earliest accounts of their journey — Betty's letter, the first reports of Webb and the Air Force — include virtually nothing about the bulk of the Hills' trip to Montreal. Perhaps it seemed irrelevant. It is true that quite apart from the bizarre experience that was its climax, in their later interviews the Hills described the trip as disappointing. Barney told John Fuller that he had a curious sense of disquiet before leaving; he remembered an "ominous feeling that I should carry something as a device for protection." He packed a pistol in the car's trunk. On the way west to Niagara Falls his mood lifted, and Barney sang as he and his wife traversed New York. They stopped at an ancient fossil bed, chipped away a memento, and placed it on the dashboard as a souvenir. Looking at it left Barney with something of a wistful feeling.[2] And then, after a day or two of winding their way through upstate New York, they crossed the Canadian border, stopped for the night, and approached Montreal the morning of Tuesday, September 19.

Under hypnosis both Hills told Simon that Montreal wore them out, though for different reasons. Betty felt stymied by the language, remembering that a waitress was "sure I was French, but I'm not." Barney seemed more on edge, though his wife did not seem to recognize it. He said he was distraught by the crowds and chaos of the city. "I do not particularly like the thought of staying there," he told Simon while under hypnosis. His tension seemed magnified by his language; while his wife used the past tense with Simon, Barney kept slipping into the present: "It's a big city. There's much confusion." He described bafflement at the French street signs and admitted that he bought two dollars of gas at a fuel station so as to have a pretext for asking directions — a story that signals the desire of a Black man to indicate that he was a legitimate customer.[3]

His wife seemed not cognizant of Barney's stress. Alarmed by reports of an oncoming storm, the Hills decided in the afternoon of the nineteenth to head home. Again, though, Barney felt threatened even after they crossed the border and stopped for a late dinner in Colebrook, New Hampshire. He recalled a young man outside a restaurant whom he identified as a potential threat and a waitress who seemed unfriendly. Back in the car, he remembered breathing deeply and thinking, "I should get ahold of myself, and not think that everyone is hostile." While her husband stewed, Betty's only memory was of the food not being very good. They left Colebrook a few minutes after ten o'clock.[4]

They drove for perhaps an hour, perhaps two.[5] And then they saw a light in the sky.

Across all the accounts the Hills gave at different times and in different places, the first time either of the Hills recalled mentioning their experience to anybody was after they awoke the next day. While under hypnosis in early 1964, Betty told Benjamin Simon that she and Barney invited Dot and Henry, a couple who rented the apartment in their house, to share a breakfast after the Hills awoke late in the day on September 20. The two had suggested Betty and Barney take their new handheld video camera to Montreal, but Barney declined. Betty recalled her husband making a somewhat dry crack. "If he had the movie camera, maybe he could have taken some pictures," Barney joked. The two asked what he meant, and Betty said, "He saw a flying saucer and doesn't want to admit it. And if he had pictures, he'd have proof of it." Neither Barney nor his wife mentioned this interaction to Simon or John Fuller again, but the bare bones of the story are there, laced with two facts that might have made this story significant to Betty. The first: Dot was interested. As Betty recalled, she believed in "these strange flying objects." The second: Betty marked even this early memory with anxiety. "Barney and I kept saying we weren't going to talk about it, that we were going to forget it," she said. "But I couldn't."[6]

After the meal, late in the afternoon, Betty called her sister Janet Miller, who lived with her family in Kingston, New Hampshire, twenty miles south. Again, anxiety. As Janet's daughter Kathy remembered, Betty reported that she "was starting to feel an uneasiness" about the night before. Later, under hypnosis, Betty recalled telling Janet that she and Barney had seen a light in the sky, moving as no normal light should. She told Janet that the object seemed to have fins. She also told her sister about some strange spots that had appeared on the Hills' Chevrolet and was intrigued when Janet advised her to hold a compass to them. The needle began spinning madly. Even more, the Hills' clothes were damaged: Barney's shoes scuffed and Betty's dress torn.[7] As Betty worried to her sister, Janet told Betty that a family friend, called "Buz" in the record, was in her home. Buz, who according to Betty was a police officer, told Janet that "if anybody reported a strange object in the sky, they were to report it to Pease Air Force Base."[8] Betty chewed this over, talked to her husband, and then did it.

UFOs as Science

The military's provenance over strange lights in the sky was not an inevitability. Neither was the determination that they were a scientific problem. Many veterans of World War II remembered the phenomenon American pilots called "foo fighters," glowing lights that pursued, paced, and danced around their planes in the night skies over the European theater. One man described them as "red balls off his wing tips" and said they chased him as he accelerated to 360 miles an hour. At the time some speculated they were some sort of German psychological weapon. Others thought they might be hallucinations, or "gremlins," supernatural creatures like faeries or demons that harried and harassed humanity. The options for interpreting such weirdness seemed wide open.[9]

Then, beginning in the summer of 1947, an eruption of reports of strange objects and lights in the sky emerged from the American press. There had been isolated such incidents before—even early that year—but by mid-summer the story began to gather momentum, each attracting more interest in the wake of the last. On June 24, Kenneth Arnold, a respected Boise businessman and licensed pilot, landed his private plane in Yakima, Washington, and reported that he had seen nine strange shiny discs arranged in loose formation near Mount Rainier, hurtling through the air like "a saucer skipping over water." He estimated they were moving at some 1,700 miles an hour. Arnold's story was irresistible, and headline writers seized upon his description to coin the term "flying saucer." In July there were a wave of sightings around the Pacific Northwest and Missouri. Six months later, in January 1948, Captain Thomas Mantell of the Kentucky Air National Guard died pursuing a cone-shaped object reportedly 250 to 300 feet in diameter and moving south past Louisville. As it rose into the atmosphere Mantell eagerly followed, only to lose oxygen and plummet to his death. Then, in July 1948, Clarence Chiles and John Whitted, the pilots of an Eastern Air Lines flight traveling from Houston to Atlanta, were startled to see a light above Montgomery, Alabama, at 2:45 in the morning. As the object hurtled past their plane, the shocked pilots noticed a pointed nose, what appeared to be two rows of windows, and a plume of orange exhaust. Upon passing the Eastern DC-3, the object pivoted upward into a cloud bank and simply vanished.[10]

These stories and a dozen more reported during the same months seized the attention of the American government for several reasons. Edward Ruppelt, an Air Force officer who would soon be assigned to investigate saucer reports, said later that Chiles and Whitted's story "shook [the military] worse than the Mantell incident. This was the first time two reliable sources had been really close enough to anything resembling a UFO to get a good look."[11]

Ruppelt's analysis of the case points to two concerns that consumed the military in the early years of the Cold War. The first was the question of security. Ever since World War I, the federal government had been turning to trained experts in economics and social sciences to guide policymaking. Franklin Roosevelt had taken the practice to new heights, consulting with experts in the natural sciences on weapons development even before World War II began. But even so, the Manhattan Project was an unprecedented collaboration between American scientists and the federal government, mounted for fear that foreign scientists would create a working nuclear weapon first. That fear persisted after the war. In the age of nuclear weapons, security was a scientific issue. If the United States was to remain free, the country that had successfully developed the atomic bomb would also need to stay a step ahead of Soviet scientists.[12]

Over the 1940s and 1950s, in starts and stops the federal government transformed the hasty and jerry-rigged Manhattan Project into an establishment of sorts, an increasingly complex set of relationships between the federal government, on the one hand, and scientific institutions like research laboratories, industrial contractors, and universities, on the other. A participant, the physicist Alvin Weinberg, dubbed this web of funding and contracts "Big Science." The adjective might simply refer to finances. In 1940 the U.S. government spent $97 million on scientific and social scientific research; by 1953, it was allocating $2.1 billion. But even if science was big, it was never unified. Some of the more influential figures in American science at the time, such as the engineer Vannevar Bush, who had served Franklin Roosevelt in several posts that made him, essentially, Roosevelt's chief science advisor, were suspicious of federal oversight. In *Science — The Endless Frontier,* his famous manifesto calling for continued government funding for scientific research after the end of the war, Bush argued that a federal agency overseeing science should be granted great amounts of funding but largely direct its own affairs, as scientists required independence to work properly. Eventually Congress did allocate incredible funding to scientific research, but contrary to Bush's wishes the vast majority of this money ended up flowing through the tight control of the military.[13]

But such efforts did not necessarily endow Americans with confidence in the scientific establishment. As early as 1947 Americans were seeing media coverage of Soviet spies caught while attempting to pilfer American nuclear secrets. In 1943, the federal government identified the engineer Arthur Adams as a spy who had passed nuclear information to the Soviet Union. Adams fled to Russia in 1946, narrowly evading arrest, and the press began to publish fearful stories about him the next year. In 1948, the former Communist Party member Whittaker Chambers accused the high-ranking State Department official Alger Hiss of being a spy, and the resulting Congressional hearings and eventual criminal trials dominated the news media for the next two years, until Hiss was sent to prison for perjury. By 1950, a steady drumbeat of names was appearing in the press. Klaus Fuchs, Julius and Ethel Rosenberg, Harry Gold, Irving Lerner — all were Soviet agents who had stolen or tried to steal American nuclear secrets. Some were themselves scientists. It seemed only logical to fear the potential of Soviet technology.[14]

At apparently reliable reports of strange lights in the sky, then, it was no surprise that the military was "shook." Though Americans today instinctively link unidentified flying objects to extraterrestrial technology, that was not true for those who lived through those intense months in the late 1940s. For a couple of years, Scandinavian nations had been reporting strange "ghost rockets," objects or lights in the sky that seemed to behave like the infamous German V-1 missiles that bombarded the Allies during World War II. Though little physical evidence was found, President Harry Truman received a memorandum warning that these lights might well be a "deliberate demonstration for political effect." The Soviet Union could be seeking "intimidation" of European nations. In a poll taken in August of 1947, the Gallup organization reported that while 90 percent of Americans had heard of "flying saucers," most people did not believe they were extraterrestrial craft. Rather, most pointed to misidentifications or had no answer. But many worried that they were secret weapons, perhaps developed by the United States or, more worryingly, the Russians.[15] Kenneth Arnold himself believed the latter. In spring 1948 he published an article describing his sighting and recounting counsel he had received from "a former Army Air Force pilot." The man told Arnold that what he had seen was "some type of jet- or rocket-propelled ship that is in the process of being tested by our government, or it could even be by some foreign government." Arnold closed the piece by calling for "an investigation by the Army and the FBI."[16]

He got what he wanted. Military reports began trickling up from local bases by July 1947. On the Fourth of July, an Air Force spokesman dismissed the Arnold event and stated that the sightings had "not produced enough fact to warrant further investigation." But by the end of the year the Air Force had received 156 reports and was quietly referring them to the Technical Intelligence Division of the Air Materiel Command (AMC)—the branch of the Air Force responsible for research and development—at Wright Field outside Dayton, Ohio. In September, Lieutenant General Nathan Twining, head of the AMC, signed a report to the commanding general of the Air Force that said "the phenomenon reported is something real and not visionary or fictitious." He took quite seriously the possibility of advanced technology. Twining's report noted these things might be of "domestic origin," or it might be that "some foreign nation has a form of propulsion . . . outside our domestic knowledge." On January 22, 1948, the Air Force launched Project Sign. Its purpose was to determine whether these objects were a threat to national security. But the project's report, issued the next year, largely punted. "No definite and conclusive evidence is yet available that would prove or disprove the existence of these unidentified objects," the report began. But its authors were reasonably convinced that the things were not Soviet weaponry. "An objective evaluation of the ability of the Soviets to produce technical developments so far in advance of the rest of the world results in the conclusion that the possibility is extremely remote," they claimed. Nonetheless, Project Sign recommended that study of these things not be abandoned. "Such sightings are inevitable," noted the report. And 20 percent of the sightings the project had evaluated remained unexplained.[17]

The end of Project Sign marked a turning point. The Air Force had been primarily interested in whether or not these craft were weapons, and they did not seem to be. For the most part, the Sign report ascribed such sightings to mistaken identifications of natural phenomena. But they remained, in the Air Force's estimation, a national security threat. Their concern now pivoted to the second reason why Ruppelt thought the Chiles-Whitted sighting was so important: the two men were, as he had put it, "reliable sources." How could such steady men see something the Air Force was persuading itself did not really exist?

UFOs as Pseudoscience

James Bryant Conant was worried. The chemist and Harvard president had played a major role in the government's sponsorship of scientific research during the war. He helped shepherd the Manhattan Project to a successful conclusion. But rather than rest on his laurels, when the war ended Conant launched a campaign for better public education about science. In his estimation, Americans did not understand what science was or how it was supposed to work as well as they should, and that could prove dangerous. If national security depended upon maintaining American scientific and technological dominance, how could citizens in a democracy make intelligent choices if they did not understand what maintaining that dominance would require? As Conant put it, once the bomb dropped, "The scientist was no longer thought of as a man in an ivory tower, gradually unraveling the secrets of nature for his own spiritual satisfaction, but as a miracle-worker."[18]

At least since Vannevar Bush argued for the possibility in *Science — The Endless Frontier* American scientists had been worrying that the public's ignorance about their work might pose a security threat of its own. Bush himself observed that "while there must be increased emphasis on science in the future training of officers for both the Army and Navy, such men cannot be expected to be specialists in scientific research."[19] This was why Bush believed that if a national agency for science were to be created (as it was in 1950, as the National Science Foundation) it should be self-governing, insulated from pressures from politicians who did not understand the work. But others were not so sanguine. In 1957, an editorial in the flagship journal *Science* made almost precisely the same point that Conant had. "To the consumer of scientific knowledge, that is to say, to the man who rubs the lamp and commands the jinni, the achievements of science are nothing more nor less than feats of magic," the author wrote. He suggested one might as well rename the National Science Foundation the "National Magic Foundation."[20] William Laurence, *New York Times* science columnist, thrust such worries into the public view, warning repeatedly in his column what he had told an audience of teachers in May 1950: they needed to better teach science because an "accurate and objective dissemination of science news would play a major role in preserving our democratic society."[21]

Almost as soon as the war ended, Conant began to devote resources, time, and energy into revising science education in America. Harvard issued widely adopted curricula, and Conant himself compiled a textbook. And after the Soviet Union launched its satellite Sputnik in October 1957, the federal government embraced both his fears and his aims. A month after Sputnik launched, a University of Colorado physicist offered the American scientific community faint praise: "If you consider science as an instrument of the cold war, then maybe we are lagging a bit—but if you are talking about science itself, America is doing all right." But his article as a whole endorsed the more dire predictions of the famous Edward Teller, who had worked on the Manhattan Project and who believed the Soviet Union was outpacing the United States. "They will advance so fast in science and leave us so far behind that their way of doing things will be the way," Teller glumly predicted. Congress responded in the same way as Conant had: in 1958, the National Defense Education Act plowed millions of dollars into science education in American universities and secondary schools.[22]

Conant and other scientists tried to reorient popular understanding of science away from the once popular notion of the "scientific method." They feared too many Americans believed science was simple and foolproof, and thus were dangerously gullible. Instead, people should respect how complex and often tentative science was. This would both gain prestige for scientists and lower expectations about what science might accomplish. As Bush put it in a 1946 speech, "I am certainly not one of those who speak of the scientific method as a firm and clearly defined concept and who regard it as a mystical panacea immediately applicable to any trouble and immediately productive of a complete cure."[23] Bush was pointing at a major problem many scientists were beginning to fear: what they would start in the next decade to call "pseudoscience," a word that warned of dire threats that would prey on Americans' gullibility and challenge democracy itself.

And here we return to the problem of Chiles and Whitted, apparently reliable sources. Several students of science in the Cold War have invoked Thomas Gieryn's notion of "boundary-work" to describe disputes over what was "genuine" science and what was "pseudoscience." For Gieryn, scientists (like, for instance, Bush or Conant) govern the boundaries of legitimate science in social and cultural ways because there is no normative definition of what "science" is. Instead, "science" is something identified through consensus and institutional weight. Daniel Thurs and Ronald Numbers have argued that during the Cold War, the institutionalization of Big Science in the interest of national security created "an enhanced sense that there was a scientific orthodoxy" whose boundaries were governed by the academy, military, and industry. Michael Gordin has pointed out that the idea of pseudoscience is less useful as a way to identify a body of ideas or a method than it is as a way to mark where the boundaries of "science" as a professional discipline are at any given moment. Surveys of magazines and books show the use of the term "pseudoscience" skyrocketing in the years after World War II.[24]

The Russian-born psychiatrist Immanuel Velikovsky illustrated the problem. In 1950, Velikovsky published a book titled *Worlds in Collision* with Macmillan. Even before it was published the book was infamous. Velikovsky thought that the planet Venus originated as a comet-like object from the planet Jupiter. Around 1400 BCE, en route to its present orbit, Venus had a near miss with Earth and disrupted the orbit of Mars. These brushes wreaked havoc on Earth. Velikovsky argued that many stories from ancient civilizations — the

—

biblical flood narrative, for instance, or the vanishing of Atlantis — were really describing those disasters.[25]

Horrifyingly to people like Conant, Velikovsky called himself a scientist. So did his defenders. The journalist and Velikovsky defender Eric Larrabee declared, in a letter to *Scientific American,* "Respect for the scientific method does not require blanket acceptance of all the current orthodoxies."[26] Velikovsky himself insisted that he followed what he believed the scientific method to be: methodical, rigorous analysis of data. As he put it, he would "investigate one planet, the one under our feet, in order to learn its past; and then by the deductive method [seek] to apply the results to the other members of the solar system."[27]

In a pungent retort, the science writer Martin Gardner reeled off a dozen of reasons why this was "pseudo-science." Velikovsky treated the Bible and carbon dating as equal sources of information, for instance. His math was occasionally wrong. But Gardner also touched on a reason for using the term far more useful to people like James Conant. Velikovsky, along with other "cranks," he said, worked "in total isolation from his fellow scientists." Science, for Gardner, was not simply about particular methods but about legitimate auspices. Pseudoscience, on the other hand, was isolated and therefore dangerous. "A renaissance of German quasi-science paralleled the rise of Hitler," Gardner said. "If the German people had been better trained to distinguish good from bad science, would they have swallowed so easily the insane racial theories of the Nazi anthropologists?"[28]

Gardner's equivocation of Nazism and pseudoscience with credulity was telling. It explains in part why he, and many trained scientists, labeled Velikovsky religious rather than scientific. Gardner was careful. He expressed appreciation for "informed and enlightened Christianity," like the Hills' Unitarianism. By that Gardner meant religion that positioned itself in consonance with the consensus of contemporary science. "A theist can regard evolution as God's means of creation," Gardner explained. This was respectable religion. But what he believed to be bad religion, what he called "religious superstition" was something else entirely, and he thought Velikovsky was afflicted with a desire to defend a "cruder Biblicism" that would ultimately lead to national degradation. The Harvard astronomer Cecelia Payne-Gaposchkin, among others, agreed. After reading Velikovsky's book, she shrugged. "There always have been, and always will be, well-meaning people who defend the literal interpretation of Scripture," she said. Like Gardner, she was careful: it was not just Velikovsky's Judaism in question — it was that he interpreted the Bible in ways contrary to scientific consensus. As these arguments show, "science" and "religion" are not discreet objects with impermeable boundaries; rather they are constructed categories people use to claim different sorts of authority.[29]

Because of fears like Gardner's, the bulk of those affiliated with the national scientific establishment began to doubt that UFOs were scientific. Thus, the Air Force began to worry about those who claimed to have seen one. Almost invariably these witnesses sought the approval of scientists and claimed to be scientific; their use of those words themselves can be read as a bid for legitimacy. But to the Air Force such assertions often seemed naïve, isolated, and not in step with "science" as a national project. And hence, a threat.

This was why the Air Force began to seek ways to draw the boundaries of science in such a way as to exclude UFO believers. For a time, the Air Force tried to convert UFO sightings into empirical data. After Project Sign issued its final report, the Air Force's investigation was reorganized as Project Grudge, which became Project Blue Book in 1952. In 1955, the Air Force issued its crowning accomplishment in the investigation: Project Blue Book's *Special Report Number 14*. Long in the making, the report was Blue Book's attempt to rationalize what it called "the subjectivity of the data." Attempting to winnow out as much of the human factor as possible, the study took the data of some four thousand UFO sightings and submitted them to a panel of experts who managed "the reduction of data contained in sighting reports into a form suitable for transfer to IBM punched cards." In other words, Blue Book sought to transform the impressionistic experiences of UFO witnesses into a form interpretable by an IBM computer by turning each report into a punch card. This was, the report noted drily, "extremely difficult and time consuming." *Special Report Number 14* concluded that "scientifically evaluated and arranged, the data as a whole did not show any marked patterns or trends." The social sciences worked hard to embrace this sort of mathematical rationality in the early Cold War. It was a way to mark their work as truly scientific, and in the case of *Special Report Number 14,* to draw UFOs out of that circle.[30]

The Air Force's investigations also invoked the social sciences, particularly psychology. This grew increasingly common. In 1949, Project Grudge reported that only 23 percent of its cases remained unexplained. But Grudge also warned that the problem was not one of the natural sciences. Rather, the problem lay inside the witnesses themselves; it was psychological, not empirical. Grudge's report listed some possible reasons one might report a UFO: "misinterpretation of various conventional objects. A mild form of mass hysteria and war nerves. Individuals who fabricate such reports to perpetrate a hoax or to seek publicity. [Or] psychopathological persons."[31] Only months after Grudge issued its report, the Air Force collaborated with Sidney Shallett of the *Saturday Evening Post* for an article that some officials devoutly hoped would put the issue to rest. Shallett's thesis: "It is a jittery age we live in . . . it is small wonder that harassed humans, already suffering from atomic psychosis, have started seeing saucers and Martians." To soothe nerves, Shallett recounted the stories of a number of Air Force generals, steady men who were not falling for the jitters. General Hoyt Vandenberg, the Air Force chief of staff, told Shallett he once saw "a strange, disk-shaped lighted object" buzz past his aircraft window. But "instead of getting rattled, he just experimented a bit by moving his head at different angles, and sure enough. . . . It was merely a reflection of a ground light on his window."[32]

Despite such efforts, in 1952 the nation saw another rash of UFO sightings, and the phenomenon drew more attention than it had since 1947. For two weeks in July, strange objects appeared on radar and in the skies over Washington, D.C. President Truman himself asked for Project Blue Book's assessment, and the Central Intelligence Agency formed a special study group to address the problem. A September 1952 CIA memo expressed worry that Project Blue Book was working on a piecemeal basis and called for a more thorough solution. In January 1953, the CIA designated the Caltech physicist Howard Robertson to chair an investigative panel. Robertson and CIA officials recruited a half dozen other scientists, most of whom had little familiarity with the phenomenon, and in January 1953, the panel gathered in CIA offices. They spent four days reviewing two dozen cases gathered by the Air Force and deliberating. After the last day, the panel signed off on a report declaring that the major threat of unidentified flying objects was not the objects themselves but their potential to cultivate "a morbid national psychology in which skillful hostile propaganda could induce hysterical behavior and harmful distrust of duly constituted authority."

The report observed that most Americans were undereducated in science, and it urged a "program of education" that would "reduce the gullibility of the public." The panelists indicated that they "felt strongly that psychologists familiar with mass psychology should advise on the nature and extent of the program."[33]

And so, finally, the Air Force drew the veil of secrecy over UFO investigations, in one more effort to prevent the sightings and a credulous public's misinterpretation of them to damage national security. It is hard to overestimate the impact of the Robertson Panel on the federal government's assessment of the situation. Project Blue Book would continue in the Air Force for another sixteen years, before shuttering in 1969, but its staff was reduced. The Air Force issued Regulation 200–2, which required Air Force officials to discuss UFO investigations only after cases had been resolved, so as to avoid stoking further public fear. "It is permissible to inform news media representatives on UFOB's when the object is positively identified as a familiar object," the regulation stated. "For those objects which are not explainable, only the fact that ATIC [Air Technical Intelligence Command] will analyze the data is worthy of release."[34] If UFOs could not be rendered into the language of physics or metallurgy, they would be turned into psychological phenomena, and the solution became preventing the gullibility of the American people from misinterpreting the scientific questions involved.

Secrecy was in vogue. As the Cold War heated up in the later 1940s, the Atomic Energy Commission, which governed American nuclear science, felt pressure from Congress and the military to treat secrecy as a matter of national security. This "secrecy regime," as Alex Wallerstein has called it, was neither monolithic nor totalizing; rather, it was an organizational and rhetorical effort to equate secrecy and security and to enforce secrecy through regulation and cultural pressures. Though they might harm the United States in different ways, the American military worried about making both nuclear secrets and UFO data public.[35] That is what the Hills encountered when they called the Pease Air Force Base.

CHAPTER 5

NICAP AND ITS CRITICS

Barney Hill did not want Betty to call Pease Air Force Base. At least initially, he seemed to hope that if the Hills simply did not discuss their encounter, it would vanish from their lives. He had many other concerns, after all.

But Betty believed it was important to call, and her reasons why showed that she held a distinctly different understanding of how science in the United States should be organized than did the federal government, one that she shared with many other Unitarians and other liberal activists in America. Her call to the Air Force set off a chain of events that drew the Hills into tension not simply with the government, but with their long-held liberal beliefs about their ability as citizens to affect American policy. But they also connected her with a host of other people who shared her concerns and began to show both Betty and Barney other ways of imagining how American society might be organized.

The Henderson Report

Betty Hill called Pease Air Force Base on September 21, 1961. She remembered the first man she spoke to seemed initially confused, but he took her story in stride, gathered her information, and spoke briefly with Barney. Later Major

---

Paul Henderson, who had been assigned to collect the Hills' information for Project Blue Book, called the Hills back. He spoke to the Hills several times over the next day and quickly produced the earliest written account of the couple's experience. He recorded that the Hills told him that between midnight and 1:00 a.m. on September 20, on New Hampshire Route 3 near Lincoln and the towering stone hills of Franconia Notch, they observed through the windshield of their car a strange object in the sky: "They noticed it because of its shape and the intensity of its lighting as compared to the stars in the sky. The weather and sky was [sic] clear at the time."[1]

Henderson noted that the Hills described the object as "a continuous band of lights — cigar shaped at all times, despite changes of direction." It was large; "when first observed it appeared to be about the size of a nickel at arms length. Later when it seemed to be only a few hundred feet above the automobile it would be about the size of a dinner plate held at arms length." At one point, "wings seemed to appear from the main body. Described as V shaped with red lights on tips. Later wings seemed to extend further." The thing produced no noticeable exhaust nor sound. If it was a machine, it was unlike any they were familiar with.

When the Hills saw the object, Henderson wrote, it was at about a 45-degree elevation above their car, "traveling north very fast"; that is, toward the Hills, who were moving south on Route 3. "Shortly thereafter it stopped and hovered in the air," and the Hills stopped the car and used binoculars to observe the object. Its wings emerged at that point, and the object began to descend toward them. "At this point," Henderson wrote, "they decided to get out of the area, and fast. Mr. Hill was driving and Mrs. Hill watched the object by sticking her head out the window." It left them with a last oddity: "While the object was above them after it had swooped down, they heard a series of short loud 'buzzes' which they described as sounding like someone had dropped a tuning fork. They report that they could feel these buzzing sounds in their auto." About thirty miles south, near Ashland, New Hampshire, they again heard the buzz.[2]

For Henderson, the interview satisfied the concerns of the Air Force after the Robertson Panel. By this point the Air Force was primarily interested in mobilizing the language and authority of science to defuse reports of unidentified flying objects before they turned into rumors that could stoke civic worry and unrest. His report accordingly revealed a suspicion of the Hills themselves — not of their motives, necessarily, but of their competence as average, scientifically unqualified citizens. Henderson noted that neither Barney nor Betty "possess any technical or scientific training" and thus their usefulness as witnesses was low. He filled out the forms and filed his report away. Its cover sheet asked the official to mark off whether the object was a "balloon" or an "aircraft" or an "atmospheric disturbance."[3]

Soon after Henderson filed his report, Project Blue Book filed its own record card on the Hill case. The Blue Book report connected the Hill sighting to an anomalous radar hit: at 2:14 a.m. on September 20, Pease Air Force Base radar operators saw an "unidentified A/C [aircraft] come on PAR [precision approach radar] 4 miles out," though no one saw anything with a naked eye.[4] Such ghost radar hits were hardly uncommon. The report stated, "Actual source of light viewed is not known but it has all the characteristics of an advertising searchlight." Under "conclusions," a Blue Book staffer had marked a box for "other" and written in "optical conditions." Someone crossed that out and wrote in "inversion," which itself was crossed out and notated with "insufficient data." Nonetheless, the card concluded that "there is not evidence which would indicate that the objects in these sightings were due to other than natural causes."[5] So far as the Air Force was concerned, the Hill event could be filed away.

But the Hills themselves were not done with the Air Force.

For Barney Hill the problem had less to do with whether the sighting was mechanical or atmospheric than with his stark awareness that his credibility sat under Henderson's eye. He initially told Betty he didn't want to speak to Henderson at all. Under hypnosis Betty claimed that when she suggested calling the Air Force, Barney kept telling her, "Forget about it! Forget about it!" When the major insisted that he wanted to speak to both Hills and Barney finally took the phone, Barney was relieved to find Henderson friendly and interested. He told John Fuller he remembered "at no time did I get the impression that [Henderson was] impatient." When he took the phone, Barney indicated apologetically that Betty took the experience more seriously than he did. As Henderson observed, "He says that on looking back he feels that the whole thing is incredible and he feels somewhat foolish — he just cannot believe that such a thing could or did happen. He says, on the other hand, that they both saw what they reported and this fact gives it some degree of reality."[6] For Henderson, this would have spoken to the Air Force's belief that the real worry was inside the heads of people like the Hills, not in the sky.

Barney's anxiety and embarrassment marked a deep dissonance. On the one hand, he did not want to call the military; he felt foolish doing so. Perhaps behind his strain and behind his relief that Henderson was willing to take him seriously lurked deeper issues; the memory of a Black father hoping to advance in the world; the experience of a Black man hungry for esteem from institutions like the Air Force and careful to manage the image of his own respectability, because as his teachers to his parents to Robert Bagnall had taught him, his goal should be integration and uplift.

But Betty felt differently, and her motivations speak to an alternative way of imagining what science should be in postwar America. When she spoke about Henderson later her confidence in her own perceptions was only bolstered by disappointment with the Air Force. Like Barney, she, a divorced woman who struggled for an education and a respectable career, wanted to be taken seriously. But whereas Barney felt validated by Henderson's interest, Betty remembered being less enamored with the officer. She remembered that she "was disappointed because I thought someone from Pease would come out." She told Fuller in their interviews that she thought the Air Force was not treating their experiences with the gravity they deserved; Henderson to her seemed "in a rush," like he "wanted to get this over with," sentiments that echoed earlier complaints under hypnosis to Simon that Henderson's "whole attitude was one of a skeptic." She even accused him of speaking "very sarcastically."[7]

Betty's description of Henderson emphasized those things her husband only alluded to: frustration about not being taken seriously, annoyance with a government that did not listen to its citizens, and a worry that scientific discussion in the United States was too separated from the liberal democratic processes of debate and discussion and public involvement that both Betty and Barney had grown up valuing. Disgruntlement with the Henderson call set the Hills on the path toward relinquishing their faith in the American state.

Radiation

After returning to their home in the early morning of September 20, both Hills had taken long baths because they felt "unclean." As Betty told John Fuller, she and Barney didn't know "what dangers we'd been exposed to . . . cosmic rays, radioactivity, these things." The strange markings on the car seemed ominous.[8] Under hypnosis Betty said she had called Pease Air Force Base "for our own protection . . . I don't know anything about radioactivity."[9]

The words Betty used pointed to two things in particular she might have been thinking about. The first was the space race. A few months before the Hills' encounter, the Soviet Union became the first nation to put a human being, Yuri Gagarin, beyond the earth's atmosphere. The National Aeronautics and Space Administration (NASA) followed, launching Alan Shepherd into outer space a few weeks later. That accomplishment gave President John F. Kennedy the confidence to declare that the United States would put a man on the moon by the end of the decade. Americans in the 1960s were living with the frenzied rush of the space race on a day-to-day basis, in part because the federal government wanted to turn astronauts like Shepherd into living demonstrations of American scientific superiority. But, frighteningly, as astronauts ventured forth to colonize the "final frontier," they were beset with dangers like "cosmic rays," which received extensive coverage in the press. In 1961 the phrase was in the headline of a heavily reprinted Associated Press news story that described astronauts' vulnerability to "potentially heavy doses of cosmic rays," enough to "sicken or perhaps kill a man." So far, the story reported soberly, Alan Shepherd seemed all right. But the story nonetheless underscored the potential dangers of outer space.[10]

Similarly, the Hills were far from the only Americans to worry about radiation closer to home. Throughout the 1950s, the US government had been testing, off and on, a series of thermonuclear weapons far larger than those used in 1945. The fallout, literal and figurative, from these tests was massive. The Japanese protested when testing in the Pacific Ocean began sickening citizens in Tokyo. In 1957 Japanese audiences flocked to the movie *Godzilla*, a thinly veiled allegory in which nuclear testing woke a monster from the oceans. By 1959 Americans were worried too. An article in the *Saturday Evening Post* asked, "How concerned, then, should we be about the amounts of radioactivity in the air we breathe, the water we drink, the food we eat?" Titled "Fallout: The Silent Killer," the article warned of the horrendously long half-life of the radioactive element strontium-90 and quoted the Nobel laureate chemist Linus Pauling speculating that for every nuclear bomb tested, fifteen thousand children would be born with birth defects. Later that year strontium-90 began showing up in milk, and terrified parents started calling Congress.[11]

In 1960, John F. Kennedy was elected to the presidency in part on a promise to renew negotiations for a test ban with the Soviet Union. Three months before the Hills' experience, he met personally with Soviet leader Nikita Khrushchev to push for such a ban but failed to gain an agreement. On September 15, the same day Barney decided to ask for time off to take his wife to Montreal, Kennedy announced that the US would renew testing in an attempt to gain leverage ahead of future negotiations. Many Americans were unhappy.[12] Five years later Betty would still be writing to scientists describing her recurrent bouts with pneumonia, worrying over how sick her dog Delsey was, and asking about "certain radiation dangers connected with UFO sightings."[13]

Watching other Americans deal with concerns about radiation would probably have encouraged the Hills to call the Air Force and voice their concerns. By 1961, nuclear energy had been, for a decade and a half, the ground upon which many Americans had been fighting for what historian Kelly Moore has called a "liberal" approach to scientific policy. These Americans, scientists among them, believed that Big Science was itself a threat to democracy because, swathed in expertise and secrecy, it constrained the ability of American citizens to make educated choices about their government. They encouraged public education, organization, discussion, and transparency about national science research.

In the immediate aftermath of World War II, a number of scientists organized and pushed for international regulation and global transparency about the atomic bomb, a position that Vannevar Bush and James Conant had supported as the war wound to a close. Their encounter with the security regime that controlled American nuclear power was painful; many of these scientists were accused of disloyalty or sympathy to communism and called to testify before Congress. Some, like J. Robert Oppenheimer, who was instrumental in the development of the bomb, lost security clearances and jobs. But their ideas persisted. By the late 1950s, a new movement led by the biologist Barry Commoner was pressing the federal government to be more forthcoming with nuclear information, particularly given the hazards of nuclear testing. Commoner and several other scientists, including Linus Pauling, collaborated on a petition urging greater dissemination of nuclear information. It declared, "As scientists we have knowledge of the dangers involved [in nuclear testing] and therefore a special responsibility to make those dangers known." In September 1961 Commoner's group was nationally known for its campaign to make data about atomic weapons, radiation, and nuclear testing more widely available.[14]

Betty and Barney Hill's Unitarianism stoked their sympathy for a liberal conception of science. Unitarian faith in democracy was rooted in a belief that all human beings were essentially rational, and that they were therefore capable of understanding and debating scientific policy (or any other sort of politics) if they were given the chance. Jack Mendelsohn, a popular Unitarian writer, called for "snatching reason from the hands of textbook scientists, logicians, and technologists." He pointed at the danger of something he called "scientism," warning that when scientists grew too enamored of their own esoteric knowledge and technological expertise, a democratic society would suffer. What was needed, then, was a robust conversation about science and scientific policy that kept all American citizens fully informed.[15] Unitarians thought they were uniquely equipped to foster that dialogue. "When a man goes to a Unitarian church he does not leave the scientific method behind him," declared Stephen Fritchman, editor of the Unitarian *Christian Register.*[16] Even in Portsmouth John Papandrew, the Hills' minister, preached that science and democracy should stand as models for each other. "As in science, a single fact in isolation is an illusion, so too the liberal ministry and church must think of itself in terms of process," he said, "where the different elements may come together in challenge providing creatively for growth."[17]

Some Unitarians were involved in the debates over atomic weapons and nuclear power as well. The Unitarian Charles Coughlen, a scientist at the federal atomic facility at Oak Ridge, expressed optimism about the prospects of Unitarianism at Oak Ridge because many scientists there were affiliated with the scientists' movement pushing for a loosening of the secrecy around nuclear weapons. Given all this, Coughlen said he believed these "scientists are Unitarians at heart, and would welcome the opportunity to affiliate with a Unitarian church if they knew it existed and understood what it stands for."[18]

More famous than Coughlen was Harlow Shapley, an astronomer who directed the Harvard College Observatory until his retirement in 1952. Shapley was a Unitarian fellow traveler; though not formally a member of the faith he often published in Unitarian periodicals and attended Unitarian gatherings. Repeatedly in the 1940s, Shapley endorsed proposals for national scientific organizations that emphasized transparency, responsibility of scientists to elected politicians, and national and international exchange of ideas. He once sneeringly alluded to the "kept men of the industrial friends of science," warning that Big Science was hardly as apolitical as it imagined itself to be.[19] As the war drew to an end, Shapley called for citizens to commit themselves to embrace the responsibilities for understanding and participating in debate over control of American science. At a lecture in New York City in June 1944, he said, "The post-war responsibilities and opportunities for professional men and women, scientists and artists of all kinds include a social duty at a high level." But two years later at MIT he worried that this had not happened. He called for a national "exchange of ideas and understanding which would control the real enemies of the world—poverty, disease, ignorance. . . . Science had [*sic*] won the peace but is being excluded from the enforcement of the peace."[20]

In May 1957 Shapley reviewed James Conant's book *Science and Common Sense* for the Unitarian *Christian Register* and praised the Harvard president for reaching out to nonscientists who were dangerously underinformed. As Shapley put it, the nation needed "skillful bodies of unspecialized thinkers and specialized technicians for the single-minded purpose of evaluating progress and proposing steps that will smooth the advance" of science, which would in turn foster a democratic and progressive culture.[21] It would be science, in Shapley's formulation, that brought true democracy to the entire human race: not through ensuring American supremacy or promoting economic growth, but by expanding knowledge and communication to as many people as possible. Education, he said, was "indispensable if democracy is to prevail and the dignity of the individual is to be respected."[22]

Betty Hill had read Harlow Shapley and had once heard him speak.[23] His feelings were hers. She was annoyed with the Air Force precisely because it seemed to her as though it was not taking her seriously as an informed and competent citizen. She told John Fuller that the sighting had made her believe that the human race was "on the threshold of science now," and that she believed that of course the Air Force would want to know about what she had seen. But it did not.[24]

Two days after her call with Henderson, restless for validation, she went to the Portsmouth Public Library and checked out the 1955 book *The Flying Saucer Conspiracy,* by a former Marine pilot named Donald Keyhoe.

That visit to the library would eventually introduce Betty to figures who offered her and Barney help as they sought to shake off the disappointing (for Betty) encounter with Henderson. In Donald Keyhoe and the astronomer Walter Webb, she and Barney would find allies who believed that the problem of flying saucers required greater public discussion and respect for witness testimony, like that of the Hills. But both Webb and to a lesser extent Keyhoe were also invested in maintaining the respect of conventional authorities in government and science. In their advocacy for a more liberal approach to the scientific conversation about UFOs, then, they worried about elevating the influence of a third figure, George Adamski. Adamski claimed to have interacted with creatures from flying saucers who had given him a message for Earth. To Keyhoe and Webb, he was a pseudoscientist.

Donald Keyhoe

As they recounted to the police officer, the two farmhands were driving down an empty state highway near Levelland, Texas, just west of Lubbock on the night of November 2, 1957. It was closing in on 11:00 p.m. when a burning light erupted from the sky above and to the right. "It looked like a torpedo, about 200 feet long," Pedro Saucedo said to Officer A. J. Fowler, when he called him from the nearest pay phone down the road. As the thing passed overhead, the engine and lights of Saucedo's truck abruptly went out. Fowler later told the Air Force he assumed Saucedo and his friend were drunk and hung up. But an hour later there was another call. A motorist reported that he had seen a gigantic glowing object sitting in the middle of a highway north of Levelland. As he approached, his engine sputtered and died. When he got out of his car the object rose into the sky, and his engine woke. Then Fowler received another call, and another, and another. Glowing objects sitting on the road; flaming torpedoes overhead; engines dying and roaring back to life for miles around Levelland.[25]

In all, poor Officer Fowler spoke to fifteen people about strange lights before he crawled into bed at 5:30 the morning of the third. But he was not able to sleep much. Reporters began to call. The next day, November 4, the Soviet Union launched the first spacecraft to carry an intended passenger (a dog named Laika), and despite — or perhaps because of — the news that the United States was losing ground in the space race, by the next morning, newspapers, local and national, had picked up on the stories out of Levelland. Fowler found himself answering his home phone again and again and again. Reporters linked these civilian sightings to anomalies picked up on radar and reported by pilots in the area, and they worried that these sightings were simply another indication of failures in American science.[26]

Many members of the scientific establishment concluded that the problem was scientific illiteracy. Harvard astronomer Donald Menzel insisted that the sightings were simply natural phenomena. "The evidence leads to an over-whelming probability," he said, that "the fiery unknown at Levelland was ball lightning." More important, Menzel thought that believing UFOs were something other than readily identifiable atmospheric phenomena was a threat to the nation. It called into question Americans' trust in their leaders and could lead to dire consequences. "An open mind does not mean credulity," Menzel warned. "The security of the country" depended upon accuracy in "these identifications." Project Blue Book sent an investigator to Levelland, and his report mirrored Menzel's assessment.[27]

Another organization, though, felt differently. The National Investigations Committee for Aerial Phenomena also studied the case. It was the country's largest and most vocal group arguing that UFOs were a consistent category of phenomenon and deserved investigation. Such effort would, in NICAP's estimation, build a robust democracy through involving the American people in conversations about scientific questions. Its assessment of Levelland was not merely that Menzel and Project Blue Book were wrong; NICAP argued that the deeper problem was the state's lack of faith in public deliberation about science.

"The American people should know the facts," the leaders of NICAP declared. They called for respect for the testimony of "CAA tower operators, airline pilots, and members of the armed forces whose duties require cool-headed thinking and an absolute lack of hysteria." Democracy, NICAP's leadership declared, relied on "public enlightenment."[28]

Donald Keyhoe was NICAP's most prominent public advocate. Born in 1897, he trained as a pilot at the US Naval Academy during World War I. With other Americans he devoured stories of the aces of the European theater, solo pilots like the German Manfred von Richthofen—the famous Red Baron—or the American Eddie Rickenbacker. In small biplanes or triplanes these men spied over enemy lines, harried opposing armies, and, most dramatically, sparred with each other in the skies, dogfighting with guns mounted on their planes or even with handheld pistols. The newspapers romanticized them, painting the sky as the last vestiges of the Old West and the aces as its cowboys. Keyhoe longed to join their ranks, but he graduated from the academy in 1919, the year after the war ended. After being injured in a plane crash in Guam, he ended up in a clerk's job with the federal government. But in 1927 the secretary of commerce, searching for an employee with relevant experience, assigned Keyhoe to escort Charles Lindbergh on a publicity tour celebrating Lindbergh's successful solo flight across the Atlantic Ocean.

Keyhoe turned the experience into a memoir called *Flying with Lindbergh*. The book paints Lindbergh as a romantic hero, the last of the aces. Keyhoe writes about chastising a "matronly woman" who complained to Lindbergh's handlers that the man meant too much to the world to be allowed in a dangerous airplane again. "You oughtn't begrudge him that little freedom," Keyhoe lectured her. He had been writing since his long months in bed recovering from the crash in Guam, churning out pulpy supernatural thrillers for cheap magazines. But after the success of *Flying with Lindbergh,* he realized his audiences loved flight for the same reasons he did. So he invented two superheroes, the World War I pilots Philip Strange (the "Brain Devil") and Richard Knight, who in a series of stories used their psychic powers, their planes, and their wits to defend freedom against the great war machine of the German state, knights of the sky. In December 1941 he volunteered to return to the military and served until the end of World War II. Donald Keyhoe clearly still longed to be an ace.[29]

—

In 1949, Keyhoe — again working as a government bureaucrat and freelance writer — received a telegram from an editor at *True* magazine. It read, "HAVE BEEN INVESTIGATING FLYING SAUCER MYSTERY. . . . LOOKS LIKE TERRIFIC STORY. CAN YOU TAKE OVER WASHINGTON END?"[30] The age had found its man. The UFO chase was another battlefield where a hero might confront a war machine of a different kind.

Keyhoe began calling his friends in government and in quick succession — in January and March 1950 — published an article in *True* and a book, both with the same name: *The Flying Saucers Are Real*. As he sought to breach the Air Force's secrets, the responses all mirrored the one he had with his old friend Orville Splitt, a Pentagon publicist:

"Look, Don," said Splitt, "why do you want to fool with that saucer business? There's nothing to it."
"That's a big change from what the Air Force was saying; in 1947," I told him.
He shrugged that off. "The Air Force has spent two years checking into it. Everybody from Symington down will tell you the saucers are bunk."[31]

In his article and book, Keyhoe developed a philosophy not so different from that of his earlier fiction. In fact, the book reads like fiction. It is written from a first-person perspective, with Keyhoe himself as one of the heroes investigating the shadowy nooks of the Air Force, the reader encountering evidence not of mathematics or probabilities but of individual testimony, and Keyhoe as a reliable witness. At the end of his book, Keyhoe named his conclusions. "1. The earth has been under periodic observation from another planet, or other planets, for at least two centuries. 2. . . . Air Force officials still fear a panic when the truth is officially revealed."[32]

With the final point, Keyhoe zeroed in on the problem. The question was whether the American government trusted the population sufficiently to include them in the serious conversation about flying saucers that Keyhoe was convinced must be happening. He rejected the Air Force's denials that there was very little actually to investigate; instead, he grew convinced that, as with nuclear weapons, the government was relying on secrecy. He saw distinct connections between the two presumed conspiracies. "The Army, Navy and Air Force are working secretly on all sorts of things," one of Keyhoe's informers told him. The old pilot wondered if "some solar-planet race discovered the dangers long ago. . . . There may be some other atomic weapon we don't suspect, even worse than the A-bomb, one that could destroy the earth." He connected the dots. Alien spacecraft had increased their observation of Earth upon detecting American nuclear weapons. This was why the government was seeking to cover up the reality of flying saucers. Military officials feared the panic among the American populace that they assumed would come at the twin revelations of their own culpability and the existence of such superior technology.[33]

In 1956 Keyhoe helped found NICAP. It was never large; Keyhoe at times funded the group out of his book earnings. But Keyhoe learned from Velikovsky's mistakes. He read the psychiatrist, and observed that while "this particular account [that is, Velikovsky's theory] is not accepted" widely among academics, it was important to gain the legitimacy of respectable figures in order to make a strong case. So Keyhoe recruited academics, retired military figures, and prominent journalists to NICAP's board. Its newsletter, the *UFO Investigator,* positioned its work as the logical result of a desire to defend American democracy. As one board member wrote, "There seems to be a great fear among the powers that be that the American people will panic if told the truth. How little they know and understand their countrymen." Another stated, "I have been raised on a rugged philosophy which holds that the American people can be trusted with the truth."[34]

It is no wonder, then, that Betty Hill—a believer in public debate herself— found an ally in Donald Keyhoe when she picked his book up at the Portsmouth Public Library the day after she called Pease Air Force Base. *The Flying Saucer Conspiracy* was Keyhoe's third book about UFOs, and in its opening lines Keyhoe declared, "For several years the censorship of flying-saucer reports has been increasingly tightened." The gauntlet was thrown. Then Betty learned of mysterious satellites, silenced Army officers, and the possibility that alien civilizations were using the moon as a base for the investigation of Earth. Finally, at the culmination of the book, Keyhoe proudly presented to the Air Force "a witness list, naming hundreds of pilots, radar experts, and other reliable witnesses." A friend admiringly observed, "There's no arguing with all that evidence."[35]

And yet of course there was. Keyhoe's appeal got him nowhere.

But Betty devoured the book. Three days later, she sent Keyhoe a letter telling him that his book has "been of great help to us and a reassurance that we are not the only ones to have undergone an interesting and informative experience." It is the first known written account either of the Hills would create describing their experience. She reported substantially the same story they had given Henderson: a "bright object in the sky which seemed to be moving rapidly," reversing its directions and "flying in a very erratic pattern." But perhaps bolstered by Keyhoe's evident trust in his witnesses as opposed to the doubt she perceived from Henderson, Betty continued beyond what Henderson had written down. Just south of Franconia Notch, in the vicinity of Indian Head, a small resort near a large rock formation, the couple stopped their car and got out to "observe it more closely with our binoculars." Barney walked forward, "standing in the road, watching closely," while the object's wings extended. He noticed a row of windows, extending from wing to wing. And then.

> He was able to see inside this object, but not too closely. He did see several figures scurrying about as though they were making some hurried type of preparation. One figure was observing us from the windows. From the distance this was seen, the figures appeared to be about the size of a pencil (held at arm's length), and seemed to be dressed in some type of shiny black uniform.[36]

Betty's experience with Henderson had left her with the first hints of suspicion that some authorities would not listen to her. But Keyhoe seemed to her an adequate replacement. She addressed him by his title — "Major Keyhoe," the same rank as Henderson — and told him, "We did not report my husband's observation of the interior as it seems too fantastic to be true." Then she requested better information on "flying saucers" than she had gotten from the Air Force. "We should," she wrote, "have more recent information regarding development in the past six years," since Keyhoe's book had been published. Contrary to Henderson's reports, which presented Barney as alternately sheepish and hearty, Betty sketched Barney as driven to anxiety at his inability to understand what had happened to him. According to Betty, Barney remembered his own fear, but not what had caused it. After sighting the creatures, Betty wrote, Barney leapt back into the car "in a hysterical condition, laughing and repeating that they were going to capture us." She pled with Keyhoe for help, writing, "We are searching for any clue that might be helpful to my husband in recalling whatever it was that caused him to panic."[37]

When Betty's letter reached NICAP headquarters in Washington, D.C., it was sent right back to New England, to a young man named Walter Webb, a NICAP volunteer. Webb was only five years out of college. He had settled in Boston after graduating from Ohio's Mount Union College and worked briefly at the Smithsonian Astrophysical Observatory near Harvard before joining the city's Hayden Planetarium, where he worked as a lecturer. He had been interested in UFOs for more than ten years. Late at night on August 3, 1951, while still in college and working as a counselor at Camp Big Silver, a summer camp in southern Michigan, Webb had been caught off guard. While showing two boys constellations through his telescope he saw a strange yellowish light drifting westward along an undulating path. He could not identify it. The sight stuck with him enough that when he arrived in Boston he sought out J. Allen Hynek.[38]

Hynek was an astronomer. He had also come to Boston from Ohio, leaving a professorship at the Ohio State University to work on a project tracking satellites at the Smithsonian Observatory. He had already spent years consulting for Projects Grudge and Blue Book and was probably the most prominent scientific investigator of UFOs in the United States in the fall of 1961. Short and dapper, the son of Czech immigrants, he was fond of pipes and maintained a van Dyke beard and a mustache throughout his life. All he needed was a bow tie to take on the spitting image of a nineteenth-century German philosopher. Struck by his look, Steven Spielberg cast Hynek in a small role in his 1977 film *Close Encounters of the Third Kind*. Spielberg owed Hynek a favor because Hynek had devised the famous classification that gave Spielberg the title. Later, Hynek would muse about which category the Hills fell into. The story they had told Paul Henderson was a close encounter of the first kind: a sighting of a craft at a short enough distance to note detail. Observing the strange marks on the car would upgrade the encounter to one of the second kind, in which a craft left a physical mark on the world. In her letter to Keyhoe, though, Betty described what Hynek would call an encounter of the third kind: one in which a human being saw a creature.[39]

When Webb met Hynek the scientist's satellite work was eating up most of his days. His consulting work was part time. But he was growing steadily more interested in UFOs. He had agreed to consult with the Air Force because UFOs were, he had thought, "a golden opportunity to demonstrate to the public how the scientific method works." He was frustrated with the Robertson Panel's conclusions and, most of all, the government's "lackadaisical and irresponsible" disinterest in open conversation on the topic. But at the same time, he could not bring himself to buy Keyhoe's theories of extraterrestrial visitors and moon bases. "I cannot presume to describe," he said, "what UFOs are because I don't know, but I can establish beyond a reasonable doubt that they are not all misperceptions or hoaxes."[40]

Unlike many other scientists, Hynek was torn between not only two camps of opinion on what UFOs might be but also two ways of imagining science, one which viewed it entirely as the province of trained experts and another that worried that erecting such walls would lead to antidemocratic stultification. He did not want to leap to the same conclusions that Keyhoe had, but he did think public conversation about UFOs important. And he was not only torn; he knew the dangerous position he occupied. Upon learning Webb was interested in the phenomenon, Hynek invited the young man to his home for dinner and showed him his files. But — sensitive to the concerns for respectability that plagued the Hills — he cautioned Webb not to talk too excitedly about these lights in the sky or to write publicly about them. After all, he warned, they did not want to be perceived as "flying saucer enthusiasts."[41]

George Adamski

The enthusiast par excellence in 1961 was George Adamski, who, to Walter Webb, might have seemed like Betty and Barney Hill gone wrong. By the time of the Hills' experience he was a silvery-haired widower in his sixties. He owned a small ranch, Palomar Gardens, in the mountains north of San Diego and led a relatively quiet life — until he began giving lectures around Southern California about UFOs in the late 1940s. He turned out to have an offbeat charisma, a knack for publicity, and a vigorous rhetorical style. In 1953 he published a book, *Flying Saucers Have Landed*. He had been involved in California occultism for much of his life, and his book blended his esoteric fascinations with a brash intellectual populism. It was full of broadsides against the federal government, a "City of Experts" that churned out "tons of paper" in support of "Dogmas."[42]

Adamski also claimed to be scientific. He presented photographs of flying saucers he said he had taken at his ranch and called them "scientific" evidence. He claimed to have "proof," in the form of measurable astronomical data, of extraterrestrial "activity on or near the moon." He embraced his ostracism from expertise as a sign of clearheadedness. "I have no college degrees," Adamski observed proudly. "The layman is left to use his own perspicacity." He and a few friends spent much of the early 1950s in the dry deserts and high plateaus of Southern California around Mount Palomar, looking for UFOs to photograph. On November 20, 1952, they were eating lunch off the shoulder of a road near Desert Center, California, when a large, silver-colored, cigar-shaped craft drifted overhead, followed by a small flying saucer. Adamski followed. The saucer settled itself in the shadows of a nearby mountain, and a small, humanlike figure disembarked and greeted Adamski.[43]

Adamski learned that the creature came from Venus and was named Orthon. He believed Orthon was male and said he stood about five foot six and had blonde hair and tanned skin. Over a series of meetings, Orthon warned Adamski of nuclear destruction and taught him that all intelligent species were destined for eternal progress if they embraced harmony with the universe. Adamski spread these messages in a chain of books and a seemingly never-ending lecture tour until his death at age seventy-four in 1965.

To many other people in the UFO community, Adamski was not scientific at all. Like Velikovsky, he was branded a pseudoscientist, somebody motivated by religion rather than by genuine science and who had not, as Unitarians had, found a way to reconcile the two. Edward Ruppelt, a former director of Project Blue Book, described people like Adamski with religious terms. "They seek salvation from outer space, on the forlorn premise that flying saucer men, by their very existence, are wiser and more advanced than we," Ruppelt wrote, and he linked such "religious" implications to a lack of scientific expertise. "To such people a searchlight on a cloud or a bright star is an interplanetary spaceship."[44]

NICAP agreed. Frequently in its journal, the *UFO Investigator*, editorialists used the word "religion" to distance their own scientific work from the claims of Adamski. NICAP writers made a distinction between "UFO observers," who were "honest, intelligent, and reliable," and "UFO believers" — the "cultists, the mystically inclined, pseudo-religious unscientific people." Keyhoe and his organization were careful to specify that they did not mean to be perceived as "anti-religious," rather, they were simply opposed to religion that seemed to them unscientific. In 1960, Keyhoe dismissed a volunteer for claiming "mystic-religious links with UFOs." Unfortunately for Keyhoe, one of Adamski's great fans was the treasurer-administrator of NICAP, Rose Campbell, who had often worked for free to keep the organization running. But in fall 1958 she threatened to resign if NICAP did not devote at least half its resources to investigating accounts like Adamski's. Keyhoe held the line. He had already asked Adamski to submit for evaluation the negatives of his photographs of Orthon's saucer and a chunk of metal Adamski had been saying came from the Venusian's ship. Adamski declined, and Keyhoe lost his patience. "The sensational nature of his claims has kept many people from seriously considering the verified UFO evidence," Keyhoe wrote, and so Rose Campbell walked away.[45]

The ways some UFO advocates, for example those at NICAP, carefully used the language surrounding religion illustrate, more than anything, the desire to be taken seriously by members of the American scientific and cultural establishment. But Adamski did not mind the label "religion," for the same reasons the Hills believed that their Unitarianism made them confident in science. Like the Hills, he believed that science and religion might go hand in hand. A being he called "the Master" once told him that he would "tell you [Adamski] of the physical life on other worlds, as well as spiritual or religious truths, although we do not make that kind of division. There is but one life." He discussed the Bible at length, claimed that "religion is the science of life to be lived as taught by Nature," and pronounced himself a friend to all religions, because "all faiths are founded upon a pearl of wisdom." Adamski was deeply influenced by the fin-de-siècle Theosophical movement, which taught that human beings were destined for spiritual progress under the guidance of enlightened beings; his work translated Theosophical philosophy into the language of science, technology, and alien spacecraft.[46]

George Adamski, Walter Webb, and the Hills alike believed that science was a pathway to human dignity and evolution. The difference for the moment was the authorities that each looked to and the cultural boundaries they drew around science in the context of American life in the early 1960s. The words "science" and "religion" did not have intrinsic meaning but were tools for claiming or denying respectability.

When Webb received Betty's letter, forwarded from NICAP headquarters along with a suggestion that he drive up to New Hampshire and interview the Hills, he was a bit hesitant. As he wrote in the report submitted to NICAP on October 26, five days after his interview with the Hills, he was committed to a "proper skepticism whenever occupants or creatures are involved in UFO cases simply because of the sensational nature of the claim."[47] Like his mentor Hynek, Webb was struggling to stay within the boundaries of science as he understood it.

On October 21, Webb drove up to Portsmouth from Boston and sat with the Hills for six hours. He eventually turned the interview into a six-page report he submitted to NICAP. This was Webb's first report, describing what he called "the first encounter."[48] He was relieved when, upon meeting the Hills, he "was impressed with their intelligence, apparent honesty, and obvious desire to get at the facts and to underplay the more sensationalistic aspects of the sighting." Indeed, Webb seemed to very much like the Hills, so much so that he downplayed a few details that seemed to him tending toward credulity. He later confessed that he found Betty's confusion about the strange, seemingly magnetic spots on her car uncompelling and was pleased to learn that Barney harbored doubts about them as well. To Webb, the spots were the sort of thing foul weather might create, and he knew that a large piece of metal might confuse a compass. He did not mention the spots in his report.[49]

Nonetheless, the story the Hills told Webb was more dramatic and fuller than the ones that either Henderson or Keyhoe received. They told him it was just after midnight and they were near Groveton, New Hampshire, when they saw a "bright moving star-like object" below the twin lights of the moon and Jupiter. It seemed to Betty like a falling star except that it fell upward, moving west of the moon and then heading north. Betty said it was brighter than Jupiter. She was excited and curious, and for the next forty minutes or so she persuaded Barney to stop "several times" for a better look. Barney remained skeptical, saying that it was probably an airliner. As the object veered around and approached them, they saw that the band of light across the object's middle did not extend all the way, creating a twinkling effect as it rotated.

Just south of Franconia Notch, a stony, narrow passageway through the White Mountains, and near the resort called Indian Head, Barney pulled over. He left the car on and stepped out. Betty handed him binoculars, and he watched as the object began to descend toward the car. He "could see eight to eleven separate figures watching him at the windows." Barney told Webb there was a "burst of activity." All the figures but one rushed toward the walls and appeared to take hold of various tools, and the wings on either side of the object, dotted with red lights, began to descend. As far as Barney remembered, it was perhaps fifty to eighty feet in the air by this point. He remembered himself saying, "I don't believe it."[50]

Barney was seized with fear. The figures seemed human, "dressed in shiny black uniforms and black caps with peaks or bills." The uniforms seemed like glossy leather. And Barney, the World War II veteran, panicked. "The figures reminded the observer [Barney] of the cold precision of German officers," Webb wrote. "They moved smoothly and efficiently and showed no emotion except for one fellow operating a lever, who, Mr. Hill claims, looked over his shoulder and smiled." Barney called the single figure who did not move the "leader." This one "held a special attraction for the witness and frightened him terribly. The witness said he could almost feel this figure's intense concentration to do something, to carry out a plan. Mr. Hill believed he was going to be captured." Again, Webb quoted Barney directly: Barney used the phrase "like a bug in a net." Webb wrote that Barney, at this point, called the ship "something alien and unearthly containing beings of a superior type."

Barney leapt back into the car. Webb, like Betty, records him as "laughing in a hysterical manner," crying out, "They're going to capture us!" The Hills ripped down the road. After "five or six blocks," they heard the strange beeping sounds. About thirty-five miles farther down the road, they heard them again. Betty turned to her husband. "Do you believe in flying saucers?" she asked. "Don't be ridiculous," Barney replied. "That wasn't a flying saucer."

This final incongruous detail illustrates Barney's own boundary-making. What he had seen could not be a flying saucer, because flying saucers were the stuff of eccentrics and fools, of Adamski and his ilk. Just as Hynek warned Webb not to be perceived as a "flying saucer enthusiast," so was it important to Barney to maintain the boundaries around his reputation: to associate himself with

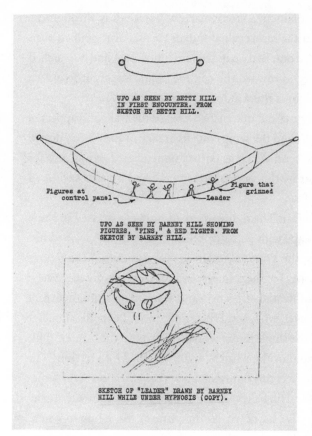

UFO AS SEEN BY BETTY HILL
IN FIRST ENCOUNTER. FROM
SKETCH BY BETTY HILL.

Figures at
control panel
Figure that
grinned
Leader

UFO AS SEEN BY BARNEY HILL SHOWING
FIGURES, "PINS," & RED LIGHTS. FROM
SKETCH BY BARNEY HILL.

SKETCH OF "LEADER" DRAWN BY BARNEY
HILL WHILE UNDER HYPNOSIS (COPY).

A series of sketches by the Hills of the craft and the beings inside it, produced shortly after the sighting, and later in 1964 while under treatment with the psychiatrist and hypnotist Benjamin Simon.
From "A Dramatic UFO Encounter in the White Mountains, New Hampshire, Sept. 19–20, 1961," Box 5, Folder 14, BBHP, University of New Hampshire. Used with permission.

"science" because science was respectable. Indeed, he remembered that when Betty's sister Janet had told them about her UFO sighting a few years earlier, he had sat quietly, scorning her in silence although he wanted to debunk her. He said later that he found the phrase "flying saucer . . . detestable." Because of that he had worried that Walter Webb, who used the phrase, was a "kook" until he met the young astronomer.[51]

Barney Hill knew very well he could not afford to be seen as irrational, nor was it his inclination. But he was sure he had seen something, and he trusted that his perceptions should be taken seriously. The tension would weigh on him for the rest of his life. It was evident in his reluctance to speak with Major Henderson and in his careful interactions with Walter Webb. Webb seemed to understand this. He reported that Barney assured him that he had been a "complete UFO skeptic before the event," and he praised Barney as a "careful, accurate, scientific person."[52] It was in the interests of both men to present their ideas and interpretations as something other than what Adamski was doing. To label their work "science" was to make it something respectable.

Validation

Robert Hohmann and C. D. Jackson were members of NICAP, and both worked at IBM, which in the early 1960s sat near the center of the military-industrial complex. For a time Jackson had worked at an IBM plant in Huntsville, Alabama, near the Redstone Arsenal, a major rocketry research facility. IBM's tabulating equipment not only enabled the production of Blue Book's *Special Report Number 14,* it also managed the US government's Social Security database. Its engineers had successfully programmed a computer to play checkers, and they were poised to run the American space flight effort. Hohmann was a technical writer and Jackson an electrical engineer, and both were eager to mobilize the scientific legitimacy of IBM to prove UFOs were alien craft. As they wrote to Donald Keyhoe, "We have attempted to pursue this subject objectively, in the hope of collecting sound, reliable, quantitative data."[53]

During the first week of October 1961, the two attended a professional conference in Washington, D.C., and had lunch with Donald Keyhoe. Over the table, Keyhoe showed them the Hills' letter; later he asked Webb to forward them a copy of his report. On November 3, Hohmann sent a letter to the Hills designed to awe them. "We are mature people associated with a major electronics and engineering corporation," Hohmann wrote. "Our discussion would be entirely objective." He and Jackson hoped the Hills could help them "verify the origins of these vehicles according to existing scientific theory maintained by Professor Hermann Oberth," a German rocket scientist who had worked at Redstone Arsenal. Hohmann also offered "assistance in answering your questions," gathering that the Hills had many of those.[54]

Hohmann struck every note the Hills, hungry for scientific validation, could have hoped for. He invoked his association with institutions that commanded the aura of science. Indeed, it was telling that the Hills seemed to believe that Hohmann and Jackson worked on behalf of the federal government. Betty later wrote that they were "scientists, working at top level government jobs." Barney said, employing a favored slur, "They were not kooks. They were businesslike, professional." Given the era, the Hills' mistake was perhaps forgivable — particularly because it confirmed their hopes. It also signaled that they believed the sort of conversation about science they had hoped for all along might now be coming to pass.[55]

Hohmann and Jackson arrived in Portsmouth around noon on November 25 and spent the rest of the day interviewing the Hills about their experience, point by point. To John Fuller, Barney said, "They pursued the subject purely scientifically, by giving us information about projects that scientists had been interested in." Sometimes this meant that the Hills had trouble following their train of thought. They asked if Barney or Betty "had ever come into contact with or worked with nitrates or fertilizer." The two could not think why, but after Jackson and Hohmann poked around their garden the Hills realized Betty had a bag of fertilizer in the trunk of the car. And then Barney remembered that he had grown up on a farm, around nitrate fertilizer, and that there were nitrates in the shotgun bullets he sometimes handled. Marveling, he said, "we would never have put any significance on it," when Jackson revealed that he believed exposure to nitrates might be a common link among various UFO sightings. As they departed, Jackson and Hohmann promised to be in touch, and later they forwarded the Hills material about Alpha Centauri, explaining that they believed the famous scientists Nikola Tesla and Guglielmo Marconi had tracked radio signals from the star system.[56]

The authority Jackson and Hohmann claimed meant a great deal to the couple. They offered both a language and a set of authorities that seemed to offer validation. That was why Betty and Barney began seriously considering hypnosis when one of their visitors — perhaps either Jackson or Hohmann, perhaps another friend named James MacDonald — suggested that they might want to look into it. They had been toying with the idea for several weeks, but a few years later both the Hills credited this meeting as the moment the idea seriously took root. Americans had heard a lot about hypnosis in the previous few years, and the Hills believed that now there were hypnotists who were, as Betty put it, "really professionally trained."[57] Respectable scientists, in fact.

—

CHAPTER 6

THE INTERPRETATION OF DREAMS

In 1949, Project Grudge suggested that the majority of UFO sightings were due to "a mild form of hysteria and war nerves" or the fantasies of "psychopathological persons."[1] The suggestion inaugurated a grand tradition of transforming UFOs into psychological phenomena, moving them from the sky into the minds of those who observed them. The authors of the Grudge report and many psychological professionals saw this as a way to delegitimate their physical reality. Many of the Hills' critics used psychology in this way. But for the Hills, and for many UFO believers who followed them, psychology could validate their experiences and demonstrate that they rested within the boundaries of science.

Since the interwar period, when Freudian psychoanalysis had become famous in the United States, the sciences of the mind had proven increasingly popular. As with other sciences, they benefitted from heavy state subsidies. During World War II the US military appointed committees to wage psychological warfare on Germany and Japan, and the state-funded Emergency Committee on Psychology worked hard to understand and promote the morale of American citizens. Impressed by these agencies, after the war Congress passed the 1946 Mental Health Act, allotting $7.5 million to bolster education and training in psychiatry and psychology, and in 1951 President Harry Truman created the Psychological Strategy Board, responsible for the "coordination and evaluation of the national psychological effort."[2] In the thirty years between 1940 and 1970, membership in the American Psychological Association surged from 2,739 to 30,839; membership in the American Psychiatric Association similarly shot from 2,423 to 18,407.[3]

As with the other sciences, experts in the field linked its proper maintenance to healthy democracy, and its proper maintenance to recognition of their own authority. Harvard psychologist Gordon Allport claimed that "national problems . . . are nothing but personal problems shared by all citizens." In 1943, Allport led the Society for the Psychological Study of Social Issues, a networking organization that bridged academia and government, in drafting a statement titled "Human Nature and Peace." It declared flatly, "War can be avoided. . . . The frustrations and conflicting interests which lie at the root of aggressive wars can be reduced and re-directed by social engineering."[4] Soon these promises seemed vindicated. Thurgood Marshall won the landmark Supreme Court case *Brown v. Kansas Board of Education* in 1954 with psychological arguments. "Separating children from others of similar age and qualifications solely because of their race generates a feeling of inferiority," Chief Justice Earl Warren wrote, in the court's order that school segregation was unconstitutional. "Whatever may have been the extent of psychological knowledge at the time of *Plessy v. Ferguson* [the 1896 case that upheld segregation], this finding is amply supported by modern authority."[5]

The Hills believed in psychology's power. Barney Hill echoed Earl Warren's arguments about the link between psychology and racism in speeches he gave against segregation, arguing that "we can see the psychological damage" of racism in "Negroes becoming discouraged early in life."[6] Betty Hill, trained as a social worker, had been introduced to the work of Sigmund Freud in college. By the end of World War II, Freud's methods of psychoanalysis, premised on the notion that painful memories manifested in psychological or even physical distress, had reached social work programs. Social workers in training were commonly instructed to be alert to the psychological needs of their clients and to be aware that their struggles might derive from forgotten trauma. As Betty later wrote in a letter, as "a professionally trained social worker" she was familiar with the theory of psychoanalysis.[7]

———

Showing their faith in the field, Betty and Barney agreed to receive couples counseling before their marriage. Betty had suggested counseling to Barney in the summer of 1956, when she first met Barney and his then-wife Ruby. She suggested it again when, after dating for several years, Barney proposed. They saw a therapist for several months, and Betty believed that the counseling had done them both good. "The lines of communication were always open," she said. Counseling had revealed to them that though their personalities were quite different, "we complemented each other." As historian Rebecca L. Davis has argued, marriage counseling gave many postwar couples, as it did the Hills, the assurance of expertise, the possibility that they could confront a confusing problem and — importantly — cooperate with a therapist to solve it. It was perhaps natural, then, that the Hills expected the same when they turned to psychology to help them puzzle out what they had seen in the sky.[8] In her letter to Donald Keyhoe, Betty wrote that the Hills were "considering the possibility of a competent psychiatrist" to learn more about the event.[9]

Unitarian Psychology

Jackson's and Hohmann's suggestion that the Hills try hypnosis came not a moment too soon. Betty was having nightmares. They began ten days after the sightings; disturbing and confusing dreams for five nights in a row. A co-worker at the state welfare department, Jane McLaughlin, told Betty the dreams must indicate some real trauma — a suggestion that reflected the influence of Sigmund Freud on American culture. After Hohmann and Jackson visited, Betty began writing down her dreams.

But the language the Hills used to describe their experience with psychiatrists as they sought to figure out what had happened to them reflected ideas about the discipline more prevalent among other Unitarians than among Freudian practitioners. At precisely the time the Hills were looking for a competent psychiatrist, an earnest Unitarian minister and PhD candidate named Carl Wennerstrom was completing his dissertation at the University of Chicago. He was interested mostly in the intersection between his faith and psychological practice, and he spent weeks in clinical work as a chaplain and counselor at hospitals and clinics. By his own account his work with "persons confronting deep suffering and pain, and often the prospect of an early death," convinced him that a deep paradox lay at the heart of Unitarianism in the United States. On the one hand, Unitarians professed allegiance to the expertise of psychologists and psychiatrists. But on the other, he observed, they shied away from the "mysteries" of the mind. They did not want those experts to tell them that patients' problems could be confusing or unfathomable. They wanted only challenges that could be understood and mastered. In a striking parable, Wennerstrom wrote in frustration that when Jesus was crucified the Unitarian was not there; "perhaps he was off to the Circuit Court, hoping against hope to get a reversal of the conviction." Or, "he might have been investigating the future support of Jesus's family." But regardless: "at the place of crucifixion, he was absent." The inevitable pain of the cross was intolerable. Unitarians searched instead for problems they could fix.[10]

Wennerstrom died abruptly in August 1963 at thirty-six. His advisors edited his nearly completed dissertation and published it to wide attention in the Unitarian press. Wennerstrom might have been surprised. He had believed many Unitarians would resist his ideas. He had interviewed a wide range of Unitarian ministers and reported consistent responses. One minister "of deserved distinction," confessed to Wennerstrom that he was "appalled upon confronting Freud's idea of the unconscious." He insisted, "I believe in Man. It is he alone who has the power to overcome the evils within him through the powers of reason and intellect." Wennerstrom recounted the conversation with mixed admiration, writing, "Here is wisdom, insight and above all courage. And yet I think there is also a clinging to naïve rationalism."[11]

The Unitarian press of the era illustrates Wennerstrom's conclusions. Unitarians consistently reported familiarity with psychological theories and a certain discomfort with the idea that human beings might be beyond their own comprehension at times, or that the mind might produce anxiety or neurosis that could not easily be cured. They insisted that the "unconscious" Freud posited could not overpower rationality. The Unitarian psychologist Rudolph Druikers was among the most vehement. "A new mysticism, clad in scientific language and using mechanistic formulations, degrades man by assuming the existence of a cesspool within each individual containing all the repressed urges and drives," he warned of Freud's theories. "Such premises would never permit man to gain full dignity, to become fully responsible for himself."[12]

This did not mean, though, that Unitarians rejected psychology and psychiatry. By the 1950s Unitarians were using such metrics to gauge the potential of ministers. Instead they insisted that proper psychology would allow people to understand themselves and solve their problems. Molly Harrower, a noted psychoanalyst, ran a ten-year study on the uses of various psychological tests to judge the sort of personalities that would be successful in the ministry and concluded that ministers with what she called an "above average" or "average personality endowment" would be able to resist "psychological weakness" and function well in the ministry, while those with a "below average" endowment would need counseling to get to the point where they could "protect themselves in times of stress." The popular Unitarian writer Jack Mendelsohn believed psychoanalytic techniques "are excitingly useful techniques for helping to clear away some of the debris of anxiety, guilt, and hatred which keep us from enlarging our precious margins of freedom." But he, like Druikers, warned of "a total psychological view of human behavior based on mechanistic principles." Mendelsohn advised his readers to measure their therapists' counsel against their own reason and rationality.[13]

That was how Betty Hill approached the problem of her dreams. They were not terrors to manage but puzzles she could solve with the assistance of a competent therapist. This confidence was evident when she turned her dream notes into a five-page document she titled "Dreams or Recall?" Probably in November 1961, assuming that her dreams must reflect a comprehensible single event, she wrote, "I will attempt to tell my dreams in chronological order, altho they were not dreamed in this way." What followed was a comprehensive narrative, far more logical than a dream.[14]

Betty's Dreams

Betty's document "Dreams or Recall?" seems to be the first written account of what Walter Webb would later call the Hills' "second encounter," in which Betty and Barney interacted with creatures from the craft they had seen. Betty uses the language of psychology throughout: altered states of consciousness, trauma, and forgetting. Her opening sentences distinguish between events the Hills had forgotten and "events of which we are consciously aware." She then describes a story she had not told Henderson, Keyhoe, or Webb. After seeing the light in the sky the Hills came upon "a huge object, glowing with a bright orange light, which appeared to be sitting on the ground." Barney swung the car off of Route 3. At that point came the series of beeps.[15]

Then, Betty begins describing events that the Hills could not consciously re-member. She associates that forgetfulness with trauma, saying that she was "ter-rified" and that she felt "at the bottom of a deep well . . . fighting to become conscious . . . I am dazed and have a far away feeling." Barney likewise "does not appear to be conscious of what is happening." There were eight to eleven figures standing in the road. Their car's motor died. The figures approached and re-moved them from their seats, and took them to the glowing object, a "disc, almost as wide as my house is long."[16]

Betty frames the events onboard the craft in a repeating pattern: a search for knowledge punctuated and thwarted by trauma. She was separated from Barney "and objected to this." In response the leader of the creatures, whom she identi-fied as male, showed "exasperation." The creatures told her they wished "to find out the basic differences between them and us" and promised she "would not experience any pain." Her dress was removed and her body minutely examined—strands of hair and fingernail clippings removed, mouth and ears peered into, skin poked and gently scraped. A small machine that "resembled the wires of an EEG" was touched to different parts of her body. She settled into complacency. And then a long needle—four to six inches—was, "with a sudden thrust," inserted into her navel, and "suddenly I was filled with great pain, twist-ing and moaning." The creatures were startled and the leader quickly relieved her of the pain by passing a hand before her eyes. She felt inordinately grateful to him. They told her it was a pregnancy test.[17]

This pattern was then repeated. After her examination the leader said he "regretted this fright" and offered to answer any questions Betty might have. She asked to take an object back with her, a book with "symbols written in long, narrow columns," as proof of her experience. He agreed. She asked where they were from. He then "pulled down" a star map from the wall and asked her if she knew where Earth was; she admitted that she didn't, and he said he could not tell her where they were from if she couldn't locate her own planet. At one point, creatures came into the room and examined Betty's teeth. The leader told her they were puzzled because they had found Barney's dentures. Betty explained dentures were something older human beings used, and the leader seemed puzzled. "What was old age," he asked her. Then other creatures came into the room with Barney, who was "still in a daze." They took the book from Betty, and the leader told her they had decided the Hills would forget the experience. She "became very angry" and said that she would "somehow, some way remember." He laughed and warned that if the Hills tried to remember the events "it would lead to confusion, doubt, disagreement . . . it could be very upsetting." He then walked them back to their car, and Betty picked up their dachshund Delsey, who had been cowering there the whole time.[18]

The language of memory and forgetting, of trauma and fascination, of sleepwalking and trance and unconsciousness showed Betty's translation of her dreams into the language of psychoanalysis — but of a very Unitarian kind, because it also shows her confidence that the events might be decoded in a quite literal way. From her very first letter to Donald Keyhoe she was sure her nightmares and her husband's anxiety pointed beyond themselves to some genuine memory of trauma and suffering. But that letter also indicated that Betty Hill thought that this encounter might be explained. Before he dismissed them from the spacecraft, after all, Betty tried to persuade the leader to agree to "a quiet meeting with scientists."[19] While a Freudian might have read Betty's dream for its symbolic nature, Betty instead read it as straightforward recall that had given her a mission and a purpose.

Barney's Anxiety

Barney likewise leaned on the language of psychology, but his traumas were earthly. In many ways, his experience with psychoanalysis was typical of a postwar American. "Anxiety" was a powerful term in the mid-twentieth century. While Freud had identified anxiety as the product of unconscious grappling with the libido, by the postwar period neo-Freudians such as Karen Horney,

Harry Stack Sullivan, Erich Fromm, and Alfred Adler were more influential in the United States. They emphasized that anxiety derived from outside pressures as much as internal tensions. Thus, many of the counselors Barney would consult explained that his anxiety, which seemed to his wife and friends to be spiking in the months after the encounter, was the product of his environment: his familial relationships, his job, and his identity as a Black man.[20]

His two sons lived with his ex-wife Ruby in Philadelphia. The divorce had been a hard one, and even a decade afterward when Barney spoke to John Fuller it nagged at him. "Divorces can't be a happy occasion, but this was a crime," he said. He missed his sons a great deal. Barney III and Darrel were then teenagers, and Barney felt as though Ruby offered "no encouragement for the boys to accept me as their father." He saw them once a week and more in the summers, but this grew harder when the post office transferred him from Philadelphia to Boston. He was anguished that the boys "seemed that they were indifferent" to him and responded to his letters only sporadically. Betty the social worker assured him most teenagers were lackadaisical about familial relationships. "They are like many children of that age," she told him, trying to persuade Barney "they knew [him] as the father and they would never forget."[21]

That helped, but by then Barney was driving sixty miles each way five days a week to his post office shifts in Boston. His blood pressure began steadily to rise. By early 1962, he was suffering ulcer pains, which would at one point require a week's hospitalization. More oddly, what Barney called "small warts" and "little pimples" started to grow on his "lower abdomen." He later told John Fuller that at the time he did not associate them with the encounter with the UFO — at this point the experience seemed to be little linked to his other anxieties — but he was sufficiently troubled about them to consult other doctors. Eventually a skin specialist in Portsmouth speculated they were teratomas, a relatively common and often benign tumor, and removed them. But it was yet another thing to worry about. By the spring of 1962, Barney Hill was drinking more than his doctors thought wise.[22]

Weekends, he and Betty would get in the car and drive back up to Franconia Notch.

Walter Webb had asked the couple if they could pinpoint the spot where they had first seen the light. On November 11, in between their visits from Webb and

Hohmann and Jackson, they returned to the area and looked around. Upon ascending a rise, they saw a large round orange object hovering on the horizon and after a burst of awe realized it was the moon. They told Hohmann and Jackson about the trip, and the two encouraged the Hills to make another visit, this time at the same time of day as the encounter. As the four of them tried to calculate what time that had been, Jackson and Hohmann noticed something odd. As Betty recounted it in a letter to Walter Webb written a few days later, after some thumbnail arithmetic the group realized that "it appears that this part of the trip took 3 ½ hours and is quite puzzling to us, as we believe we drove quite rapidly toward home." The drive from Franconia Notch to Portsmouth was slightly more than a hundred miles.[23]

The Hills began to worry their memories were incomplete, and they came to believe that returning to Franconia Notch might help restore them. Barney estimated they returned twenty or twenty-five times. Betty had vague memories about a diner they had seen on the route. Sometimes they would stop and get out of the car and stare up at the constellations, as Barney put it, looking "for anything we might see that we could possibly identify." They found little. On one trip they stopped at a lodge in Vermont (having gotten fairly lost) for dinner and asked other patrons about UFOs. "Their first reaction to our presence was one of overwhelming friendliness," Barney remembered. But after bringing up lights in the sky, "it was almost as if we had the plague." The strain followed them home. A letter arrived from Hohmann saying he was unable to find a psychiatrist who could help them. Tension was rising. Barney, worried about far more than the UFO, once grew "furious with Betty for driving me up into the mountains," where one night they got stuck on a snowy road, looking for the elusive moment their lives had changed.[24]

Exploring having failed, in March of 1962 Betty asked friends for the name of a competent psychiatrist and received a referral to Patrick Quirke, an MD who ran a practice in Georgetown, Massachusetts, a small town thirty miles south of the Hills' home. The Hills' interactions with Quirke illustrate the links they drew between expertise, authority, and their search for respectability; their belief that the boundaries of science as they understood it should include and legitimate them.

Betty wrote Quirke a letter requesting an appointment and enclosed a brief summary of Walter Webb's report. "Many puzzling aspects remain," she said,

---

"so it is believed that hypnotism could clarify these." The Hills very much wanted to signal seriousness, and so Betty pointed out, "We have been interviewed by Mr. Webb and by two electronic engineers, Mr. C.D. Jackson and Robert Hohman [*sic*]." Betty told Barney that "this is a place where many of the professional and wealthy people" went, and when they were there he was astonished when a woman in a floor-length mink coat swept through the waiting room.[25]

That the Hills seemed a bit starstruck indicates the profound trust they—like other Americans—invested in experts, and more, how much they perceived Quirke to be capable of ushering their experience into the borders of reputable science. Barney remembered Quirke "seemed to have a lot of knowledge of UFOs." The Hills took that as a comfort: they understood the doctor to be assuring them that he was not merely familiar with such events but also, as Betty put it, "a complete believer." Barney recalled him informing them that "we had nothing to be alarmed about . . . this was not too unusual . . . we weren't psychotic." Quirke urged them simply to "wait a while" to see if their anxiety subsided on its own. Betty wrote to Webb that the doctor saw them out with a joke: his "advice—next time take a camera with us!"[26]

Quirke seemed skilled enough with people that regardless of his intention the Hills took from him not only reassurance but reinforcement. Whether or not he had intended to gently dissuade them from taking their experience seriously, the Hills understood him to be legitimating their story. Each fixated on a different piece of the doctor's advice that revealed their divergent concerns. Betty crammed a stray Quirke observation into a small addendum to her letter to Webb: "It is impossible for two people to have the same hallucination at the same time." She took this as validation and encouragement in her quest. "I simply had to find out just exactly what happened," she wrote Webb.[27] She believed this was possible, and she expected professionals to help her on the way.

Barney, for his part, remembered another comment of Quirke's. "The fact that we were interracial . . . would have been nothing uncommon to these creatures if they did exist because they would have long solved the problem if there had been racial conflicts wherever they had been from." For Barney, this was less reassuring than the doctor perhaps had meant it; as he said, "Possibly this is one reason we had answered the encounter." The idea that the Hills' racial identities somehow marked them to the craft's occupants seemed suddenly an unnerving possibility.[28] Quirke shrewdly recognized the impact of white supremacy on Barney's anxieties.

Whatever his intention, though, Quirke did not resolve the Hills' worries. They wrote to Walter Webb uneasily about a member of NICAP who politely pestered them by phone and mail. "We do not want any publicity," Betty emphasized. Meanwhile throughout the summer of 1962 Barney tried to persuade his son Darrel, who was graduating high school, to attend the University of New Hampshire in nearby Durham. His ulcer continued to act up and he continued to drink. Finally, in late 1962 he began seeing Duncan Stephens, a distinguished psychiatrist who had offices in nearby Exeter. Barney liked Stephens, who identified Barney's worries as stemming from issues of work, family, and race and helped him deal with those problems. Barney did not initially bother bringing up the September 1961 experience.[29]

But the UFO did not leave them, nor would Betty have expected it to, disciplined as she was in the language of Freud. She continued to correspond with Webb, whom she trusted, and began a hobby that would persist for the rest of her life: she began tracking UFO sightings. In January 1962 and again in September she reported to Walter Webb that her sister, her husband, and various other acquaintances reported strange lights in the sky. And slowly, slowly the Hills began to share their experience with more people – Jackson, Hohmann, Quirke, and others they judged to be experts who might validate their experience. In August 1962, for instance, Webb persuaded Barney to talk with him about the experience on a Boston radio show. Barney agreed because he also trusted Webb and because he was assured he would appear anonymously.[30]

In October the year following, the Hills met Lorraine D'Allessandro, a member of NICAP from Massachusetts who drove to Portsmouth to see them. She invited the two to attend a meeting of UFO investigators in Quincy, Massachusetts, on November 3. The Hills went, and when they arrived, they found a crowd of two hundred people and themselves reluctant celebrities. The crowd asked to hear their experiences. Barney did most of the talking, and a man named Howard Roy took notes, which he later turned into a report he titled "The Off Beat." Roy captured Barney's desire to be perceived as reasonable and sensible. He wrote Barney was a "quiet and well-spoken fellow" who said he hoped he would not be perceived as "a fugitive from the twilight zone," a refer-ence to the popular TV series about the bizarre. Barney claimed to be a "firm skeptic and firm disbeliever in unidentified flying objects." He told largely the same story Major Henderson had recorded, adding a description of the figures he saw inside as "human-like," bathed in "a shadowless blue light." Upon seeing the figures he started "laughing perhaps a little hysterically," Barney admitted, and closed by assuring his audience he had sought a psychiatrist's help.[31]

The experience was frustrating for Barney and Betty. They had attended the meeting hoping to find experts who might help them and instead found them-selves the center of attention. As Betty wrote in her diary, they had attended in hopes that "someone, somewhere could give us information so that we could have some understanding of what had happened to us. No one could."[32]

They had better luck closer to home. One night when their minister, John Papandrew, was visiting, Betty and Barney told him about their experience, seeking his advice. The minister suggested they tell the story at the next meeting of what he called "Couples' Club"—a small gathering of his parishioners who came together for vigorous discussion of "controversial issues as well as current events." The dynamic Papandrew thrived on such conversation, and so did the Hills. On November 23, 1962, he asked them to tell their story after another presenter spoke. Papandrew was so interested that he invited them to bring Walter Webb to the group to give a presentation on the possibilities of "life in the universe," as Webb described it, the following March. The Hills were so gratified for the favorable response that they recalled Papandrew telling them that he "believed in UFOs."[33]

At that November meeting the Hills met the scheduled guest, an army offi-cer and poet from Pease Air Force Base named Ben H. Swett. Swett was also an amateur hypnotist. The Hills told John Fuller that after the formal presentation most of the crowd left, whereupon Papandrew drew those who remained, in-cluding Swett and the Hills, into a discussion about the Hills' story. Betty wrote the same in a letter to Webb soon after the meeting. Years later, however, Swett remembered hearing their story in private conversation as the gathering was breaking up. All agree, though, that their conversation lasted long after the rest of the group went to bed.[34]

Swett remembered that the Hills seemed anxious, while they, hungry for validation from a military officer who also understood psychology, remembered him as a font of helpful information. Their recollections paint a somewhat different picture of the event. "As they told their story, Barney's face kept twitching spasmodically on one side. I didn't like the looks of that," Swett recalled. In his memory he tried to be measured about UFOs, merely saying, "There are a lot of reports by credible people." Betty, though, reported to Webb that Swett affirmed "that the Air Force does know of the existence of UFOs." The two pressed Swett to hypnotize them, but Swett was uncomfortable with the idea. He said that "recovering those memories might reveal a lot of trauma, and cautioned them against going to an amateur hypnotist, such as myself, or a half-baked hypnotherapist." Swett hoped to discourage them, but Betty said he sounded to them much like Patrick Quirke. The two men "asked about the same questions [and] came to the same conclusions," she told Walter Webb.[35]

That the Hills associated an amateur like Swett with a professional like Quirke illustrated that ideas of what counted as expertise and who was able to claim it remained, to many Americans, constantly confused and contested. But the Hills' trust in Swett indicated their confidence that the scientific establishment would eventually confirm their experience, and their faith that they could have a conversation with a scientist like Quirke as equals, interpreting their experience together. Indeed, at this point, regardless of what Quirke or Swett might have intended, Betty and Barney Hill believed that every expert they consulted assured them hypnosis would reveal they had encountered aliens.

CHAPTER 7

THE PROBLEM OF HYPNOSIS

In May 1956 the Santa Monica Assistance League, the local chapter of a charity devoted to aiding poor children with the cost of school, sent out an invitation to its annual Spring Spree.

> Reincarnation is sweeping the nation
> So we thought we would try the latest sensation
> League members, get ready, come one and all
> You're having a real Bridey Murphy Ball.[1]

Similar events were happening in places as far flung as Delaware and Houston. "Reincarnation cocktails" were served, and décor was designed to evoke "some other life." One event promised that "Spanish moss will dangle from ghostly trees." Attendees were instructed to "come as you were"— that is, to dress as somebody they might have been in a previous life. All in tribute to "Bridey Murphy."[2]

Bridey Murphy was an Irish woman who reportedly lived in Cork and Belfast from 1798 to 1864. She married a lawyer, raised children, and died in a fall. Hers was the sort of unremarkable life that would have been forgotten were it not that in November 1952 the Colorado housewife Virginia Tighe submitted

—

to hypnosis and began describing, in Irish brogue, her memories of a past life as Bridey Murphy. In January 1956 Morey Bernstein, her self-taught hypnotist and a professional salesman, published *The Search for Bridey Murphy* with Doubleday.

As did Donald Keyhoe in his books about UFOs, Bernstein told his story as a first-person investigative adventure, the bold hero himself (not, notably, Tighe), a determined American of commonsensical bent, traveling the country to learn the science of hypnotism — something, he explained, Americans could do themselves. He claimed his discovery of Bridey Murphy had proven "how much we can all do with our own minds." He cured his wife of headaches, a friend of stage fright, and a local woman of paralysis in her right arm. His book sold hundreds of thousands of copies its first year in publication, and Bernstein had a movie deal before it came off the presses. Forty newspapers printed excerpts. By March 1956 *Life* magazine was reporting that the book had conjured a "hypnotizzy."[3]

The weighty stakes of psychology give some hint as to the origins of Bernstein's enthusiasm and the urgency of his debunkers. Just as Air Force scientists and the Robertson Panel explained that UFO sightings were the result of untrained imaginations that might become dangerously overstimulated, so did Lewis Wolberg, noted psychotherapist, tell *Life* magazine that the solution to Bridey Murphy was not in Ireland or history books but in Virginia Tighe's own "childhood and development." He also believed she was evidence Morey Bernstein didn't know what he was doing. As Martin Gardner labeled Immanuel Velikovsky a dangerous pseudoscientist, so did Wolberg caution readers of *Life* of "very serious danger through the amateur-hypnosis craze." Problems like "acute anxiety or other disturbances of the psyche" were possible. Even worse, the problem could affect national defense. The reporter who interviewed Wolberg told the story of a young Air Force pilot whom an amateur hypnotist inadvertently immobilized to make that point.[4]

Wolberg's frustration with Morey Bernstein's book revealed a dynamic similar to the arguments about whether UFOs were pseudoscience. Various government reports had concluded that though UFOs were not real, belief in them could harm American society. Similarly, when periodicals sent reporters to Ireland with orders to dig for information, they could solve nothing. Tighe recalled that Bridey Murphy shopped from a grocer named Farr — who turned out to be real. She said Bridey worshipped at a church, St. Theresa's, which did exist — but was built after Bridey's death. Tighe claimed Bridey lived in a wooden house, which were rare — but not nonexistent. It was all frustratingly and, if one were intrigued with Bernstein's story, tantalizingly inconclusive. But Wolberg shifted the grounds of the argument. The problem was not one that history could solve. Rather, it was a question of Bernstein's pseudoscientific understanding of hypnosis. Tighe's mind formulated Bridey Murphy in response to Bernstein's questioning, and in so doing revealed the dangers of amateur hypnosis. Belief in UFOs had become a dividing line between real science and pseudoscience. The power of hypnosis to work wonders like Bridey Murphy became a similar point of distinction between expert and layperson, and therefore between who could be trusted and who could not.[5]

In December 1964 the Hills visited a professional psychiatrist who was willing to hypnotize them for the first time. Their expectations for the experience were in line with Bernstein's, who believed that hypnosis was an uncomplicated route into the hidden realities of the mind, and characteristically Unitarian in that they expected this psychiatric treatment to reveal genuine memory, to clear away the rubble of anxiety and forgetfulness and restore them to complete control of their selves. But this was not what their psychiatrist understood hypnosis to be. Indeed, when the Hills emerged from his office fully believing that they had been abducted by beings from another world, their psychiatrist chastised them for not submitting to his expertise. When the Hills realized this disjuncture, it confused and frustrated them for the same reasons Henderson's apparent dismissal of their experience had frustrated Betty. And their confusion eventually curdled into anger and doubt, and they began to distrust medical authorities as they were beginning to distrust the state.

Hypnosis in Theory and Practice

The post–Bridey Murphy "hypnotizzy" existed in large part because the technique was not well understood and did not enjoy a consensus definition. Sigmund Freud had famously abandoned the technique in favor of the "talk" therapy of free association, and it was not until World War II that it began gain-ing a reputation in the United States. It proved a useful treatment for soldiers suffering from a variety of issues, for example, conversion disorder (neurological problems like numbness or paralysis linked to psychological triggers) or psychoneurosis (distress, anxiety, fears, or confusion linked to trauma—what would later be called post-traumatic stress disorder). Dentists also found it valuable for mitigating pain. And it was generally agreed among professionals that, as Milton Kline, one of the most respected students of hypnosis in the 1950s and 1960s, put it, "training in hypnosis itself without adequate training in psychodynamics and psychotherapy cannot provide an adequate background for hypnotherapy."[6]

But Bridey Murphy was not the only reason why hypnosis seemed to be escaping expert control in those years. In the spring of 1952, in the midst of the Korean War, Chinese radio began broadcasting two American voices, those of captured Air Force pilots. Both accused the United States of using biological weapons in "this war against capitalism." It was a tremendous news story, and it seemed to confirm fears about the psychological powers of communist nations. Throughout the Korean War the journalist Edward Hunter churned out a series of books that described a Chinese technique called "coercive persuasion," which Hunter translated as "brainwashing." In *Brain-Washing in Red China*, published in 1951, Hunter described watching a stage hypnotist with some friends and musing that "we might regard such things as great fun, but apparently they were being taken seriously by other countries." For Hunter, hypnosis posed a threat both to national security and to individual autonomy. He presented hypnosis as a seemingly irresistible weapon. "On a battlefield, if you make believe a rifle isn't there, you get shot," he warned.[7]

By the end of the decade, William Joseph Bryan, great-grandson of the famed politician William Jennings Bryan, was appearing regularly on television, in courtrooms, and on Hollywood sound stages touting the powers of hypnosis. He became famous for working on a number of high-profile murder cases. In 1960 he hypnotized serial killer Henry Busch, who stabbed three women to death in Hollywood, California. In 1964, he hypnotized Albert DeSalvo, who after his confession to the murder of thirteen women became known as the Boston Strangler. Bryan claimed that hypnosis could reveal unrecoverable details about their crimes. He taught actors in a variety of horror movies. He said that *The*

Manchurian Candidate, the controversial novel and 1962 film about prisoners of war hypnotically programmed to be assassins, drew on his work. Bryan was a trained psychiatrist and was careful to warn of the "dangers of stage hypnosis." Yet he also insisted that hypnosis was a precise, almost surgical tool for recovery of memory. "Under the proper hypnotic medical treatment," he declared, "every bit of this memory can be brought back." Lawyers Bryan worked with celebrated his successes. Al Mathews, a former chair of the Los Angeles County Bar Association, said that Bryan had proved to him that hypnosis produced reliable results. "Hypnosis achieves belief without doubt," he wrote admiringly.[8]

The notion that hypnosis was a thoroughly reliable process that worked with measurable precision certainly fit Morey Bernstein's claims. "Hypnosis enormously extends the memory," Bernstein wrote, citing Sigmund Freud for support. In the famous case of "Anna O," Freud and his colleague Josef Breuer had used hypnosis to relieve the symptoms of a young woman haunted by traumatic, repressed memories of her father's death. He and Breuer concluded that traumatic memories might cause symptoms despite being forgotten. They wrote, "Not until they [patients] have been questioned under hypnosis do these memories emerge." Bernstein cited this study with triumph. Freud had proven conclusively, he said, that memory was like a gemstone buried in the earth, waiting to be recovered. He and Bryan and Hunter popularized the idea that hypnosis was an altered state of consciousness in which the mind gained abilities it otherwise did not possess.[9]

That belief reinforced the Hills' Unitarian conception of psychology's job: to restore clarity and rationality to the human mind. Barney Hill described hypnosis functioning with the precision of a machine. He told John Fuller that one reason he agreed to hypnosis was his belief that it was "one valid way of extracting information; I understand more so than the polygraph machine, the lie detector machine."[10] Betty wrote to Donald Keyhoe that they were "searching for any clue that might be helpful to my husband, in recalling whatever it was that he saw." It was for this reason that they were "considering the possibility of a competent psychiatrist that uses hypnotism."[11] To the Hills the links between hypnosis and memory were clear and evident.

But for the most part experts disagreed. Trained psychiatrists like Robert Jay Lifton worried that the media had developed a "lurid mythology" surrounding hypnosis. Another expert, Milton Kline, co-founded the Society for Clinical and Experimental Hypnosis and edited a volume titled *A Scientific Report on the Search for Bridey Murphy* in order to put people like Bernstein and Bryan to rest. In the volume, a host of PhDs and MDs declared that the Murphy saga had "produced a distorted and confused picture of hypnosis." Kline warned that the story encouraged Americans to experiment with something that they didn't really understand. "One doesn't go around inserting hypodermic needles in one's friends," he said, frustrated. For him, hypnosis required management by experts, and layfolk should not attempt to understand what was happening on their own.[12]

The gap between lay and expert understanding was particularly acute in the case of memory. It is generally agreed that memory does not function as Bernstein believed it did. It does not simply sit on a shelf in one's mind waiting for recovery but is formulated and reformulated each time it is brought to consciousness. Recall is affected by the context in which it takes place. By the twenty-first century, experts were arguing that hypnosis was not a special state of consciousness but rather a state of deep relaxation and cooperation with a hypnotist. Such a state would encourage what the psychiatrist Martin Orne, a contemporary of the Hills, called "confabulations" — knitted together memories comprised of actual recall, suggestion, and fantasy assembled to answer a hypnotist's request. Milton Kline agreed, pointing out that "fragmentary exposures to experience can not only be recalled under hypnosis but can be reformulated into a meaningful cohesive story." He believed Virginia Tighe suffered from cryptomnesia, a phenomenon quite similar to confabulation.[13] This was, more or less, what the Hills' own psychiatrist eventually concluded had happened to them. His name was Benjamin Simon, and he was one of America's leading practitioners of hypnosis.

Doctor Simon

In the summer of 1945, the Army Signal Corps commissioned the filmmaker John Huston — already famous for his work with Humphrey Bogart on *The Maltese Falcon* — to make a documentary, which Huston would title *Let There Be*

Light. It was designed to convince the skittish public, in the Army's thinking overly fearful of psychology, that psychological treatments were effective and safe. The film follows several soldiers at Mason General Hospital, a War Department psychiatric facility on Long Island. One had "hysterical amnesia" from surviving a shelling in the battle of Okinawa; another had suffered from a stutter since seeing his comrades killed; a third had lost his sight to conversion disorder rather than from any physical damage. Among the doctors at Mason General was a stocky, balding man in his early forties with a natty mustache named Benjamin Simon. His remarkable feats make him emerge as the star of the show. At one point he briskly hypnotizes a soldier with conversion paralysis in his legs, probes his psyche with a few pointed questions, and then, Jesus-like, commands him to walk and draws him upright from the bed. The stunned soldier staggers forward.[14]

Born in Russia in 1903, Simon migrated to the United States with his family when he was two years old. He excelled at a series of prestigious universities, including Johns Hopkins and Stanford, before receiving his MD from Washington University in 1931. While an undergraduate he served as a subject for experiments in hypnosis, and he refined his technique while a resident in psychiatry. During the war he served as a lieutenant colonel in the US Army and chief of neuropsychiatry at Mason General, and afterward moved to Massachusetts, where he worked at several different hospitals and taught at Harvard and Yale. In his early sixties he retired to private practice in Boston. By then he was a well-known expert on hypnosis. It was for this reason that when Barney Hill finally told Duncan Stephens about his sighting and requested hypnosis, Stephens sent Barney and his wife to Boston. Barney called ahead to set up a consultation, and early in the morning on December 14, 1963, the two drove to Dr. Simon's Boston office. They were on time for an 8:00 a.m. appointment.[15]

By that point in his career, Simon was thinking about hypnosis much as many other specialists were. They rejected the notion that hypnosis was a distinct state of consciousness in which subjects could perform feats of memory or physiology otherwise impossible. Instead, they argued that hypnosis was best understood as a cooperative relationship between the subject and the hypnotist in which the subject entered a state of great concentration and desire to enact what that subject believed hypnosis to be. Milton Kline, one of the many experts

Benjamin Simon poses for *Look* magazine in his office, 1966.
Look Magazine Collection, Prints and Photographs Division, Library of Congress, LC-L9 66–2889-C-26A.

to debunk Bridey Murphy, rejected the notion that hypnosis was a special state of consciousness and explained "the patient in the hypnotic trance is not a passive but an active agent," not operating like a machine but responding to the therapist. "Little or no therapy at the present time is considered to be done by hypnosis, but rather within the framework of the hypnotic relationship," Kline concluded.[16]

Benjamin Simon agreed with Kline. He understood the relationship between counselor and subject to be essential to hypnosis, because it was also the relationship between other dyads: expert and layperson, scientist and amateur. For Simon the expert should be in control both in the process and in the interpretation of hypnosis. By this time Simon had cultivated an assertive and exquisitely calibrated bedside manner premised on his own authority. When reviewing the Hills' case with journalist John Fuller, Simon was quick to express irritation when the journalist used the metaphor of a "tape-recorder" to describe how the hypnotized Hills seemed to be playing back their lost memories. "You picture me operating like a mechanic or computer," he complained. "Everything should be more tentative." Simon preferred to describe hypnosis as an expression of the therapist's ability to manage his patients. He told Fuller it was "a state of close relationship between the two of us," himself and his patient, "in which they are going to be very cooperative."[17] Evident in this small dispute was the broader disagreement over hypnosis generally and the tension between expert and lay understanding the Hills were struggling with.

Simon explained to Fuller that he adopted the persona of a "stage magician," in part because imitating such well-known techniques would awe patients and thus induce hypnosis easily, but also because it suited his sense of himself as in command of his patients. Simon would seat his patients in a chair in front of his desk and then come around the desk to stand right in front of them and talk softly and urgently, telling them to clasp their hands tighter and tighter, or that their head was growing heavy, or that they were getting sleepy—a phrase he confessed to using "out of old custom." All of this was to impress the patient. "I use these physiological things that I know are going to take place naturally, and that convinces them, and the more convinced they are of my power, the less they're going to resist," Simon explained. Such a technique demanded, he said, modestly, "a rather strong personality, a man who's got to have not only the capacity to command but the feeling of it himself." That was Benjamin Simon.[18]

His method certainly worked with the Hills. As with Patrick Quirke's, the Hills found Simon's office "very impressive," and they were a little intimidated. Barney worried about Simon's thirty-five-dollar fee for each appointment but was reassured that his insurance was good. All in all, Barney told Fuller, after the initial conversation Simon had "completely captivated me to the point that I felt this was a person I could trust." Awe was Simon's goal. He was happy when patients "don't have much to say," he told Fuller. It meant that "they have already put themselves in my hands." The Hills were satisfied with this because so far, experts had validated them, and they expected the same from this man.[19]

That first meeting was brief. Simon introduced himself, asked a few questions, and explained that he saw his hypnotic treatment as an adjunct to Barney's long-term work with Duncan Stephens. He stressed his aim was not recovery of memory but the relief of anxiety. Then he induced hypnosis in both Hills, briefly, to ensure it could easily be done. Afterward he read Walter Webb's report—the Hills had brought him a copy—and spoke with Stephens at a professional conference. He was not rattled by the odd story. Such were "almost routine" in his office, as he put it to Fuller, and he said he was "quite neutral" on the question of unidentified flying objects (though the journalist pressed Simon on that, suspecting him of maintaining a professional facade). Simon did admit that the case intrigued him; it seemed an "intensive bit of therapy that may be unique." He bought a recording device. And he called the Air Force and NASA to see if there was anything he might have been missing.[20]

After talking with Stephens, Simon believed he had determined his challenge. "The essential problem here," he concluded, "was their anxiety over this period of amnesia," the stretch of time following Barney's panicked jump back into the car after seeing the craft's occupants that he could not remember. Barney's drinking and Betty's dreams were products of that anxiety. "I was dealing with an anxiety state in two people who had had a very traumatic experience," he explained. "In opening the amnesia . . . I would expect to bring out the source of the anxiety."[21] Talking with Fuller, Simon agreed that the Hills were not so different from the soldiers at Mason General, and his work with them comparable to his work with the Army.

At the same time Simon was careful to specify to anyone who cared to ask that the Hills' "emotionally disturbing experience" was not necessarily an encounter with an extraterrestrial spaceship. He was less interested in what they encountered than in their emotional relationship to the experience. Annoyed that Fuller seemed to be mischaracterizing his position in a draft of *The Interrupted Journey,* Simon sharply insisted that "hypnosis will confirm a fantasy as strongly as it will a reality. In other words the fact that they proved it under hypnosis does not prove that it was a reality. It only proves that they believed it."[22]

It was not that the Hills were lying about seeing a strange craft in the sky; it was that Simon believed memory might reflect both, or either, actual and emotional reality. But as the sessions went on, a contest emerged over the question. For quite a while Simon readily asserted his professional authority, and the Hills, as patients, trusted him and submitted to it. But as Simon attempted to persuade the couple that the events they believed they recalled had not actually happened, the Hills began to resist. They were becoming aware that scientists might draw the lines between legitimate and illegitimate evidence, between real and pseudoscience in ways differently than the Hills themselves did, and the growing disjuncture made them uneasy.

Dr. Simon held three preparatory sessions with the Hills beginning January 4, 1964, testing their responses to hypnosis. Later Simon gave Fuller a copy of a lecture he often delivered titled "Hypnosis: Fact and Fancy." Therein he described three stages of hypnosis. A light stage produced "a certain degree of general suggestibility." In the second stage, "paralysis of the volitional control of the larger muscles" was possible, as was insensitivity to pain. The final stage, what Simon described as somnambulism, was what he hoped to produce in the Hills. In this stage it was possible to direct amnesia, to slow the pulse, and to produce hallucination. The Hills were both easily led into somnambulism, though Barney somewhat more than Betty.[23]

Barney told Fuller that he felt silly when Simon asked him to clasp his hands together, as though "I'm just humoring this man." But Simon kept talking. Barney thought, "I'm not hypnotized, and he said you can't pull your hands apart, and I was struggling to pull them apart, and yet I knew that if I opened my fingers I could pull them apart." And then Simon woke him and Barney was stunned and all the more compelled by Simon's authority. In later sessions Simon pricked him with a needle and convinced him that a small dog had come into the room. Betty posed a bit more of a problem. At one point in the process she started giggling and her induction was broken. She remembered Simon was surprised and seemed somewhat annoyed. Later, though, he successfully persuaded Betty that her cigarettes tasted foul. Simon also gave each Hill what he called "cue words" to prompt hypnosis quickly and suggested to both that they would not remember what they said under hypnosis until he made them aware of it. Then he was ready to begin.[24]

CHAPTER 8

IN DR. SIMON'S OFFICE

On February 22, 1964, the Hills arrived at Simon's office at their customary time of 8:00 a.m. After briefly reinforcing her cue word, Simon directed Betty into the waiting room and took Barney into his office, where he induced hypnosis. For the next hour, Simon asked Barney questions about their interrupted trip to Montreal. He spoke again with Barney on February 29. On March 7, the Hills' roles were reversed: Betty entered the office and Barney, after brief reinforcement, remained outside. On March 14, he separated them again but induced hypnosis in and interviewed each. By the time the Hills arrived on March 21, he had formulated a theory of the case, and again he interviewed each. On March 28, he induced Betty for some final discussions but spoke with Barney out of hypnosis. On April 5, he brought the Hills into the office, sat them down, and began playing the tapes of their hypnotic sessions.

Simon's choice to begin with Barney was intentional. Later, in the comments he wrote on Fuller's manuscript, Simon outlined his reasoning. "I began with the presumption (prejudice!) that Barney, the more suggestible might be the origin of the abduction business."[1] Simon believed that Barney, who appeared more anxious than his wife and who to Simon's mind suffered more from social discrimination and pressure, probably had more repressed trauma. So Simon began with Barney.

Barney's responses revealed a man who lived with the constant fear of racial hostility, who worked ceaselessly to prove his respectability to authority in order to mitigate that fear. In their first session Simon asked Barney to "tell me in full detail all of your experiences, thoughts, and all of your feelings beginning when you left your hotel." Barney started even earlier, describing their arrival at the motel, "approximately 112 miles from Montreal," the night before and worrying "would they accept me? Because when they say that they were filled up and I wonder if they were doing this because [they] was prejudice [*sic*]." Simon asked, "Because you're a Negro?" and Barney responded, "Because I'm a Negro." Simon tugged upon this thread, asking how often Barney worried about being discriminated against and whether he shared such fears with his wife. "She does not share my concerns about this matter," Barney said, and he confirmed that he had shared his fears with Betty, but that "I never express them to her when we are actually seeking a place." Not only did Barney fear discrimination, he seemed to believe he sometimes experienced it alone. His wife certainly was not consciously racist, but she appeared to Barney sometimes blind to what he faced. This disjuncture would deeply mark how each Hill perceived their experience.[2]

Slowly, slowly over the course of the session Simon hunted possible trauma and fears. He asked how much Barney and Betty had to drink while on their trip home (one can of beer each, much earlier in the day). When Barney expressed worry about getting across the US border, Simon asked why, and Barney confessed he had brought a gun, because "I believe in the hostility of white people, particularly when there is an interracial couple." When Barney said that in "New Hampshire I will be in mountain areas, and I don't like that," Simon asked, "Do you fear mountains?" At both the restaurants the Hills stopped at, in Coaticook, Canada, and Colebrook, New Hampshire, Barney was on edge. A "not very friendly" and "dark skinned" waitress in Colebrook stared at the couple, and Barney could not help but wonder, "Is she a light-skinned Negro or is she Indian or is she white?" In Coaticook he remembered a man, "the stereotype of the hoodlum with the ducktail haircut and I immediately go on guard against any hostility."[3]

Both Barney and Betty recalled stopping three times after they first saw the light in the sky — once at a picnic area north of Franconia Notch; once in the Notch, near the rock formation called the Old Man of the Mountains; and once just south, near Indian Head. It was at this last stop that Barney recalled seeing figures through the binoculars. As Barney described what he saw, to his doctor's eyes he grew visibly agitated. "During the explosive parts of the patient's discussion he showed very marked grimacing, twisting, tears rushed down his cheeks," Simon said into the tape recorder after Barney left. "He would clutch his face and his head, and writhe in considerable agony." The two spoke about whether the craft was an airplane. Barney said he wished it were because he enjoyed watching small planes, Piper Cubs, landing on a local lake in wintertime. "I want to hear a jet. I want to hear a jet so badly," he said. But this light seemed more dangerous. It was not making a noise, and it was moving strangely, "coming around toward us." As he had feared persecution at the restaurant and hotel, so did he feel it again here. "I am wondering if these pilots are military, and they shouldn't do that," he told Simon plaintively. "And what if they drive at me?"[4]

Suddenly he started screaming. "I've gotta get my gun! Ugh! Ugh! I've gotta wake up!"[5]

Simon tried to soothe him, as he had soldiers convinced that the shell blasts they saw so vividly in their minds' eye would harm them. They should remember these things — remember them, because they were in the past. "Calm down. It's there. You've seen it. It's not going to hurt you."[6]

It worked for a time. Barney calmed, and over two sessions — on February 28 and 29 — he told Dr. Simon about the figures he saw on the craft. Consistently while under hypnosis Barney described them by way of analogy to human groups he associated with fear or hostility, signaling his sensitivity to racism. The figure he saw through his binoculars, looking at him over his shoulder — "He's smiling. . . . I think of a red-headed Irishman. I don't know why. Oh, I think I know why. Because Irish are usually hostile to Negroes, and when I see a friendly Irish person I react to it by thinking I will be friendly." But the other figure he noted, the one Barney called "the leader," he said "looks like a German Nazi. He is a Nazi." Barney gave little physical detail explaining these analogies. Most of the figures on the ship "were dressed something like lieutenants." The leader, on the other hand, wore a black scarf, a hat with a visor, and a jacket. Simon, seeking associations, asked Barney about the "hoodlums" he had described in Coaticook. "There was no resemblance between them and this leader?" Barney said no. Yet the anxiety lingered.[7]

—

111

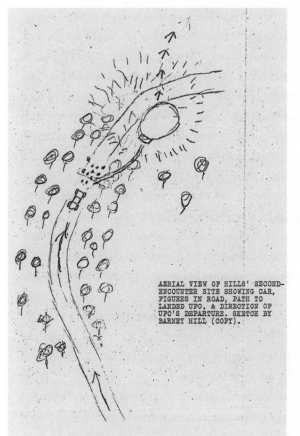

AERIAL VIEW OF HILLS' SECOND-ENCOUNTER SITE SHOWING CAR, FIGURES IN ROAD, PATH TO LANDED UFO, & DIRECTION OF UFO'S DEPARTURE. SKETCH BY BARNEY HILL (COPY).

Sketch by Barney Hill. In 1964, after recovering memories of being abducted by aliens, Barney drew the layout of the moment late at night in 1961 when the car he and his wife were in was stopped on the road by figures and a burning craft.
From "A Dramatic UFO Encounter in the White Mountains, New Hampshire, Sept. 19–20, 1961," Box 5, Folder 14, BBHP, University of New Hampshire. Used with permission.

In the sessions on February 29 and March 14, Barney pushed the story beyond what he had told Webb but still reinforced Simon's belief that Barney feared racial persecution. After describing leaping back into the car and fleeing the craft, he suddenly paused and asked Simon a question. "Are we being robbed?" Simon asked, "What makes you think you're being robbed?" There were, Barney said, "a group of men and they were standing in the highway and it was brightly lit up as if it was almost daylight." A light he described as "orange-red" glowed from the road. The men were "all with black jackets," he said, like Navy pea jackets. And then pleadingly, "And I don't have any money."[8]

Barney thought there were three to six men, and when Simon asked if they were white, Barney said, "I don't know about the color but they did not seem that they had different faces from white men." He said nothing more about their appearance but was overcome with a feeling of helplessness. He was lifted out of the car. He compared his situation to that of a "man being carried to the electric chair." Whether he was afraid or not he could not seem to decide. As had Betty in her dream, he recalled entering a strange state of consciousness. "My eyes are tightly closed and I seem dissociated." Simon perked up at that word, asking Barney what he meant by it. "I am not afraid. I feel like I am dreaming," Barney replied. "I am there and I am not there." But at the same time, as he described being smoothly hoisted up a short incline, he abruptly declared, "I don't want to be operated on."[9]

Just as the figures in the window evoked racial threats, he told Simon that being carried along by the men evoked feelings that he associated with the discomfort and defenselessness of past medical procedures — an ear examination, his tonsils being removed. In his interview on February 29, he described feeling that his pants zipper was open and a creeping coldness around his genitals. He wondered, "Are they putting a cup around my private parts?" On March 14, he described a small tube about the size of a cigar inserted into his rectum and the eerie sensation of a single finger pressing against the base of his spine. Fingers reached into his mouth and something scraped his arm. He opened his eyes once, glimpsed what looked like an operating room painted sky blue, and closed them tightly again. The creatures were making noises that he imitated as "mum, mum, mum, mum." Finally, he recalled being returned to the car.[10]

He kept his eyes closed throughout all of this. Eyes were at the center of Barney's experience. In his hypnotic regression he fixed on the eyes of the leader, a phenomenon Simon found curious. "His eyes were slanted," Barney said, and his voice filled with fear. "It was not like a Chinese. Oh, I, I feel like a rabbit." When Simon asked Barney what he meant Barney recalled how he and his cousin would trap rabbits in the bush while he was a sharecropper's son in rural Virginia. The sense of vulnerability haunted him. "Oh those eyes," Barney moaned. "They're there in my brain. Oh please, can't I wake up?" Simon said no, so Barney continued. The men said nothing as they removed Barney from the car. "Only the eyes are talking to me. The eyes don't have a body. They're just eyes. . . . The eyes are telling me, 'Don't be afraid,' " he remembered. As had happened earlier in the interview, the story drove Barney to terror, writhing and crying. Simon suggested that Barney sketch the eyes, and this calmed him somewhat.[11] Simon resumed the interview on February 29 and spoke briefly with Barney again on March 14 and 21, reviewing some of the same events. On those days Barney showed less distress.

The story Betty told under hypnosis closely mirrored the narrative she had cobbled together from her nightmares a few years before, with a handful of expansions and distinctions. Dr. Simon induced hypnosis in her on March 7 and March 14, and again briefly on March 21 and 28. His discussions with her husband were a volley of back-and-forths, but Betty needed less encouragement. With a few exceptions, Barney's story was a series of impressions, emotions, and reactions. By contrast Betty offered Simon arresting detail, extensive dialogue, and a developed plot. Most striking, though, was the distinction in the mood of the spouses. Barney's story was shot through with wariness and terror, Barney himself constantly coiled in anticipation. Betty's story, on the other hand, was marked with fascination instead of fear. Though occasionally punctuated with fear or pain, overall her mood was one of awe. For Barney, the world was dangerous. For Betty it was benign — and most of all, an educational experience. She believed she was learning.[12]

While her husband's memory of their time in Montreal was filled with frustration and wariness, Betty's was gentle, puzzled, and fond of the people who alarmed Barney. They got lost. She was hoping for a motel, but "somehow we just didn't see one, or we passed it before we noticed it, or something." The people, though, "were quite friendly," even though they assumed she spoke French. The customs agent at the border was helpful, and the servers at the restaurants were chatty. She recalled "they talked to us for a few minutes."[13]

As Barney noticed the light in the sky his apprehension grew and grew, like a shadow around the edges of his calm. He feared pursuit. Betty, in contrast, welcomed the sighting with curiosity and interest. There was a "bigger star" just below the moon that "seemed to get bigger and brighter looking," she remembered. "I was puzzled about it." She asked Barney to stop so they could let their dog Delsey out, but also because she wanted to look more closely. Their respective moods drew them into a small conflict. Barney suggested the thing was a satellite or a plane. "But it wasn't," Betty said defiantly. It began to flash colors.

Barney edged closer and closer to panic, getting back in the car, driving on, saying that the object seemed to be coming toward them, but Betty "laughed and asked him if he had watched the Twilight Zone recently." She stared through the car window, "wondering if they were as curious about me as I was about them." Finally, she grew fed up with Barney's worry, snapping, "You've got to stop! You've never seen anything like this in your whole life! It's amazing!" So Barney stopped again. They passed the binoculars back and forth. Barney got out of the car — and this was when he saw the figures within. He panicked, leapt back into the car, and the Hills' Chevrolet whipped through the darkness of New Hampshire Route 3.

"I was sort of afraid, but I wasn't that afraid," Betty said.[14] But then she was.

From this point on, her hypnotic recall closely mirrored her dreams, punctuated with three moments of fear or pain: when the figures approached the car, when the needle plunged into her navel, and when the leader took the book from her. She would sob in Simon's office when she remembered the first two events, and the doctor tried to calm her. As in her dream she felt a loss of mental control when the six "men" (three to each car door) approached, and she told Simon she felt that she was "asleep and I've got to wake up. I've got to wake up." Speaking into the tape recorder after Betty left for the day, Simon observed that when she described the needle "tears were running down Mrs. Hill's cheeks. Her nose was running." She showed "marked agitation" that calmed only when she described the leader relieving the pain with a gesture. As he had with Barney, Simon probed for possible underlying fears and asked her if the men made "sexual advances" toward her. Betty said no, but when she asked the leader why they had used the needle, he told her that it was a "pregnancy test." She whimpered, "I don't know why they put that long needle into my navel," and Simon thought it best to end there for the day.[15]

But, for the most part, the transcripts of her hypnotic sessions, even more than the dream narrative, tell a story of wonder. As in her dream, when the men drew her from the car, she said that she was feeling like "I'm asleep and I've got to wake up." And yet unlike Barney, who clenched his eyes shut in fear, she kept her eyes open and spoke to the figure next to her. She said her husband's name; he did not respond, but the figure did. "Oh, is his name Barney?" he said, in "a sort of foreign accent." This one she called the leader, but the casual affability of his question set a mood profoundly different than that of Barney's first impression of the staring, uniform-clad creature with the terrible eyes.[16]

Her hypnotic recall of the events on the vessel mirrored those of her dream, with additional detail and expansion and a great emphasis on her curiosity and the relationship she cultivated with the leader. When Barney was taken away, the leader assured her that her husband would be fine, and that "as soon as we get done testing the both of you, you will go back to the car." So she calmed. She was sat down on a "stool," which might have been white or chrome, and the tests began. They examined her arm with a machine like "a microscope with a big lens." They scraped the arm with something that looked like a letter opener and pressed something that looked like plastic upon it. They examined her mouth and ears and shoulders and feet and took samples of hair and ear wax and fingernail. A man she called the "examiner" fumbled with her dress zipper and laid her on a table. They brought over another machine with wires and a screen and touched her all over the body with the thin, narrow points at the ends of the wires. And then they slid that needle into her navel, and Betty screamed.[17]

Simon ended the first session there. Her remaining sessions elaborated on her relationship with the leader, and the transcripts of those sessions unfold in long, fluid paragraphs with only occasional prompting from Simon. Her native good spirits and curiosity began to reassert themselves. While the events mirrored her dream, she elaborated on the leader's humor and warmth. She recalled him helping her to dress and laughing when she told him, "This was quite an experience." He was helpful when she asked for proof of it, asking "what kind of proof would do." When he agreed she could take the book she was "delighted." Then she emphasized her own curiosity about the universe. She had once seen the Harvard astronomer and friend to Unitarians Harlow Shapley (though she misnamed him "Harold") speak and saw "photographs that he had taken of millions and millions of stars." She wished she knew more. She described the leader drawing the star map from a holding place in the wall, and Simon prompted her to draw a copy.[18]

Betty then expanded her recounting of the leader's puzzlement over Barney's dentures and the concept of age. This expansion emphasized the leader's confusion and their growing closeness. In order to clarify the need for dentures she tried to explain how humans ate and found herself knotted in confusion: the

———

116

leader did not understand the concept of vegetables and trying to explain that led to the impossible task of describing what the color yellow was. In frustration, Betty pled with him to meet with people who "could answer all his questions." She begged him to come back. And he said, "If we come back, I'll be able to find you all right. . . . We always do find those we want to." Betty was again baffled, and again he laughed.[19]

Her recounting of her departure from the craft became almost emotional. When the leader took her down the ramp, she insisted to him, "You can never, never, make me forget about it, because I'll remember it if it's the last thing I ever do." His response was gentler than it had been in the dreams. "Barney won't remember one single thing. And not only that, if he should remember anything at all, he's going to remember it differently from you and all you're going to do is get each other so confused you won't know what's going on." He then led her back to the car and apologized if she had been frightened. "I was very badly frightened in the beginning," Betty confessed, but she assured him that "I certainly wasn't afraid now and that this had been an amazing experience." Again she invited him back. "He would try," she reported.[20]

Harlow Shapley published frequently in Unitarian venues. In 1957 he wrote in a popular Unitarian periodical, "To many the picture that science paints is dismal. To us, however, the awakened ones, the cosmic facts are wonderful. How glorious that man is a part, no matter how small and brief, of the mighty play of the universe."[21] This is how Betty Hill felt. Her husband experienced the abduction as terror and oppression, Betty experienced it as wonder and awe. She thought she was learning about the universe Barney was fleeing persecution when he returned down the ramp.

Abduction as Pathology

The inevitable disagreements over what happened to the Hills reflected differing ways of thinking about authority, and the first dispute was between the doctor and his patients. Though the Hills readily submitted to Simon's authority, soon they began to perceive a disjuncture between his interpretation of their experience and their own. In a sense, the disagreement was between Simon's professional training and the Hills' Unitarian, popular understanding of science. According to Simon's training, hypnosis was a way to access the kaleidoscope of emotion that refracted into memories. For the Hills, believers in their own rationality and in hypnosis that could extract genuine memory like a scalpel, their memories were real.

Simon ruefully acknowledged that this was precisely the state of affairs that drove him to believe in patient submissiveness, particularly in a situation like this. As was Paul Henderson, Simon was sure the Hills were not educated enough to fully grasp his method or interpretations; he did not consider their opinions worth engaging. Simon later wrote to UFO debunker Philip Klass that he declined to comment publicly on the Hill case because "I thought a confrontation would be undignified and Betty would be at a disadvantage based on her own inadequacies in scientific knowledge." He concluded that the Hills "were out of my class." Simon mused to Klass about writing his own book on the case, but he never did. In 1975, though, he began appearing on television to explain why he did not consider the abduction story reliable.[22]

Simon was willing to stipulate that the Hills had seen something in the air. "Leave it open whether an unidentified flying object as such exists," he told John Fuller, "whether it comes from the Russians scouting here, or whether it's a misinterpretation of some kind of balloon or God knows what." But at the same time, he was convinced that the abduction was "completely unlikely . . . because there are many inconsistencies in it." Ten years later he wrote to Klass that "I have never deviated from my conviction that the 'sighting' took place. What was sighted I don't know; nor do the Hills know. I am also sure that the 'abduction and examination' did not take place except as Betty's dreams."[23]

This kind of benevolent paternalism reflected broader trends in the American social sciences since the end of World War II. Just as the US military and foreign policy establishment relied more and more heavily upon experts in the hard sciences as the early years of the Cold War dragged on, so did domestic policymakers lean more and more upon psychology and other social sciences. And just as with the physical sciences, social scientists like Simon were growing increasingly protective of the boundaries of their profession and the inability of those they deemed incompetent to participate in their conversations. Social scientists had begun to gain access to the wealth of funding and support from federal agencies in part through arguing that they were as equally rigorous as the hard sciences. It was the job of social scientists to engineer society in ways that required specific technical mastery, just as in physics or biology. These arguments led social scientists to assert their authority over the untrained, as hard scientists had already done.[24]

This strategy was dramatically illustrated in the War on Poverty, a massive legislative program proclaimed by President Lyndon Johnson at the very time the Hills were making their trips to Benjamin Simon's office early every Saturday morning. In his 1964 State of the Union address delivered on January 8, a few weeks after the Hills' first session with Simon, Johnson called for a society in which each citizen had "a fair chance [at] a full-time job on full-time pay." He denounced "our failure to give our fellow citizens a chance to develop their own capacities." This diagnosis implied failure in economic structures but also in citizens who failed to seize opportunity. The president was articulating a complicated genealogy of ideas about poverty in America, combining liberal faith that poverty could be solved through study and training with a much older belief in an "unworthy poor" who could not care for themselves. It was a common position to take. The Gallup poll reported at the time that most Americans favored more aid to the poor but also believed that poverty was at least in part due to lack of individual effort.[25]

Johnson's generalizations represented an emerging theory that captivated many of those in his administration, what anthropologist Oscar Lewis and socialist journalist Michael Harrington dubbed the "culture of poverty." There is "a language of the poor, a psychology of the poor, a world view of the poor," Harrington wrote.[26] But what Harrington argued was a symptom of structural inequity, many of the War on Poverty's advocates read as a cause. The poor suffered from pathologies and hence could not be trusted with direct monetary aid. Instead they required rehabilitation.[27] In the same way, during the War on Poverty many psychologists came to insist that people suffering from psychological ailments required treatment that they might not understand or might even resist. Indeed, Theodore Sarbin, a professor of psychology at Harvard, wrote that the poor were trapped in a belief in their own inefficacy; they would require therapists to help them understand that their worldviews were incorrect before poverty might be alleviated. As Ellen Herman has observed, psychology in the War on Poverty became a vector for expressing the authority of trained professionals over a variety of areas of public life.[28]

These patterns were evident in Dr. Simon's office. Simon believed that the Hills' lack of understanding of hypnosis made them incapable of fully understanding what their memories represented. It was his role as expert to interpret their psyches for them. During their sessions, he tried to persuade them that their story was not logical. But over and over the Hills rebuffed him. When he pointed out to Barney that he and Betty described the craft differently — shaped either like a cigar or a pie — Barney said "when it was flying in the sky it gave the appearance of a cigar," but when it was close enough he realized that "what I thought was a straight row of lights on a plane, turned out to be a curved series of lights." When Simon asked Betty how the leader might speak English but not understand the concept of age, she said that they communicated through "thought transference" rather than in spoken language. Both strenuously rejected Simon's notion that Barney had absorbed Betty's dreams.[29]

When Simon pushed Barney, he seemed to find a smoking gun. In the March 21 session Barney said, "She would say that she had had a dream and the dream was that she had been taken aboard a UFO and that I was also in her dream, and was taken aboard." Simon was puzzled, though, because only a few minutes before, Barney had said Betty had not told him of the dreams. Barney clarified. "When someone would ask us about our sighting of a UFO, and then she would mention this." She told friends about her dreams in Barney's presence.[30] Almost immediately, though, Barney deflated the solution. Hoping he had proven his theory, Simon asked Barney if Betty told him about the aliens' tests. "September the twentieth I was lying on a table," Barney said. "She dreamed, but this is not what she told me was in her dreams." Simon was stymied. "There were men down in the road that actually stopped you?" he asked. "Yes," Barney said.[31]

Because the Hills would not concede that their lack of expertise meant that they were not capable of judging whether their memories were genuine, Simon came to believe that their conviction that they were really abducted — indeed, their insubordination to his authority — pointed to a host of unaddressed psychological incapacities. When he began the Hills' hypnosis on February 22,

Simon believed that Barney had unconsciously generated the story. By March 21, having spent weeks discussing the abduction with each of the Hills, he had formulated a new theory. While waiting for the two to arrive, he wondered into the tape recorder about the "possibility that she had a dream experience, which was conveyed in some way to Mr. Hill, who seems to be the more suggestible of the two."[32]

Simon grew convinced the frustrations and fears of the Montreal trip — particularly Barney's anxiety about race — triggered anxiety attacks in both of them. They saw a strange light in the sky and argued about it. Simon put his finger on the moment where Barney turned the car off Route 3. But instead of encountering creatures in the road, Simon believed the Hills had actually gotten "lost somewhere, [on] a side road off the main way," he told Fuller. Their "fears were increasing." The intensity of the experience birthed Betty's dreams, which she passed off to her husband. In August 1964 Simon specified his diagnosis in a letter to Charles Holmes, the medical consultant to Barney's postal workers' union. Both Hills, he said, had a "psychoneurotic reaction" to the light in the sky, manifested in two ways: an "anxiety reaction" and "amnesia for an emotionally disturbing experience."[33]

Simon also pointed to Barney's anxiety about his manhood. He was struck with Barney's anxious relationship with authority. Barney's frustration with his wife over the object in the sky was one example, but Simon also looked closely at Barney's fear of the leader's eyes. He told John Fuller that he believed that worry reflected their doctor-patient relationship. After all, he said, "It's my eyes that were important in the hypnosis."[34] This pattern — anger at authority coupled with fear of confrontation — seemed plausible to Simon, especially in light of the physical experiences Barney reported on the craft, and they pointed to another diagnosis. In the summer of 1965 Walter Webb began an expansion of his original report, and with the permission of the Hills he went to Simon's house to hear the tapes. In conversation afterward Simon told the young man he believed Barney showed indication of "latent homosexual feelings."[35]

At the height of the Cold War the phrase was less a description of Barney's sexual inclinations than it was an observation about his success at living up to common expectations for men. Freud developed the notion of "latent homosexuality"; he believed it was a normally unconscious reflection of repressed trauma. By the time of the Cold War many American psychologists and psychiatrists concluded latent homosexuality derived from shame over a man's failure to properly fulfill his masculine responsibilities of providing for children, governing a family, and taking a productive role in society. As the psychiatrist Abram Kardiner explained: "They cannot compete. They always surrender in the face of impending combat. This has nothing to do with their actual ability, for many of them have extraordinary talent. It does have to do with assertiveness and pugnacity and the way in which they interpret the cultural demands for accomplishment." Men incapable of performing their gendered duties would consciously or unconsciously drift toward homosexuality.[36]

The theory did not seem ludicrous to some who knew the Hills. In a section marked "confidential" in his new report, Walter Webb tied Simon's theory not only to Barney's personality but to his race. "Barney is passive, highly suggestible, and full of repressed anxieties and fears. She is white and he is Negro." Barney, he suggested, had spent much of his life anxious about his relationship with white authority, even in his marriage. Webb found "plausible" Simon's conclusion that "gradually, Barney's suggestibility took hold, and he, like his wife, finally accepted the dreams as a manifestation of a real experience." Nonetheless, Webb was quick to assert, he remained "far from convinced" this was a better explanation than the most straightforward interpretation: the abduction was real.[37]

Betty admitted that though she generally considered Barney "aggressive," he could also seem passive. She also said that Barney hated listening to the hypnosis tapes. It made him "very angry and upset at times." They consulted with a social worker friend, who told Barney that he was upset because "on the tapes he is fearful, crying, helpless, frightened . . . in other words, he is not very 'masculine.' " Whenever the Hills played the tapes for a friend, Barney would ask them if they believed what he and his wife were saying. To Betty's mind, though, what Barney was actually doing was asking "if the other person might react in the same way." Barney sought validation. Barney had long sought validation. Would a white Air Force officer like Paul Henderson believe him? Would scientists like Simon give his fears credibility? It was a long, long search for respect, going all the way back to the backyards and schoolrooms of Philadelphia.[38]

Of course, Webb's theory not only pointed to Barney's failure at properly enacting American manhood. It also signaled that he and Simon and many other men surrounding the Hills found Betty more assertive and outspoken than an American woman should be. According to Webb, "Betty is dominating and possessive." In the summer of 1965, in response to Webb's query about what she thought about Simon's ideas, Betty wrote, "I will agree that I am domineering," a trait she associated with being the oldest child in her family. Soon after, Leo Sprinkle, a University of Wyoming psychologist interested in alien abduction, inquired if the Hills would be willing to fill out a personality test. The couple agreed. Betty confessed traits of "competitiveness," rebellion, and justice, admitting her capacity for great "constructiveness or deconstructiveness." Her scores placed her in high percentiles for authority and aggressiveness, higher than those of her husband's, which sat in the middle of the pack.[39]

Simon unpacked all of these theories to John Fuller, explaining in an interview why it was he thought that the Hills resisted his explanations. "They're not psychotic," he said, meaning that he did not believe the Hills were delusional or a danger to anybody. But they had, he worried, thought of hypnosis as a sort of "magical thing," like many Americans with no more than a casual knowledge of the practice did. They also, he suspected, were unconsciously "trying to deny a very terrifying experience," not, perhaps, an alien abduction – but the regular pressures of a tense moment in their marriage, lost on a strange road, squabbling, haunted by potential threats.[40]

Betty and Barney's 1960s

The Hills' treatments with Simon ended in the summer of 1964, but their confidence in the veracity of their recovered memories only increased as time passed. That confidence triggered a significant shift in their worldview. Though they had not unquestioningly accepted whatever authority set in their way, their activism was premised on the notion that the state could be a force for benevolence; that the American system should, fundamentally, work; and that they themselves, as competent citizens, would be its allies. They repeatedly had expected those they took to be scientific and government authorities – those they had grown up believing would be their advocates – to believe their story. But now they were confronted with a stark truth: all those people were holding them at arm's length. They found themselves grouped with the Velikovskys and Adamskis: exiled.

In a sense, though, the Hills' growing alienation from scientific authority was characteristic of the time. In 1961, three days before leaving office, President Dwight D. Eisenhower warned the country about the emergence of a scientific, military, and industrial aristocracy: "In holding scientific research and discovery in respect, as we should, we must also be alert to the equal and opposite danger that public policy could itself become the captive of a scientific-technological elite." Worried about the increasing separation between these experts and the citizens they presumed to govern, Eisenhower fretted that "the solitary inventor, tinkering in his shop, has been over shadowed [sic] by task forces of scientists in laboratories." A number of social critics, among them the sociologist C. Wright Mills and the columnist Meg Greenfield, were beginning to raise questions about the authority of the nation's scientific elite, and there is evidence Eisenhower's speechwriters were thinking of them as they had the president warn of "the military-industrial complex." "Are the scientists speaking in the interests of science or in the interest of government or in the interest of their own institutions?" Greenfield asked. "Is their policy advice, on the other hand, offered in furtherance of national objectives or agency objectives — or their own objectives based on their political thinking?" Mills denounced the "military ascendancy in the world of science" and observed that the language of "expertise" was often simply a curtain that kept the public ignorant.[41]

Other figures who were exerting influence on the Hills in these years were also expressing suspicion of the authority of the nation's scientific elite. Early in his career as a UFO investigator, Donald Keyhoe was optimistic that American scientists would eventually demonstrate that these things were alien craft. "Many intelligent persons — including scientists — believe that the saucers contain spies from another planet," he wrote in his first book. "American scientists and engineers can learn the source of the space ships' power." But by the 1960s, Keyhoe was becoming convinced that American science was controlled by the very military-industrial complex Eisenhower warned of and thus was not to be trusted. Keyhoe's 1960 book *Flying Saucers: Top Secret* warned that the CIA had taken control of the UFO investigation, and by the end of the decade he was

IN DR. SIMON'S OFFICE

writing glumly that the CIA "agents ran the whole show, and the scientists followed their lead."[42]

But neither Keyhoe nor the Hills dismissed "science" as a concept. Rather, they simply came to see that there was a disjuncture between what they perceived genuine science to be—something that the Hills, with Unitarian confidence, believed they could understand—and what Benjamin Simon was doing. They rejected Simon's understanding of psychoanalysis as a process which required a trained elite to evaluate and interpret laity who could not understand their own minds. If the 1960s were a revolt against traditional authority, for Betty and Barney Hill the decade began here.

The Hills reassured themselves that Simon was unscientific. Betty complained to Walter Webb that they were frustrated that Simon "assured us on several occasions that it is impossible to lie or deceive under hypnosis, and then discounts the tapes." She told Webb that according to her "Abnormal Psych courses at college," dreams were "a form of hypnotic recall." She asked their friend Arnold Spencer, a prominent local businessman and amateur hypnotist who had seen a UFO himself, "if it were possible to fabricate or lie under hypnosis, and he said that it is commonly believed that it is impossible."[43] Barney Hill complained to James McDonald, a physicist and UFO investigator at University of Arizona, "We feel that Dr. Simon vacillates between believing and non-believing in UFOs, and then this influences his interpretations of our hypnosis." Barney told McDonald that he had received sympathetic contact with scientists who refused to go public with their support. Barney wrote, "They fear ridicule."[44] In Barney's annoyance there was a kernel of antiestablishment populism that would only grow, both within the Hills and American culture more broadly.

The Hills began to seek out figures like Hohmann and Jackson, those whom they believed held scientific authority and would support their beliefs. Betty told Fuller in early 1966 that when they arrived home after their session with Simon on March 7, she went to her closet and removed the blue dress she had been wearing the night of September 19. It had been shoved to the back for nearly three years, forgotten for no reason she could recall. She said that "it looked as if I must have perspired so that it actually discolored the dress." It was stained around the armpits and was torn along the side of the zipper. Ten years later she described the dress more fully to a UFO investigator, Leonard

Stringfield, noting that the stains were pinkish, and that when she had taken the dress from the closet there was a dusty pink powder on it that vanished when she took it outside. Stringfield, who worked at a chemical company, offered to have the dress analyzed for her. His lab reported that it bore traces of copper, calcium, silicon, magnesium and iron. More to the point, the lab had a difficult time replicating the stain. "Whatever the reaction was" that caused the stain, the technician reported, "it was not the usual discoloration reactions that I know." Betty took this as validation, a refutation of Simon. "From the way my dress was torn," she said, I "suspect I put up quite a battle when they first tried to grab me." The dress proved to her not only that the event was real but also that she was an active agent in it.[45]

On June 27, 1964, Betty and Barney visited Ben Swett, bringing with them the tapes of their sessions with Simon. The group sat in Swett's front room, listening quietly. When the tape reached the moment when Barney spoke of the leader in his jacket staring with his glaring eyes, Swett remembered, "Barney jumped up and ran out to our kitchen and vomited in the sink." The army officer started to believe their story might be true. "I thought this would be pretty hard to fake," he wrote.[46]

The Hills thought so too. Like many Unitarians they rejected theories of sublimation, that their memories were not simply repressed but representative of something else entirely. "Dr. Simon can put this onto a Freudian thing," Barney told John Fuller, but "it is like Dr. Simon telling me, well, Barney, you must realize you never were in military service though I served four years in World War II. . . . I'm just as sure of this experience as I am that I was in the service."[47]

On the chilly, rainy night of November 8, 1965, Barney and Betty were at the center of a crowd at the Unitarian church in Dover, New Hampshire, twenty minutes or so from Portsmouth and just north of the University of New Hampshire in Durham. They had decided to tell their story to the public. Ben Swett and his wife Wyn cut past the line of people standing in the rain and were stopped by a tall, thin, bearded man wearing a tweed jacket with cameras draped around his neck. He asked Swett to introduce him to Barney Hill.

"My name is John Fuller," he told Swett. "I'm writing a book about the UFO sightings in this area, and I'd certainly like to consider his story, perhaps for another book." Swett was initially suspicious, but after Fuller's reassurances he led the author through the crowd. What Fuller told Swett was also what the Hills wanted to hear. "I'm not a sensationalist. I try to get all the information I can, and present it as accurately as possible," he said. The Hills, doubting Simon's objectivity, were impressed. They met with Fuller twice more and agreed to sign a contract allowing him to write a book about their experience.[48]

John Fuller was born in 1913 and graduated from Lafayette College, an elite liberal arts school in Pennsylvania, in 1936. He spent most of his professional career producing, writing, and directing radio and then television shows, specializing in comedy — the notorious "Candid Camera," among others. In 1957, he was living in Connecticut and picked up a weekly column called "Trade Winds" for the *Saturday Review,* a magazine specializing in the arts. Fuller's voice was comfortable, informal, and often a bit wry. He gleefully reprinted puns readers sent in and positioned himself as an advocate for common readers, skewering the establishment regularly.[49]

In October 1965, Fuller published an unusual "Trade Winds." It covered a spate of UFO sightings in Exeter, New Hampshire, one town over from Portsmouth. Fuller made a series of calls to policemen, journalists, and UFO investigators and ended the column sounding like Donald Keyhoe, praising the reliability of the police officers who reported seeing a dark object with five red lights hovering above Exeter's streets. "You can't find two better officers than Hunt and Bertrand," Fuller claimed, and wrapped it up.[50]

But he couldn't shake the story. He made more calls, got a book deal, and was in New Hampshire by November. He spoke with Betty Hill on the phone early on, while tracking down referrals, and when he heard about their story he headed to the Dover church to meet them. By that point, he was persuaded by the sort of evidence the Hills could offer. "Police, air force pilots, and radar men, navy personnel and coast guardsmen all confirmed the incredible reports that dozens of reliable and competent citizens in the area were giving me," he wrote about the Exeter craft. In February and then June 1966, writing with incredible speed, he published an article about the Exeter sightings in *Look,* one of the nation's most popular magazines, followed by *Incident at Exeter,* a book on the case. By the time the book was published he was deep into interviews with Betty and Barney Hill, Walter Webb, and Benjamin Simon.[51]

—

In February the Hills and Simon signed a contract with Fuller and his publisher. It bound all of them to make themselves available to Fuller for interviews and Simon to turn over a copy of his recordings, with the Hills' permission. Simon wanted oversight of "all medical statements and medical conclusions contained in the manuscript" and agreed a third party would arbitrate disagreements. The advance ($10,000) and royalties would be divided: 40 percent to the Hills, 30 percent each to Fuller and Simon. Fuller was again proposing a mammoth writing task for himself; his publisher wanted a manuscript by June 1, 1966. He didn't quite make that deadline, but *The Interrupted Journey: Two Lost Hours Aboard a Flying Saucer* was published in October 1966, only a few months after *Incident at Exeter*.[52]

With Fuller's aid the Hills composed an open letter (ostensibly to Betty's mother but really to be reprinted in *The Interrupted Journey*) explaining their decision to allow Fuller to publish a book about them. The letter reveals the Hills' certainty of the importance of their experience, their defense of their particular understanding of psychology as genuinely scientific, and their growing sense of alienation from the American scientific establishment. In the draft of the letter which the Hills sent to Fuller for editing they wrote, "We have met with Dr. Simon, who believes we should release this for the therapeutic value to ourselves." This claim was struck from the printed version. They described their experience as "the greatest event in the history of mankind since Columbus discovered America." This phrase was also struck; Fuller replaced it with "of great public interest." Its hyperbole can be read as reflective of the importance of the event to the Hills' inner lives — a possibility bolstered by what followed. The Hills claimed they had been disinclined to come forward because they feared "scorn, ridicule, and disbelief," but they had been persuaded it was necessary to "clarify what actually happened." Both Fuller and the Hills believed that their clear-eyed confrontation with their past had relieved them of their anxiety, and that the public would certainly react the same way.[53]

Fuller affirmed the Hills' presumptions about the relationship between hypnosis, perception, and truth. He wrote that while in a trance "the patient's memory becomes vivid and exact — details long forgotten to the conscious mind emerge sharply." In Fuller's telling, hypnosis was as straightforward as Morey Bernstein or many Unitarians believed. In his conclusions Fuller claimed that the Hills' "direct emotional response was repressed and suppressed, attaining conscious expression in diffuse anxiety, dreams of nightmarish quality, and physical symptoms – until released and discharged during treatment." This was precisely how the Hills understood psychology and hypnosis. Rather than muddying the waters, hypnosis should bring clarity and self-understanding. Fuller persuaded Simon not to state his belief that the abduction was not real in the doctor's introduction.[54]

The Hills found in Fuller the sort of confirmation Simon denied them. But that triumph was not the end of it. Despite their shared conviction that the encounter was real, Betty and Barney Hill took different truths from it. For Betty their experience was destabilizing but also liberating. It was optimistic in a very Unitarian way. The outer space of the aliens she encountered was a knowable, accessible place, inhabited by curious seekers of knowledge who intended no real harm and were willing to joke with humans. Betty's creatures were less terrifying than they were comfortably paternalistic. The story was the resolution she had sought ever since she shared her dreams with Jane McLaughlin, and the relief of its confirmation marked why Betty, at least, would not – could not – accept Dr. Simon's debunking. For her, the science of psychology revealed the universe she wanted.

But for Barney, the experience was destabilizing and terrifying, a story of haunting persecution and the fear of captivity marked by his self-consciousness as a Black man in America. The emotionally charged reactions the tapes evoked in him testified to that, as did the anger he expressed toward Simon for doubting him.

These varying responses – fascination and fear, despair and awe – marked how the Hills would engage not only with their mutual faith in their experience but also with their earlier beliefs about American politics. Like many other Americans in the mid-1960s, the Hills were coming to doubt the reliability of traditional authority, and their faith in their encounter framed their growing disillusionment.

CHAPTER 9

THE NATIONAL ASSOCIATION FOR THE ADVANCEMENT OF COLORED PEOPLE

In 1961 the Unitarians and Universalists merged to form the Unitarian Universalist Association (UUA), but the new strength the merger gave was strained by the Black freedom movement. The denomination worked hard over the next few years to lend support to demonstrators and protests for Black rights. The 1965 UUA General Assembly voted to join marches protesting school segregation in Massachusetts and Seattle. It created a permanent "civil rights worker" post in the denomination's leadership, and it issued a resolution calling on all Unitarian Universalist congregations to commit themselves "to eliminate all vestiges of discrimination." But there was fatigue in the ranks, as Homer Jack, a Unitarian minister who had long worked toward integration reported. "An interracial ministry can enrich our churches," he exhorted his fellow believers, citing concern with a recent denominational study that reported only a third of American UUA congregations would welcome a Black minister.[1]

The denomination was as white as ever, and some African Americans were growing impatient with its integrationist philosophy. In June 1966, the African American activist James Meredith was shot while on a march from Memphis to Jackson, Mississippi, and a host of other Black organizations rallied to complete Meredith's course: Martin Luther King's Southern Christian Leadership Conference, the Student Nonviolent Coordinating Committee (SNCC), and the Congress of Racial Equality (CORE) that Bayard Rustin and Homer Jack, among others, had founded years before. On the march, SNCC leader Stokely Carmichael was arrested and held by police for several hours in Greenwood, Mississippi, and on his release headed from the prison to Broad Street Park, where the marchers had gathered. "This is the twenty-seventh time I have been arrested and I ain't going to jail no more!" Carmichael said. "The only way we gonna stop them white men from whuppin' us is to take over. What we gonna start sayin' now is Black Power!"[2]

Over the next several years, both CORE and SNCC limited white participation in their organizations. Young Black leaders like Carmichael came to reject liberal faith in persuasion and the use of government as a tool to promote cultural and emotional change in the United States. To them, the call for integration ignored the practical reality that changing laws had not alleviated racial discrimination or ended Black poverty. "Integration" premised upon the sort of color blindness many white Unitarian liberals preached seemed to deny the reality of Black identity as a source of pride and persecution. The Unitarian Universalists tried to answer the call. In October 1967, Dana McLean Greeley, the head of the Unitarian Universalist Association, called to order the Emergency Conference on the Unitarian Universalist Response to the Black Rebellion. More than a hundred delegates, more than a third of them Black, attended. In his opening remarks Greeley called for the denomination to show more commitment to racial equality.[3]

And then the Black delegates withdrew. Four-fifths of them elected to join a new Black Caucus, excluding white delegates, talking among themselves about what it meant to be part of a minority in an overwhelmingly white denomination. Many of the white liberals present were stunned, finding their cherished Universalist creed under fire. Henry Hampton, a Black Unitarian Universalist and delegate to the convention recalled that a white liberal friend said to him, "I've been putting myself on the line for you for twenty years and now you want me to support a crazy kind of separatism that goes against everything I joined this church for." Jeannette Hopkins, the white chair of one of the emergency conference's commissions, resigned, denouncing the Black Caucus for "imposed discipline, secrecy, exclusivity . . . the opposite of the methods I have cherished in Unitarianism."[4] For years afterward, white and Black Unitarian Universalists fought over whether to fund Black-only organizations, and slowly, slowly Black members abandoned the denomination and the liberalism that it had claimed for its guiding star.[5]

Portsmouth's Unitarians, Barney Hill among them, felt these tensions acutely. One of the central reasons his encounter with UFOs unnerved him was fear that the story would wreck his quest for integration. But the shadow of irreconcilable confrontation between races haunted him. He invested energy in the federal government's procedural and legal efforts to promote integration but confronted a wide spectrum of resistance, from racists who rejected legal orders to violence. He committed himself to Unitarian efforts to end segregation but saw the denomination collapse under the strain. And, just as he had feared, he saw white Americans use his abduction to discredit the cause of integration. The aftermath of Barney's experience in September 1961 strained his faith in racial reconciliation.

After all, under hypnosis Barney remembered both his fear of white hoodlums and his fear of the craft's occupants, and both memories brought to mind the fact that he had brought a gun to Montreal.

Civil Rights in New Hampshire

New Hampshire was an overwhelmingly white state in the 1960s. The 1960 census reported that only about 2,500 of the state's residents were not white, less than 1 percent of the state's population. About 1,900 of those were African American. Portsmouth was the most diverse of the state's cities, home to 1,100 non-white residents — most Black — who made up about 5 percent of the city's population. Despite being home to nineteenth-century abolitionist movements and strong Union sentiment in the Civil War, by the 1960s, Portsmouth, like most other cities in the American North, allowed de facto segregation. But inspired by the growing movement for equal rights and integration across the country in the 1950s, a Black electrician named Thomas Cobbs organized the Portsmouth branch of the National Association for the Advancement of Colored People (NAACP) in January of 1958.[6]

By February 1963, Barney and Betty Hill were ascending the ranks of the Portsmouth NAACP. By 1966, they had paid off life memberships in the

—

Barney Hill delivering a speech at the Portsmouth Armory. Oversized Box 3, Folder 1, BBHP, University of New Hampshire. Used with permission.

organization. It was, after all, the same organization that had had such success in Philadelphia while Barney was growing up and that believed deeply that changed laws could stymie racism in America. In Portsmouth the organization was never large; at one meeting ten members were present; at another, an officer reported there were fifty-one inactive members on the books. Within a year both Betty and Barney were on the organization's executive committee. Betty served as assistant secretary to the branch, later as its primary secretary, and on its community outreach committee. Barney chaired the public action and legal redress committees. All this work was demanding. Barney's life in particular became a whirlwind. He grew into a polished and sought-after public speaker (joining the public speakers' club, Toastmasters, and winning awards); he helped engineer legal battles and rallies;

he was recognized in his city, and then his state, and then nationally as a civil rights leader. So much activity gradually wore down both his health and his optimism.[7]

Barney's racial liberalism committed him to a certain set of ideas. He trusted still in the NAACP's belief that government policy and education could promote not only legal integration but also racial harmony. Such campaigns were part of the long African American campaign of "racial uplift," the belief that Black leaders should pursue integration and racial equality through accomplishments white people could not deny. Such a strategy required that Black people present themselves as respectable. They needed to dress smartly, work hard, speak well, and embrace mainstream American liberal values. Integrationist civil rights leaders like the Old Philadelphians, absorbed this lesson, and Barney had learned it from them.[8]

At a February 1963 Portsmouth NAACP meeting Barney became the organization's legal redress officer, seeking to coordinate among police officers, lawyers, and community leaders to protect African American rights. He saw an opportunity. A couple of years earlier, in June 1961, after months of fierce debate, the New Hampshire legislature had passed a law prohibiting discrimination by race, religion, or national origin "in the matter of board, lodging, or accommodation, privilege or convenience offered to the general public." The law was understood to prohibit discrimination in housing and the service industry, and it was promptly and widely ignored. But Barney believed it had potential. He organized an impromptu test. On March 9, 1963, six teams of NAACP men fanned out throughout the city and visited a total of nine barbershops. "One team failed to get a haircut, and two teams met with failure on its first try," reported Barney. "From 9 barbershops actually tested, we found discrimination practiced in 4." One of those team members was Thomas Cobbs, who went to Clint's Barber Shop—only a block away from Betty and Barney's house on State Street—and was turned away.[9]

Barney and Cobbs did what the NAACP in Philadelphia had done in Barney's youth. First, they sought to rally allies to exert persuasion and encourage voluntary conformity with the law. They went to the city's Fair Practices Committee. Barney knew this organization well because his minister, John Papandrew, the firebrand for racial equality, was one of its founders. Civil rights advocates were forming Fair Practices Committees across the country in the middle twentieth century, and in New Hampshire since the late 1950s. They were private gatherings of prominent citizens in a given city or town who agreed to exert public pressure on discriminatory businesses. When Portsmouth's committee was formed Papandrew told the press that any citizen, believing he or she had suffered a lack of "equal treatment in all areas of social concern," could petition the committee, which would use "persuasion by frank talk and common sense" to resolve the problem. He called the courts a "last resort." The 1961 law was clear — and certainly, liberals believed, any reasonable citizen could be persuaded to see the virtue in compliance.[10]

Barney thought so too. In April 1963 he and Papandrew attended a meeting of the New Hampshire Advisory Committee on Civil Rights, which advised the governor on the status of civil rights in the state. There Papandrew reported the Portsmouth Fair Practices Committee had documented "six cases in which discrimination has been charged," including at the barber shop. Following the meeting, Barney filed a complaint with the Fair Practices Committee, which sent a letter inviting Charles Sprague, proprietor of Clint's Barber Shop, to a hearing.[11]

Sprague ignored the letter. The chairman of the committee wrote to Barney that "apparently Mr. Sprague, through lack of response, is not interested in any hearing with the Fair Practices Committee." He advised Barney to "take whatever steps you deem appropriate."[12]

Barney and Cobbs still trusted the system. They went to the city attorney, who charged Charles Sprague with violating the 1961 antidiscrimination law and summoned him to a hearing before Judge Thomas Flynn of the municipal court. Inconceivably to Barney, in court Sprague willingly admitted — and proudly — that he had broken the law. He believed it unconstitutional. Judge Flynn granted him an appeal to the New Hampshire Supreme Court. Before that court in April 1964, Sprague complained, oddly, that the 1961 law violated the Thirteenth Amendment — passed in 1865 to abolish slavery and "involuntary servitude" in the United States — because it compelled him to serve those he did not wish to serve. The court rejected this argument out of hand and returned Sprague to Flynn for sentencing. The maximum penalty the 1961 statute allowed was a one-hundred-dollar fine. Sprague was fined fifty dollars.[13]

On the face of it, it was a victory of the sort Barney had long hoped for. The government had come through. New Hampshire courts were willing to enforce their laws. But there were ominous signs beneath the triumph. Sprague had simply rejected outright the premise of the Fair Practices Committee. He was not interested in reasonable debate. He did not share Barney's commitment to respectability. His punishment might be satisfying but his intransigence was worrying; it showed not only the persistence of racism but the fragility of Barney's trust that reform and law could resolve racism in America. Barney began to feel the nagging pessimism and anxiety that Benjamin Simon had observed tugging at his patient's mind.

Color Blindness

For Betty—as for many other Unitarians—the desire for integration manifested in an ideology of color blindness. For white Unitarians, emphasis on human rationality and equality led them to downplay race as a factor in social interaction. The denomination, heavily and self-consciously white, saw itself as the bearer of what many of its members called "universalism," the reality of human equality that led many of them to deny the importance of race. Ethelred Brown, one of the first Black Unitarian ministers, wrote that he staked his ministry on the belief that "Negroes are capable of becoming Unitarians, and that therefore Unitarianism is a universal religion."[14] Donald Harrington, minister to the famed Community Church in New York City, announced the hiring of a Black associate minister with the observation, "Mr. Dawkins happens to be a Negro. He was not hired because he was a Negro. He was hired because of the excellence of his qualifications." Harrington admonished his congregation: "For the liberal the matter of race is non-existent."[15] When the Unitarian minister Carl Seaward officiated at an interracial wedding at his church, he announced, "Racism can by minimized by Christian love. . . . Recently a unique wedding took place in a church in New England. The first Negro member of this white church was married there to a man from Jamaica by a pastor at a Negro church. The bridesmaid was a Chinese girl."[16] This panoply of diversity was for Seaward a symbol of how liberal Unitarianism might make over society, and it indicated that he and other liberals conceived of racism as a personal feeling to be over-come with religious emotion and reason.

For Betty's part, the childhood event that left the deepest impact upon her life in regard to race was her encounter with her Black neighbor, after which her mother instructed her "that some people did not like colored people, but this was not right for they were people just like everyone else."[17] This sort of liberal egalitarianism, suggesting human equality could be achieved if only enough people were convinced of its accuracy, followed her throughout her life. It blos-somed into a commitment to racial integration in her adulthood. It marked how she understood her marriage. As she boasted in a later essay about her marriage, "Our skin colors [sic] differences were a blessing, for they protected us from coming in contact with those with whom we would not want to be friends, but at the same time drew others to us."[18] She believed the latter far outnumbered the former. As she told John Fuller, race "doesn't have any more meaning to me than a person having brown eyes or blue eyes."[19]

When he began his ministry, John Papandrew, the Hills' minister, threw himself into the battle for this same sort of race-blind equality and the change of people's hearts. He was convinced, as he said in a sermon shortly before arriving in Portsmouth, "Real joy is felt only when a man's own heart is rid of all evil." He urged his congregation to "take an earnest look inside, for THERE is where the great fight between good and evil goes on."[20] When he arrived in Portsmouth, Papandrew believed that the sin of racism was the accumulation of individuals' evil or misinformed choices, and, as his tongue-lashing of the Portsmouth school board when they seemed poised to deny the Kenyan student James Karagol demonstrated, he could be aggressive in his frustration when he be-lieved people were choosing poorly because he thought human conscience instinctively understood the difference.

Soon after Barney and Betty joined South Church, they began working with John Papandrew to promote integration. Papandrew's techniques — rallies, edu-cation, and governmental action — matched his optimism, and they appealed to the Hills. Barney began speaking regularly at the South Church building. One speech was titled "Human Rights for Minorities." Both Hills and their minister joined the Seacoast Council on Race and Religion, which sought to organize Black and white Christians around Portsmouth in support of civil rights. In the summer of 1963 Papandrew led the Seacoast Council on Race and Religion in a major effort to desegregate the resorts that dotted the Atlantic coastline north and south of Portsmouth. He brought a Black couple with him as his guests to Wentworth-by-the-Sea, the most famous of these resorts, and turned down the manager's offer to give them a free meal in a back office. "Absolutely not, we want to be seated in the dining room," Papandrew said. In 1962 he wrote an impassioned letter to Martin Luther King Jr., committing himself and his congregation to the work of integration. King wrote back: "We thank you for being sensitive to these concerns and giving of yourselves that we may walk together as sons and daughters of God soon in these United States." Papandrew was moved. He read the letter over the pulpit in South Church and to his children at home every year after receiving it, and each time he affirmed his faith that such integration was possible if only people listened to their consciences.[21] In late August 1963 Papandrew collected a delegation of sixteen people to attend the March on Washington for Jobs and Freedom. They gathered early one Tuesday morning at South Church and drove to Washington, D.C., for the march the next day. Barney Hill was among them. On September 8, soon after their return, Papandrew canceled normal services at South Church in order to hold a "sermon conversation" in which he and Barney discussed the march before the congregation.[22]

The exhilaration of Washington was sustained when Lyndon Johnson became president upon the death of John F. Kennedy in November 1963. Inspired by activists like Barney, Johnson began goading Congress to pass the Civil Rights Act, a national version of New Hampshire's 1961 law. Barney joined the fray. He wrote letters to members of Congress and to newspapers arguing that "the chance to combat bigotry by all people who believe in justice, fair treatment, and equality for all Americans is now." Both he and Betty gave speeches, and Barney and the NAACP organized rallies. Johnson signed the Civil Rights Act into law in July 1964, but the Hills did not stop working. During the presidential election that fall, the Hills volunteered on voter registration drives. In October Betty reported to Walter Webb that she and her husband "have really canvassed the city." The pride was evident in her prediction that "undoubtedly this state will go to the Dems for a change." It did, and so did the country. Johnson won in a landslide, and Barney and Betty were invited to Johnson's January 1965 inauguration. Betty remembered meeting Vice President Hubert Humphrey and New York Governor Nelson Rockefeller. Betty and Barney's faith in government was rewarded.[23]

Encouraged, Barney threw himself into the work. In May 1965, he was appointed a member of his state's advisory committee to the U.S. Commission on Civil Rights. The commission had been created by Congress in 1957 to offer guidance and advice on civil rights law. Its state advisors met monthly to send recommendations to the commission in Washington, D.C. A few months later a Portsmouth city council member recommended Barney to Governor John King for a seat on the state's new five-member Human Rights Commission, a similar advisory board. He lauded Barney as an archetype integrationist, determined to work for change through the democratic process. According to the recommendation, Barney believed that "Negroes will take their rightful place in society through the educational process and steady and persistent pressure." Barney was subsequently appointed and told the press that he believed the commission should "seek compliance rather than merely mete out punishment" — that is, to change minds, not simply to exert force.[24]

Over the next few years Barney Hill became one of the Johnson administration's point men in New Hampshire. In the summer of 1964, just as Betty and Barney Hill were finishing their sessions with Benjamin Simon, the War on Poverty reached New Hampshire. In August Congress passed the Economic Opportunity Act, which created the Office of Economic Opportunity (OEO). True to the liberalism of the Johnson administration, the OEO would coordinate a vast array of programs designed not to simply redirect resources to the poor, but to provide prospects for education and training that would break the "culture of poverty" and turn these people into independent citizens. These programs included Head Start, which provided resources for preschool, summer school, and early childhood nutrition to school districts around the country; a volunteer program; a national vocational education program; and the Community Action Program.[25]

The Community Action Program sponsored more than a thousand Community Action Agencies (CAA) across the nation with the aim of improving the local economy and strengthening community. It provided funding but required local agencies to promote local innovation and seek local governance. By

1966, Barney Hill was chairman of the board of directors supervising the staff of Rockingham County's CAA. He told the *Portsmouth Herald* that his "particular emphasis will be on civil rights."[26] By 1966, the county CAA was offering a Head Start summer program for local children, job training courses, adult education courses for people seeking high school equivalency degrees, and coordination services to help poor families find available services. They also persuaded a number of physicians to offer free examinations and Dartmouth College students to offer free art classes and an after-school program for children.[27]

At the same time Barney was driving to Dr. Simon's Boston office early every Saturday morning he was embarking on a career as an activist. While he was interviewing with Simon he was working for the NAACP and lobbying both for the Civil Rights Act and for Johnson's election. By a year later, he was holding regular CAA meetings. This dizzying amount of work—and not to mention his full shifts at the post office—makes the stress he exhibited somewhat comprehensible. It also casts into new light the concern for being taken seriously that runs throughout all of the Hills' conversations about their strange encounter.

Barney felt the pressure. He told Simon after the hypnotic sessions had ended that thinking of the sighting and abduction left him in a terrible conundrum: "I would say that it is something that happened. But I put a protective coating on myself because I don't want to be ridiculed." He ascribed his reluctance to discuss the story to his stark awareness of his need to preserve his reputation and to a foreboding sense that "there was harm that could come to me and Betty by pursuing this."[28]

Betty worried too. Soon after their hypnosis she expressed concern about the damage the story might do to their work in Portsmouth. "I do not know what effect publicity would have on Barney's position in so many of the things he is doing," she wrote to Walter Webb. Not to mention her own life. If the story "were ever published in a Boston newspaper," she worried, "I would probably be fired from my job. Generally people would question my sanity."[29]

The story of the abduction that emerged from Simon's hypnosis put the Hills in a position that felt increasingly untenable. They were coming to see that the respectability they'd achieved did not necessarily mean that their story would be believed. They were beginning to worry that, quite the contrary, their confidence in their memories might actually cost them.

———

CHAPTER 10

MONOGENESIS

Betty was not wrong. In the years after their hypnosis, their case was widely shared in the press, and the Hills alternately enjoyed the publicity and recoiled from it. Much of the coverage echoed the federal government's growing certainty that UFOs were not mechanical but the product of psychological disturbance. For many members of the press, the most likely source for that disturbance in the case of Betty and Barney Hill was their interracial marriage. Some simply racist people thought this was self-evident. But other journalists, mostly liberals who supported integration, found themselves drifting toward the same position because they worried that interracial marriage in a racist society was psychologically damaging.

In August 1965 the Hills were horrified when they learned that a journalist named John Luttrell was tracking their story down. Luttrell had earned a reputation for research and fearlessness with a string of exposés on city corruption in the *Boston Traveller*, a scrappy afternoon paper with a history of publishing offbeat features.[1] He heard of the Hills' story in June 1965 and soon proved his skill. He got his hands on a recording of Barney and Betty's November 1963 presentation to the Two-State UFO Study Group, a copy of Major Henderson's report, and a statement from Project Blue Book that claimed, "The object was in all probability Jupiter." Luttrell also, somehow, located a record of the Hills' sessions with Benjamin Simon. By August he was calling friends of the Hills, and on August 19 he wrote to the Hills themselves, asking for an interview. Betty wrote to Walter Webb that she and Barney "have decided we are NOT going to be involved in his story." They ignored Luttrell's attempts to make contact. At one point they arrived home to find him sitting on their porch awaiting their return. Barney threw the car into gear and they drove around the neighborhood for ninety minutes waiting for him to leave. Hoping to stop publication of the articles, or at the least ensure that their names were not printed, the Hills hired a lawyer.[2]

Their attorney sent letters to Luttrell and his editors but failed to put a scare into the *Traveller*. Beginning on October 25, 1965, Luttrell's five-part story ran. The title of the first article was "A UFO Chiller: Did THEY Seize Couple?"[3] And with that the Hills' story ceased to be their own.

The public's response confirmed the Hills' fears that publication of Luttrell's articles would cost them. It also served as a graphic illustration of the fault lines that ran through American society. Nearly all the coverage hit the same three beats. Beginning with Luttrell himself, the media first acknowledged how professional and respectable the couple seemed to be: the very embodiment of decent Americans. Then, the media puzzled how such a seemingly solid couple could offer up such an irrational story, illustrating the success of the twenty-year campaign to delegitimate speculation about UFOs and expand the distance between individual experience and scientific expertise. Third, such coverage sought an explanation of the Hills' irrationality, and most found it in their interracial marriage. It was no surprise, then, that as Betty and Barney saw their story questioned, Barney's hopes for racial reconciliation likewise took a beating.

The Condon Committee

In the twenty years since Kenneth Arnold's 1947 sighting, the government's effort to label UFO witness testimony as unscientific and irrational had largely succeeded, and the language of mental health was key to the effort. In the fall of 1966, roughly the same time John Fuller published *The Interrupted Journey*, the University of Colorado physicist Edward Condon agreed to direct an Air Force–

sponsored special committee intended to settle the question of UFOs. In its summary report the committee worked hard to distinguish between objective, rational scientific data and the reports of regular citizens, "a notoriously unreliable source of information." Mark Rhine, a psychology professor and member of the committee, argued that UFO belief was a product of psychological problems. There are, he wrote, "perceptual distortions which are experienced by everyone. Other distortions may be peculiar to the individual because of his own psychological needs." He pointed to "mass hysteria," to hallucination, and to "the anxieties of a nuclear age." Ultimately the report reached the same conclusion as earlier Air Force studies: American citizens were unreliable. To the extent that they assigned meaning to anomalies in the sky, they were externalizing their own irrational anxieties. Edward Condon himself denounced UFO belief as not merely "pseudo-science" but "scientific pornography." He stated, hyperbolically, his belief that "teachers who teach any of the pseudo-sciences as established truth should, on being found guilty, be publicly horsewhipped."[4]

Belief that UFO sightings were the product of psychology rather than physics was evident in popular interpretation of the Hill case. In November 1965 in the *Boston Herald,* Harvard astronomer Donald Menzel explained that the Hills were so struck by the things they had seen in the sky because they were "among the uninitiated who've never seen anything like them before." Menzel insisted that "each UFO has a simple explanation" and told the paper the Hills had probably failed to recognize a planet, a shooting star, or another natural phenomenon because of their emotion and ignorance.[5]

But the Hills insisted, though increasingly alone, that they were reliable, and they used the tools available to them to spread their claims. The 1960s through early 1970s were what one historian has called "television's moment." Live coverage of events like the Vietnam War and the Kennedy assassination solidified television's power as the dominant form of American media. But at the same time, the furious competition for eyes drove many television producers to seek out increasingly titillating, provocative, and even frivolous stories, pursuing audiences increasingly narrow in interests.[6]

The Hills experienced this disjuncture. They sought to use the medium to press their respectability and credibility—but television producers often saw in them simply a spectacle of the sort that appealed to the public's fascination with their marriage and their perhaps odd psychology. In 1968 they appeared on the *Phil Donahue Show,* a talk show that had started only the year before but was already known for its host's taste for the scandalous and provocative. They appeared on Art Linkletter's *House Party,* a comedy and variety show. Perhaps most famously, Barney appeared on the game show *To Tell the Truth,* on which he appeared with two other men who each attempted to convince contestants that he was the one who had seen a UFO.[7] In one appearance in November 1965, Betty Hill insisted that "there have been over 300 scientific recordings of UFOs" by "reliable, honest people." Barney mentioned he had just received an award from Sargent Shriver, who was supervising the War on Poverty for Lyndon Johnson.[8] But more typical was an hour-long CBS special in August 1967, called "Captured by a UFO." The Hills appeared, told their story, and were pummeled by a panel of scientists who charged their story with "intrinsic implausibility," citing the improbability of long-range space travel and the Hills' inability to produce physical proof. Rather, the scientists claimed, the encounter had happened inside their minds.[9]

And finally, there was cynicism. "Whether Betty and Barney Hill spent two hours aboard a flying saucer is subject to doubt, but there's no doubt they're cashing in on the experience," stated the *San Francisco Examiner.*[10]

Most journalists were not so dismissive as that. But the more sympathetic they were, the harder it was for them to understand why the Hills believed as they did. John Barker, a features reporter for the *Portsmouth Herald,* wrote in confusion, "Barney and Betty Hill are just not the type of people that would dream up this sort of thing," crediting their activity in the civil rights movement and solid middle-class careers.[11] Poppy Cannon White, the flamboyant former editor of *Ladies' Home Journal,* herself a white woman married to a Black man (NAACP leader Walter White) expressed a sort of motherly condescension for the Hills, whom she met for coffee after reading Fuller's book. "They are the kind of people you might expect to find," she wrote, "at a meeting of the Parent-Teachers Association." She declined to signal whether she believed their story, claiming simply, "Never have I had a more exciting coffee break."[12]

Of all these stories, John Luttrell's articles explored the dilemma most thoroughly. He presented the Hills' experience as a cautionary and confusing tale, exciting because of the proximity between the respectable and the strange within it, but dangerous because it revealed the psychological chinks in democracy's

Betty and Barney Hill appear on a panel discussion after the publication of *The Interrupted Journey* made their case famous.
Box 7, Folder 12, BBHP, University of New Hampshire. Used with permission.

armor. The strange object in the sky, he wrote, "may have frightened the couple so badly, the result was an intensely realistic impression upon their subconscious that time may never erase." He paid Barney Hill the backhanded compliment of "average intelligence" and observed that the couple felt that they were "losing their minds" for months after the encounter. He worried about what their experience said about their activism. The Hills had learned from Benjamin Simon that their story transgressed the boundaries of what the American elite were willing to stomach, but to see it in print was even more devastating.[13]

Interracial Marriage

The Hills attracted a number of overtly racist attacks. For instance, John Fuller reported that "extremists in Portsmouth" targeted the couple shortly before *The Interrupted Journey* appeared in bookstores. Their "car was splattered with eggs and a swastika was painted on their sidewalk."[14] Barney's civil rights work and the simple fact of their marriage attracted such aggression.

But many who pointed to the marriage as the root of the Hills' problem were liberals who believed in integration, and their judgments indicated the deep sexual fears that lay near the heart of racism in the United States. The 1960 US census documented 51,000 mixed-race marriages in the United States, and as the decade went on liberals grappled with the institution, and not without internal conflict. Black media worked hard to normalize the institution, and the Hills served as a potent weapon. John Johnson, the Black publishing magnate who owned *JET* magazine was a strong advocate for interracial marriage, believing as did many liberals that the more contact white and Black Americans had the more white Americans would become comfortable with integration. In 1966, *JET* featured Betty and Barney Hill, under the headline "Negro, White Wife Say They Were Kidnaped, Taken in Outer Space." Reporter Bobbie Barbee went to New Hampshire to meet the two, and emphasized that, contrary to much white angst about the destructive potential of interracial marriages, the Hills were a "friendly, intelligent and engrossing pair," active in their community and leaders in the civil rights movement. Unlike many other journalists, Barbee did not cast doubt on the Hills' account.[15]

But many white liberals were not so sanguine. Many agreed with Gunnar Myrdal's claim in *An American Dilemma*: "Sexual segregation is the most pervasive form of segregation. . . . No excuse for other forms of social segregation and discrimination is so potent as the one that sociable relations on an equal basis between members of the two races may possibly lead to intermarriage."[16] In a controversial column on President Dwight Eisenhower's decision to use the National Guard to force the public schools of Little Rock, Arkansas, to obey the Supreme Court's order to desegregate, liberal philosopher Hannah Arendt observed caustically that "the Civil Rights bill did not go far enough, for it left untouched the most outrageous law of southern states — the law which makes mixed marriage a criminal offense."[17] Myrdal and Arendt agreed that southerners would inevitably and consistently resist integrated schools, integrated restaurants, and all other integration, not as an end to itself but because stopping integration would stymie interracial marriage, the great taboo. After all, interracial marriage would lead, ultimately, to equalization of power across racial lines in American society, and even many liberals struggled to imagine what that future might look like.

Because there was such vociferous resistance to interracial marriage, even many white Americans who supported integration nonetheless worried the practice would inevitably damage the mental health and social standing of any who participated in it. Repeatedly through the 1940s and 1950s American mental health professionals, integrationist liberals for the most part, warned of its dangers. Randall Risdon, for instance, studied interracial marriages in Los Angeles in 1954 and concluded that such couples "live with the feeling that social conflict in some form is always in the offing." That feeling of tension would inevitably harm their psychological health and their marriage. "The security and orderly living which most people hope to obtain from marriage are made doubly difficult by the nature of society and the cultural heritage which each race brings to it," he wrote. The psychiatrist George Little concluded grimly that interracial marriage would only be sought out by people "with an urge toward self-destruction." It was, quite simply, "spiritual death."[18]

The 1967 film *Guess Who's Coming to Dinner?* dramatized the problem perfectly. The film is a fable about the Draytons, two aging, successful white liberals whose daughter Joanna unexpectedly announces her engagement to a polished doctor, a Black man named John. Over and over, Joanna father Matt insists that he is not against their marriage per se, but rather because, as he tells her, "The problems you're going to have, they seem almost unimaginable." In the film's final speech, Matt worries to his family, "There'll be a hundred million people right here in this country who will be shocked and offended and appalled at the two of you, and the two of you will just have to ride that out, maybe every day for the rest of your lives." Throughout the film he assures himself and his wife and daughter that he is not prejudiced, that his fears are purely for the psychological and social impact the marriage will have on his child and her husband, and in so doing reveals the grip of systemic prejudice even on such an enlightened figure as himself. After all, although Matt gradually conquers his anxieties, the film goes out of its way to make John nonthreatening. He is of unimpeachable character and success; Joanna even assures her father her fiancé has insisted they will not have sex until marriage. Even with such mitigating circumstances, Matt spends much of the film in anguished worry over what such a marriage would do to his daughter's psyche.[19]

As *Guess Who's Coming to Dinner?* was playing in movie theaters around the country, American liberals who read about the Hills began acting a bit like Matt Drayton. Benjamin Simon claimed that his views on the role of race, particularly in the Hills' case, "coincided entirely" with those of the Black actor and activist James Earl Jones, whom he met while Jones was considering making a film about the case. And yet Simon confessed to John Fuller that when he went to his waiting room the morning of December 14, he was "stunned to find there was a colored man." After all, Simon explained, his was an "expensive practice."[20]

People like Drayton and Simon were theoretical believers in integration who carried ingrained assumptions that voluntary segregation, at least in the case of marriage, might save everybody a lot of stress and grief. The agony of such white liberals revealed the tensions race placed on the ideals and expectations of postwar American liberal integrationism — enough that many who observed the Hill case believed that Betty and Barney's interracial marriage would produce in them stress enough to generate psychological pathology.

Such judgments were not uncommon in the 1960s; indeed, they were part and parcel of the War on Poverty, the greatest domestic political conversation of the time. Perhaps the most famous manifesto of that effort was Daniel Patrick Moynihan's report *The Negro Family: A Case for National Action*, written in 1965, when he was a young analyst in Johnson's Department of Labor, to help guide the War on Poverty. Using the work of contemporary sociologists and psychologists — including Kenneth Clark, whose research had tipped the balance in *Brown v. Board of Education* — Moynihan argued that the trauma of slavery left Black families poor, uneducated, and reliant on mothers rather than fathers, a state of affairs that produced single-parent families and hence replicated itself. Moynihan read this as trauma, psychological as well as physical, and worried that because African Americans were trapped in this terrible cycle they could not escape it alone. He called for a massive national effort to alleviate poverty and discrimination, but the lasting impact of the report ended up being his diagnosis. African American existence in the United States was inherently pathological. Black people were helpless against it. Therefore, Moynihan argued, "the programs of the

Federal government bearing on this objective shall be designed to have the effect, directly or indirectly, of enhancing the stability and resources of the Negro American family."[21]

This diagnosis was mirrored in those the Hills received. Simon felt from the beginning that Barney was out of place and that this positioning would result in psychological damage. After all, he began his work with the Hills presuming that their distress derived from Barney. Despite placing the weight of the abduction story on Betty, the doctor remained convinced that it was Barney's racial fears that spurred his tension and thus began the story of the night. As Simon described the abduction to John Fuller, "In the abduction Barney's removal from the car by the dark coated men creates a magnificent image of the lynching of a negro. It would again emphasize and beautifully picture by the simile the fear of abduction (lynching) which can be partly resolved by accepting it under more favorable conditions."[22] For Simon, Barney's vision of the world around him was inescapably marked by Barney's own Blackness, and his ability to correctly grasp reality was therefore inevitably hampered. It was no fault of his own; he was a helpless pawn to the society he lived in.

Some variant of this explanation spread throughout the press. Again and again, white journalists painted Barney and Betty as helpless victims driven to bizarre beliefs by social condemnation of their marriage. *Time* magazine called the Hills' experience "wish-fulfillment fantasies," as when, for instance, "Barney, who generally considers the Irish to be hostile toward Negroes, remembers being treated with respect by a humanoid who looked Irish." For *Time* the dots were easy to connect.[23] Others targeted their marriage itself. Writing in *Look* magazine, the Baptist minister Daniel Tuttle declared, "In our civilization such a marriage meets with social disapproval and with deep-seated (even though often unrealized) guilt feelings in the couple themselves."[24] An Oregon journalist who wrote an extended review of Fuller's book observed, "their interracial marriage . . . made their story that much more difficult to tell to the world because of the extra hostility" that it attracted.[25] Allen Spraggett, religion editor for the *Toronto Star,* published a long analysis of the Hill case that leaned extensively on Simon. According to Spraggett, Simon believed "Barney Hill's anxiety over the interracial marriage . . . predisposed him toward some kind of emotional upheaval." As for Betty, Spraggett quoted Simon describing the long needle that the aliens inserted into her navel: "The sexual symbolism in Mrs. Hill's account is magnificent. Her story has a terrific sexual content obvious to any person who is psychoanalytically sophisticated."[26]

The Hills were furious with Spraggett's story. A sympathetic member of NICAP alerted them to its publication, sending the Hills a letter that accused the media in general and Spraggett and Simon in particular with engaging in "obvious Freudian reactions" that said more about the diagnosers than the diagnosed. Betty angrily forwarded the letter and a copy of Spraggett's story to Simon, and the psychiatrist responded with a placating letter assuring her, perhaps disingenuously, that "I was not interviewed by anyone" and "at no time have I interpreted your dreams or experience nor do I propose to." He accused the informer of being "an obvious anti-psychologist."[27]

The only one who seemed on the Hills' side was John Fuller. In his book Fuller worked hard to present the Hills' reality in fact as racially blind and integrated as many liberals imagined America should be—and in so doing he removed racial angst as a possible inspiration for the abduction story as much as he could. Early in the book Fuller claimed "their problems as an interracial couple are minimal," and "the total adjustment to their mixed marriage had been remarkably smooth." He insisted that the couple rarely was concerned with race at all, "no longer self-conscious" about their marriage. Indeed, Fuller posited that Barney's race was a source of pride. He called Barney a "descendant of a proud Ethiopian freeman."[28]

But in order to neutralize the challenge of race in the Hills' story, Fuller had to silently edit the story as the Hills told it—revealing the same tension that Barney Hill experienced in his own life. For instance, Fuller removed the pistol Barney packed into the car and later in a panic dug out. Instead, he called it a "tire wrench." Fuller also edited Barney's hypnotic description of the cup placed over what Barney called his "private parts," euphemizing Barney's language so as to obscure the long and ugly American tropes of Black male violence and Black male sexuality, to keep for Barney as positive an image as possible, and to attempt extraction of the shadow of racialized, psychological pathology from their story. Walter Webb caught the change but understood it, writing to the Hills, "I suppose there was a good reason for doing this."[29]

Alien Bodies

In *Look* magazine the minister Daniel Tuttle wrote that the strain over the Hills' marriage explained most things about their memories of the encounter. He found it fascinating that "this childless couple found their road blocked by humanoids, smaller than themselves whose skin was of a gray color. These small gray-skinned people communicated with a 'mumumum' sound, like that of small children." He concluded that the Hills' experience was "the externalization of a traumatic subconscious mental crisis." The creatures were the children — half-Black, half-white, gray — Barney and Betty would never have, the children Tuttle thought they feared to have in a society that inflicted trauma upon relationships like theirs. These small, large-headed, gray-skinned aliens have become cliché, and they have ancestors as far back as the nineteenth century and beyond, but they entered the American popular consciousness in the story of Betty and Barney Hill.[30]

Even though the abductors Barney and Betty faced were presumably extraterrestrial, nobody in the case — from observers like Tuttle to Barney and Betty themselves — could help but to place them on the racial spectrum as they understood it, drawing these creatures into conversations that sought to explain the most painful and pressing divide of their lived experience in the United States. Indeed, for some scholars the history of alien bodies in the United States, from Adamski's blonde Venusians to the Hills' small gray interlocutors, is irreducibly racialized, as humans seek to place the creatures they encounter upon a racial spectrum they have already always imagined to be real.[31] As with so much about September 19, Betty and Barney and all those who heard their story perceived the racial implications of their abductors' bodies, in ways that reflected their distinctive perceptions of that gulf.

In their interviews with John Fuller in preparation for the writing of *The Interrupted Journey*, Barney told the journalist about a frequent disagreement between the couple. He described

> many quarrels where [Betty] had in her dreams described the leader as being a very handsome person. And I would say, they are not handsome, Betty. Now this is interesting, because Betty would then say, What did they look like? And I would

reply that I just didn't know, I couldn't put my finger on it, but they are not handsome. I was very adamant about this and she was equally convinced by her dreams that they were very handsome.[32]

The dispute revealed two things. First, outside of Betty's dreams neither Barney nor Betty enunciated in print a clear description of the appearance of the creatures in the craft before their hypnosis, and even in the transcripts of those sessions what impressions they did give were glancing and analogical and weighed with emotional freight. In her letter to Donald Keyhoe, Betty described them only as "dressed in some kind of shiny black uniform" and "scurrying about" industriously. To the audience at the Two-State UFO Study Group, Barney used the phrase "human-type."[33] To Walter Webb, Barney said more, recalling figures in uniform and of "human form." He also said they reminded him "of the cold precision of German officers." Webb wrote that Barney described a "leader" who "held a special attraction for the witness and frightened him terribly." These were "beings of a superior type, beings that were somehow not human."[34]

These essential elements of danger and inhumanity echoed through Barney's hypnotic statements. He seemed to deny that these creatures seemed human, though he was willing to compare them to humans. When Simon asked if "there was resemblance" between the "hoodlum" who had caused Barney anxiety on the Montreal trip and the figure of the leader, Barney issued a flat denial. However, when Simon asked if they looked like white men, Barney said, "I don't know about the color, but they did not seem that they had different faces from white men," a convoluted description that again conveys impression without detail. He described two of the figures more thoroughly, though again eschewing precise detail for analogy. There was one "whose face is round," whose smile reminded him of a "redheaded Irishman" and the leader. When Simon asked Barney to describe the leader Barney said only that he had "an evil face . . . [he] looks like a German Nazi." He described them wearing scarves in addition to their caps and uniforms. And he said they made him feel like a rabbit, a rabbit of the sort that he hunted in Virginia as a boy. "I'm that bunny! I'm going to be pounced on!" he cried.[35]

Barney's complicated descriptions of the creatures cannot be understood apart from that terror. His emphasis on the inhuman parts of these creatures — their uniforms, the leader's haunting eyes, which Barney described as "slanted [but] not like a Chinese" — distanced them from himself. He did not elaborate on what their "human form" was, instead drawing out the military, regimented, and threatening aspects of their appearance. He also, tellingly, described them as not unlike white people, even if they did not appear like white people. By comparing himself to the rabbit, Barney implicitly asserted that if these creatures were humans, he himself was not. By comparing the aliens to segregationists and Nazis and white people, he made the same point in reverse. To Barney, these creatures were distant from his own experience and inescapably hostile because of that difference.[36]

Before undergoing hypnosis Betty did not offer a description of the creatures from conscious memory. But they came to her in her dreams, and in "Dreams or Recall?" she gave a similar, although much fuller description than did her husband.

> I would judge them to be 5' to 5'4". Their chests are larger than ours; their noses were larger (longer) than the average size altho I have seen people with noses like theirs — like Jimmy Durante's. Their complexions were of a gray tone, like a gray paint with a black base; their lips were of bluish tint. Hair and eyes were very dark, possibly black. The men were all dressed alike, presumably in uniform, of slight navy blue color with a gray shade to it.[37]

As with her husband Betty's emotional reaction to the creatures was marked in her perception of their appearance. Her dream memory was that they were "human in their appearance, not frightening. They seemed to be very relaxed, friendly in a professional way (businesslike)." The ontological gap between herself and these creatures was slight and bridged far more easily than it was for Barney. She chatted with the leader and recalled him "firmly but gently reassuring me . . . as tho I was a small child."[38] While Barney felt pursued by beings distinctly different from himself, Betty felt cared for, uncomprehending but ultimately safe in the hands of beings more like her than not.

These overriding senses of the type of relationship each had with the creatures on the craft colored the Hills' description of them under hypnosis, even after they came at that point to agree on the creatures' appearances. Their descriptions also showed how the concept of race as the Hills experienced it marked their experience and memory.

Betty Hill, convinced that racism might be best fought through equal treatment and race-blindness, thought of the aliens as simply another sort of human. Though their physical appearance changed for her while under hypnosis, the mixture of fear, anticipation, and ultimately comfort that she had experienced in her dreams did not measurably alter, from the moment the leader companionably asked her husband's name. In her dreams he was a short man with dark hair, grayish skin, and a large nose. Under hypnosis, she grew more agitated about their appearance, for when Simon asked her to describe the creatures, she showed anxiety and struggled. The first thing she came up with was that "they were out of proportion." When Simon asked what she meant, she to some extent echoed her dreams: "They were short. . . . They had a larger chest cavity, structure. They were maybe broader than we are through their shoulders." The difference seemed to be in their faces. "I want to say that their faces look like people, but I can't say that they did."[39] She did not give Simon much more detail than that.

Polygenesis

Despite the vague descriptions of the creatures the Hills delivered while under hypnosis, it was evident Betty and Barney emerged from their treatment with a clearer image of alien bodies, and one that helped Betty order their presence in her egalitarian, universalist universe. In October 1964, the Hills drove to Exeter to hear a lecture by University of Pennsylvania anthropologist Carleton Coon. Betty wrote to Webb that the title of the lecture was "The Races of Man," which drew on a seven-hundred-page book, *The Origin of Races*, that Coon had published in 1962. Coon enunciated its argument succinctly: "Over half a million years ago, man was a single species, *Homo Erectus*, perhaps already divided into five geographic races or subspecies. *Homo Erectus* then evolved into *Homo*

Sapiens not once but five times, as each subspecies, living in its own territory, passed a critical threshold from a more brutal to a more sapient state."[40] Coon conceded that *Homo erectus* had emerged in Africa, but he believed that *Homo sapiens* had evolved first in Europe (as what he called "Caucasoids") and in Asia. He thought that Europeans had some 150,000 years advantage on Africans ("Congoids"). In Coon's mind this accounted for the superiority of white civilization. "If Africa was the cradle of mankind," he wrote, "it was only an indifferent kindergarten. Europe and Asia were our principal schools."[41]

Coon's ideas were a throwback to nineteenth-century "polygenesis" theories that posited the apparent "races" of humanity (and precisely what these were — "Congoid," "Caucasoid," and so on — depended on whom one asked) were in fact different species, related but distinct in ways deeper than simple phenotype, or appearance. Coon did not go so far. By the twentieth century most such theories had surrendered the field to "monogenesis," which acknowledged that *Homo sapiens* was a single species, and Coon agreed. But Coon certainly conceived of his work as a rebuttal to what he called the "Boasinine school." Franz Boas, a towering figure in American anthropology, maintained that the seeming differences in human "races" were cultural, not biological. Coon complained to a friend that Boas's followers "have been trying to suppress me ever since Boas tried to suppress my *Races of Europe* in the 1930s."[42] Meanwhile, throughout the 1960s Coon maintained a guarded, if friendly correspondence with white supremacists who found his theories the closest scientific justification they could get to debunking the Black freedom movement. Coon, nonactivist but skeptical of racial integration, enjoyed the attention and did not mind the politics.[43]

Nothing indicates that Betty and Barney Hill were aware of Coon's entanglements. But Betty's description of what she learned from Coon bears the marks of his ideas — even as she took them in a direction that Coon would not have recognized. Betty reported her impressions of Coon's lecture in that letter to Webb and two years later recounted them to John Fuller. In *The Interrupted Journey* Fuller incorrectly attributes a lightly edited version of Betty's memories of Coon's speech to Barney. The ideas therein illustrate Betty's beliefs about aliens, humanity, and race better than Barney's.[44]

Betty reported to Webb that Coon showed a slide show. One image was

A woman who lives in a very cold climate and showed her physical adaptation to this very cold. I believe she is of Mongolian background, with very distinct slant eyes. Her adaptation is the formation of a fatty substance around her eyes, which causes the appearance of a large eye extending around to the side. Her nose is very small and flat to her face. Her mouth seems distorted by this fatty substance. . . . I do not know where that UFO was from, but I am convinced it must be a very cold climate. It was surprising to actually see a picture which resembled the men so closely — much better than we could ever begin to do.[45]

The description of the "men" in the craft here for the first time in writing implies what the Hills later enunciated more clearly: a small, almost missing nose and mouth below the large slanted eyes that Barney had remembered from the beginning.

In their interviews with John Fuller in mid-1966, the Hills gave their clearest description of the men to date, and again Betty invoked Carleton Coon. When asked about their appearance, Barney told John Fuller:

There was this grotesque kind of head with a larger cranium, diminishing as it would get toward the chin. And they [had] eyes that continued around to the side of their heads so they could look in a complete 45° angle. . . . The mouth was much like you draw one horizontal line, then draw two perpendicular lines on the end of the horizontal line, and then let this horizontal line as if it would represent the lips without the muscle that we have, would part, and whenever it would part there would come forth this membrane right there on the edge of the lips. And when the lips would part this membrane would flutter. . . . Aluminum color . . . baldish, without any hair. . . . Only two slits that represented the nostrils.[46]

After Barney's extensive description, Fuller turned to Betty and asked her to comment on it. She demurred on the sort of detailed description that Barney gave. "It's very hard for me to describe people," she said. Instead she brought up Coon's lecture. She remembered his discussion of a "group of Indians, and they lived in a very extremely cold atmosphere . . . where there's very little oxygen . . . . . there [sic] bodies had changed to adapt to the climate." They had, Betty said, "an oriental eye, but the eye socket itself gave an appearance of being much larger than it actually was because nature had developed the roll of fat around the eye, also that around the mouth. So it looked as if they had almost no opening. Also they had practically no nose . . . very very tiny ears. They did have hair and they are basically I would guess Oriental. And they were all about 4 ½' [feet tall]." Later, she would invoke her profession to Fuller, describing children with what would later be called Down's syndrome in an effort to link the appearance of the aliens to scientifically describable origins. "They looked a great deal like Mongoloids," she said, thinking of "a specific Mongoloid child I had been working with."[47]

Betty did not simply parrot Coon's ideas; rather, she seized certain of his ideas and used them in ways that might have been unfamiliar to Coon, but which helped her to place the creatures into the universe ordered as she understood it. Coon's theories of uneven human evolution and regional adaptation explained the creatures' appearance and their relationship to humanity. As she later wrote to a friend, "Barney and I had the theory that the star that the humanoids were from probably was a colder planet than the earth." Jack Mendelsohn, the popular Unitarian writer, declared his faith "affirms the oneness of the universe, the oneness of the human family, the oneness of discovered and discoverable truth, the universal validity of free inquiry, and the dawn of universal man."[48] Betty Hill found that principle in Coon's work. The beings evolved in the same way human beings did, were subject to the same laws. And as time went on Betty began to interweave the fates of the craft's occupants and those of humanity itself.

Several times in 1967 and 1968 the Hills described the creatures in specific detail for interested parties. At the end of September 1967 the two had the artist David Baker over for dinner. Energized by their conversation about the creatures, he began a series of charcoal sketches in the Hills' dining room, which he enlarged and elaborated on over the next months.

The Hills were not satisfied with Baker's initial sketches, and on Monday, October 2, he wrote to them explaining, "With my knowledge of anatomy I am endeavoring to put your detailed facial descriptions into a possible anatomical arrangement following known laws of bone structure." He explained that the Hills' descriptions of the creatures' eyes "would extend cheek bones around curve of front facial plane . . . not so much oriental as like a cat's eyes."

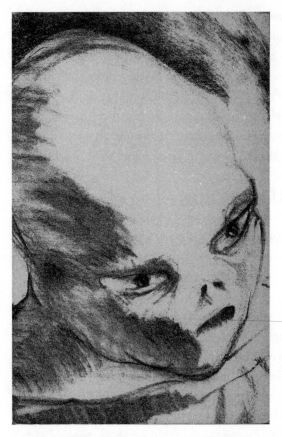

Charcoal sketch of alien head, by David Baker. Baker, an artist friend of the Hills, spent several hours with the two of them trying to capture their memories of the creatures that captured them. Oversized Box 2, BBHP, University of New Hampshire. Used with permission.

He observed, echoing Betty's impressions, that the overall description of "wide cheeked, weak chinned" creatures indeed gave a "Mongoloid suggestion to [the] face." In her response Betty compared the creatures' eyes not to a cat but to a "wall gecko," and she conceded that "whether their body build is a result of long space travel or atmospheric conditions on their home planet is speculative, but it might be indicative of a planet much older in time than we are." Betty had begun to think of these creatures as the product of the same evolutionary process that produced human beings; different less in kind than in degree.[49]

The following spring, in April 1968, the Hills invited Allen Hynek and John Fuller to a dinner party hosted by Benjamin Simon. Following the meal Simon hypnotized the pair so Hynek could question them. In these conversations the Hills largely affirmed and expanded their earlier descriptions of the creatures.

Painting of the alien leader, by David Baker.
Oversized Box 2, BBHP, University of New Hampshire. Used with permission.

Betty talked about communicating with the creatures. She said it was "like learning French when you first hear the French word, you think of it in English." Barney focused on details that horrified him: "spindly legs," "eyes with bright lights." When Hynek asked if he could analogize the aliens or the sounds they made to "represent anything you know," Barney said no. He said instead of thinking about what they looked like, "I thought if only I could get my fists up."[50]

In 1968 Betty wrote to Walter Webb, sounding slightly dazzled by the wave of attention that had overcome the Hills in the prior two years — "scientists, psychologists, psychiatrists, TV, radio, press, magazines and the general public" had all descended upon them. In the midst of this she noted to Webb, "An English psychiatrist flew over from London and was amazed at the drawings — for the occupants look like it is expected we will look in 1000 years!" She observed to Webb that the needle the occupants used to test her for pregnancy is "now in everyday usage in big city hospitals."[51] Both the creatures' technologies and their bodies were recognizable as the products of a possible human evolution and development and, hence for Betty, an ultimately hopeful vision of a possible future of her own species.

She held to these beliefs throughout her life, and they came to shape how she imagined the aliens' purpose in coming to Earth. Some years later she wrote, "The human form is the highest level of evolution. Therefore it could be assumed that this is true elsewhere in the universe." The aliens, she said, came to evaluate "my cell structure, my DNA, my genetic code," wondering what human beings were — "a different kind of mankind from them," as it turned out. She remembered from her work in child welfare and having "seen these children develop, progress, and graduate . . . [that] only mankind has these abilities." That, it occurred to her, was perhaps what these extraterrestrials were doing. She wrote to Benjamin Simon in early 1965 that she expected them to return and that her fear of such a thing was waning.[52] In old age she wrote to an acquaintance that scientists had assured her that the appearance of the creatures was that of "future man. If we continue along our paths of evolution, we will look like this in about 25,000 years." The process was beginning. She reported hearing that "in some countries babies are being born with rectangular eye sockets, some kind of mutation and a first in the history of mankind."[53]

The Collapse of Integration in Portsmouth

Though both Betty and Barney believed that the extraterrestrials were interested in human life, Barney never expressed, as Betty did, the belief that this interest derived from relationality and human evolutionary development. Instead, he told John Fuller that these creatures had to come "from other solar systems" because they had "less of this kind of knowledge of the anatomy of human beings." While his wife could communicate with these creatures, to Barney they made only a "mumumumum" sound, "some kind of sound, which had no meaning to me," said Barney. When Fuller asked if he anticipated another "UFO incident," Barney had not even considered it. "I don't have any further fear of that," he said.[54]

His sense of distance from the craft's occupants mirrored his growing frustration with racial relations in the United States, and his sense that too many white people viewed him and other Black people with the same superior, clinical distance as did the extraterrestrials. He had thrown himself into the work of the NAACP with determination, but the grumpy intransigence of Charles Sprague, proprietor of Clint's Barber Shop, had shaken his confidence that law and persuasion might succeed. Throughout the mid-1960s as often as Barney and other African Americans achieved gains, they also encountered significant setbacks. Throughout early 1964, Barney lobbied strenuously for the passage of the Civil Rights Act. His letters to Congress were confident and showed certainty that the tides of history were on his side. "The face of N.H. is changing," he advised the state's senator, Norris Cotton, a Republican who worried that the act was an overreach of federal power. "We people of N.H. have no pride in being known as the Mississippi of the North."[55]

But arguments like this had not convinced Sprague, nor did they convince some members of New Hampshire's congressional delegation. Louis Wyman, the representative for Portsmouth, announced that he believed the Civil Rights Act was unconstitutional and would vote against it. A few months later, when Wyman visited Portsmouth, Barney and the local NAACP president Thomas Cobbs were waiting. In what the *Portsmouth Herald* called a "fiery public confrontation," Barney and Cobbs cornered the congressman at an event and demanded he justify his vote. Cobbs pointed out that Wyman had justified a vote

—

against home rule for the city of Washington, D.C., "because there were too many Negroes there." Wyman, stammering, said that he believed "Negroes in Washington had not yet attained a sufficient cultural level" for self-government. Barney grew understandably angry. "I can't see how that's the fault of the Negro," he said coldly. Wyman cut the conversation off, leaving the two NAACP men unsatisfied.[56]

Such confrontations discouraged Barney. Even more distressing was the white hostility that seemed to intensify as Congress moved to pass the Civil Rights Act. On May 24, 1964, a month after the dispute with Wyman, Barney stopped at a beach in Hampton, New Hampshire, on his way home from the Boston post office and saw a group of young white people "flying a confederate flag and sitting in a ring of beer cans." They were giving another group of youths "a rough time." He called the police. But things got worse. That summer in his position with the NAACP, Barney gathered a host of complaints. There was a Black airman at Pease Air Force Base named Luther Anderson who bought a trailer in a Dover, New Hampshire, trailer park only to discover that the owners of the park would not rent him the land where the trailer rested. There was a white landlady who sought to avoid Black tenants. There was a Black woman named Geraldine Grant who was fired from a corporate position with no warning and forty-five-minutes' notice. Over and over again Barney investigated, made phone calls, sent letters — and often was unsuccessful. In June 1964, after several weeks of advocating on behalf of Luther Anderson, the city attorney for Dover copied Barney on a letter stating that he was terminating his investigation because "it does not appear to me to be a matter of racial discrimination." The NAACP's investigation of the landlady was unable to secure actionable evidence. And so on.[57]

Soon after the Civil Rights Act was passed Barney delivered a weary speech denouncing some of these injustices and claiming that more than laws had to change. He was beginning to worry that his trust in the power of the state to change minds was unjustified. "Too many people feel that New Hampshire has no problems in race relations. It is not well known that New Hampshire has a very long history of prejudice," he said. "New Hampshire has a good law. Added to this is the US Civil Rights Act. . . . But laws are only as good as the people make them," he concluded in frustration. Barney had grown up among the Old Philadelphians, people convinced that the government could, through laws and persuasion, change minds about racism. Now he was faced with evidence that social change was perhaps more difficult than he had believed.[58]

And then there was violence. White violence against Black Americans was nothing new, but it seemed only to intensify as good laws were passed. Barney had marched in a demonstration in September 1963 after Ku Klux Klan members bombed a Black Baptist church in Birmingham, killing four young girls. Two years later, in March of 1965, he found himself marching again when the Unitarian minister James Reeb and the Unitarian activist Viola Liuzzo were killed in Selma, Alabama, while participating in a voting rights march there. In August he again mourned when the Episcopal seminarian Jonathan Daniels was killed protecting a seventeen-year-old Black girl during a voting registration drive in Lowndes County, Alabama, and when police officers killed a Black man in Springfield, Massachusetts — not so far away from Portsmouth — leading to weeks of demonstrations and marches against police violence and a segregated school system. It was an "insult," Barney said in a speech, that the Springfield protestors were arrested "while the killer of Rev. Daniels was allowed to go free." Tom Coleman, who shot Daniels, was acquitted at trial by an all-white jury. And on Wednesday, August 11, only days after the passage of the Voting Rights Act, the Los Angeles police stopped a Black man for drunk driving in the neighborhood of Watts. As officers arrested him, a crowd gathered and the incident escalated into violence. The next day the mayor called for the National Guard, and Los Angeles was occupied in the face of civilian unrest, particularly among the city's Black community. Over the next six days, more than three thousand citizens were arrested and thirty-four were killed.[59]

At some point soon after that long, hot summer Barney drafted a speech. In these years he regularly spoke at the Portsmouth Naval Shipyard, which held seminars and other events on public affairs.[60] He was tired, he said, describing the "police brutality" that had sparked the "tragedies [of] summer, 1965." But most difficult to him was that despite all of the violence and suffering, he saw much less progress than he had hoped. "We still have the imposing problems of racial imbalance in the school systems, housing, job inequities, and other matters," he wrote. And he worried that the swamp of intransigence and viciousness in which the movement found itself indicated that his earlier beliefs about the inevitability of progress were naïve. The summer's violence seemed to show that persuasion

---

simply might not work. "Springfield has been particularly disturbing," he confessed. "The issue had to be forced where the authority was plainly hostile."[61]

Barney shared his jadedness with others in his congregation and denomination. John Papandrew was never content in the South Church pulpit, and as the country moved so did he. In August 1962 he went to Albany, Georgia, to join a two-year campaign to destroy the city's segregationist laws. Papandrew wrote that he found the movement's energy remarkable. It was "one of the most moving experiences of my life. Time and time again," while marching down the street or sitting in a singing congregation of demonstrators, "I had all I could do to fight back tears."[62] The experience suited Papandrew's moral zeal. He met many sorts of people in Albany, Black and white, Catholic, Jewish, and Protestant, but "we suddenly found ourselves of one accord and one heart, unified in the midst of diversity."[63] He was dismayed that those people who should have understood him best, his Portsmouth congregation, seemed not to grasp what seemed so clear to him.

Papandrew remembered that soon after his arrival at South Church, the congregation's treasurer, John Wiggin, warned him to "stop rocking the boat." A delegation of distinguished church members later came to his house to tell him that they "didn't care for my emphasis on the Negro."[64] He grew increasingly infuriated with the congregation at South Church. "The church's history is long and honorable," he wrote in a remarkable rebuke of his own flock that he published in the denominational magazine after returning from Albany. "And yet for some years its life seems to have fled." He was baffled that they seemed more concerned with boat-rocking than justice. "Someone from my own church said to me, upon my being arrested and jailed, that the terrible thing about the situation was the sensationalism," he wrote in disbelief, in words read by thousands of subscribers nationwide.[65]

Soon after, Papandrew began looking for a new church home. He quietly contacted the Unitarian Universalist denominational offices and asked for his name to be added to the pool of available ministers. In early 1963 he began speaking with other congregations. In November 1963 the First Unitarian Church of Miami extended to him an offer. He took it, and two Sundays later delivered a sermon castigating the members of South Church for moral failure. He named names, accusing the Wiggins, the Dettloffs and the Armitages, the

Evert Smiths and Pattersons – some of the most distinguished families in South Church – of moral blindness. This was "a group of people who believed, supposedly, in equality, but that somehow this meant that, peculiarly, they were more equal than others." They did not want him to preach things that made them uncomfortable. Papandrew responded with the announcement, from the pulpit, of his resignation, framed in such a way as to emphasize his masculine moral vigor: "I am leaving in truth with my independence and manhood," he concluded.[66] He and his family moved from Portsmouth in early 1964.

Barney and Betty took their minister's departure hard. And yet Barney could sympathize with Papandrew's frustration. In speech notes he echoed Martin Luther King Jr.'s famous condemnation of the "white liberals" who prized comity and peace over painful justice. It seemed evident to Barny that many white people "agree that we should advance, but not too fast. . . . The white man has not had the moral courage to face the full meaning of what he has done to the Negro and the responsibility for action which that entails."[67]

It was no surprise, then, that Barney sympathized with Black Americans who increasingly rejected liberal integrationism. For a time Barney believed the "unrealized dream of first-class citizenship" was within grasp. But given revived resistance to civil rights, he said, "Many negros have lost faith and believe that they can only expect to be treated as Negroes." He believed this was why separatist groups like the "Black Muslims," members of the Nation of Islam, had emerged. They were "directly related to the preponderance of entrenched and calcified proponents of a segregated community." Barney himself spurned the Nation of Islam; he said he frankly believed it represented "bigotry." But by the time the Black Caucus and other separatist movements like the Nation had begun to gain wide public attention, Barney had come to a point where he could recognize their radical appeal, even if he did not embrace it.[68]

Indeed, the Nation began with a UFO sighting. On June 30, 1934, its founder W. D. Fard vanished for good, but not before he held one last meeting with his chief lieutenant, a man named Elijah Poole. Fard handed Poole a reading list of 104 books, a copy of the Quran, and renamed him Elijah Muhammad.[69] Then he pointed into the sky. Elijah looked up and saw "a destructive, dreadful-looking plane that is made like a wheel." It was "a half-mile by a half-mile," a "humanly built planet," hovering ominously in the clouds. Fard told Elijah that this great Mother

Plane, this grand rotating wheel, was God's means for the destruction of white civilization. Elijah Muhammad explained to his followers that the strange objects people saw in the sky — "the small circular-made planes called flying saucers" — were dispatched from the Mother Plane to survey the world and eventually to carry the wrath of God down upon it. When the time came, Elijah assured them, the Mother Plane would wreck the world with bombs, earthquakes, floods, and new mountains suddenly jolting out of the earth. The old order of white supremacy would be destroyed, and God's true Black civilization would flourish in its place.[70]

As with other Americans who saw strange things in the sky in the mid-twentieth century, Elijah Muhammad assumed the Mother Plane was technology of some sort rather than a supernatural creature or magical manifestation. And as with other Americans, Muhammad assumed that science revealed truths about the nature of existence; Morey Bernstein argued that hypnosis had revealed scientific proof of life after death; George Adamski had claimed that alien beings hoped to teach human beings eternal progress. Elijah Muhammad believed science would reveal the bankruptcy of white America.[71] As he once declared, instructing his followers that UFOs were piloted by Black extraterrestrials: "You have people on Mars! Think how great you are. Ask the white man if he has any out there. We have life on other planets, but he don't."[72] For both Adamski and Muhammad, UFOs were associated with radical knowledge that would of necessity signal their ostracization from a society that, despite its power, was desperately corrupt.

Barney never became a Black Muslim, nor did he explicitly endorse the ideology of Black power. But the backlash he and his wife faced for their claims and their marriage and their activism seemed to him to be all expressions of the same bigotry. Like Adamski and Muhammad, he was growing less and less certain that the government that was doubting his story and the media that blamed it on his own pathology could be trusted. All this meant that as the 1960s continued, Barney Hill and Betty Hill proved increasingly willing to seek their answers outside the American mainstream.

—

CHAPTER 11

A NEW AGE

Jacques Vallée was fifteen when he first saw a flying saucer. On a Sunday afternoon in May 1955, he was with his father in the attic of their home in Pontoise, France, a suburb north of Paris, working on a carpentry project. Suddenly his mother, who was putting away her gardening tools in the yard below, shouted for her husband and son. Jacques sprinted down three flights of stairs and burst out the front door.

Above the spires of nearby Pontoise Cathedral there hovered what Jacques described in his journal as a "gray metallic disk with a clear bubble on top." Eventually it sped away, leaving "a few puffs of white substance behind." Jacques's mother thought they looked like parachutes.

Jacques's father did not follow his son outside. When his family came in, chatting about what they had seen, he insisted that they should not discuss it with anyone. No reports, no inquiries, no filings. He was worried for his reputation — he was a judge — and for his family's. "What we had seen must be some kind of new aircraft," Jacques remembered his father insisting, "something explainable."

That dismayed his son. Jacques had not only been awed by the sight. He had also assigned it meaning. "I was left with the single strong impression that we must respond; that human dignity demanded an answer," he wrote in his journal. He wrote to a UFO researcher named Aimé Michel, just as Betty Hill would

—

167

J. Allen Hynek (left) and Jacques
Vallée (right).
Library of Congress.

write to Donald Keyhoe, theorizing that the saucers had come to prod human progress. "Of course in order to educate us, they would have to find us worthy of a dialogue," he mused.

In the early 1960s he started a family, earned a PhD in computer science, became a colleague of Allen Hynek at Northwestern University, and wrote two books on UFOs at night. They were technical analyses of the phenomenon and garnered a respectful response, but his ideas soon began to drift in new directions. Perhaps it was his reading. He read John Delany's *A Woman Clothed with the Sun*, a 1960 study of miraculous apparitions of the Virgin Mary. He read Charles Fort, the American writer whose delight in strange phenomena was evident in his gleeful book titles, *Lo!* and *The Book of the Damned*, and who posited that no human discipline could explain all that was odd about the universe. He concluded that people like Fort and Delany were "the real founders of modern thought," pilgrims who grappled with the deep strangeness of the world.[1]

Then Vallée turned to Donald Keyhoe's books, and Fort's influence is notable in his response. "The Air Force's inability to think about the world in terms of anything other than the Air Force itself strikes me as particularly curious," he wrote, after reading Keyhoe. Rather, Vallée suggested, the phenomenon should "put into question both the structure of our society and the laws of our physics."[2] For Vallée, saucers were not, to put it simply, saucers. This was to say they were not mechanical devices from another planet. That notion was a product of Cold War thinking, evidence less of whatever these things might be than of the mastery of technology over Americans' imagination. Instead Vallée concluded they were a manifestation of an aspect of reality not fully understood, with more in common with ghosts than with space shuttles.[3]

This seemed a long way from Walter Webb's first report on the Hills, wherein, he assured Donald Keyhoe, that he held a "proper skepticism" of "the sensational nature of the claim."[4] To be sure, Vallée's wariness of the scientific establishment did not extend to an embrace of flying saucer prophets like George Adamski, whose books about his meetings with the Venusian Orthon Vallée called "utter fantasy, with fine fake pictures."[5] For Vallée, Adamski's stories of tall blonde extraterrestrials with opinions about nuclear war were, oddly, not strange enough—hardly so original as to explain the puzzle he had seen in the sky over Pontoise Cathedral.

Vallée sought another way. Not a middle way, exactly, but a means of learning about these craft that sought to ignore what he took to be the reductionist analyses of Project Blue Book and Adamski's dogged willingness to simply ignore whatever experts said. Both seemed to presume that the right sort of science would conclusively discover the truth. Vallée began to doubt not simply these arguments but their premise. Building on Carl Jung's psychological insights, Vallée began to pursue another way of thinking about these crafts. He wanted both to affirm their reality but also to suggest that there were more esoteric ways to learn about them.

His puzzlement and the Hills' weariness and wariness matched the mood of the nation. The way the Hills had come to understand what their experience meant in a variety of contexts—from their relationships with professional scientists to its ramifications for their civil rights work—had forced them to reorient what they believed about the world, and as it happened their reorientation mirrored that happening to many Americans across the country. For the past decade or two, the Hills had approached problems like racial segregation and even their encounter with the presumption that the right sorts of evidence or the right scientific discourse might persuade all Americans that integration was desirable, that experts sponsored by the state could solve social problems, that they really had been abducted. But increasingly, they began to wonder. Perhaps their Unitarian presumptions that science could build an equally accessible consensus about knowledge was incorrect. Perhaps instead reality was esoteric and divisive, something that splintered American communities rather than unified them. It was, after all, the sixties.[6]

In the 1950s Unitarians like Jack Mendelsohn thought issues of racism could be solved through appeals to human similarity. "I look upon all minds as one family and all men as one race," he had written. But ten years later, Unitarians were worrying that white Americans suffered from what minister Charles Merrill described as "an inability to see what is around him." In 1967, Merrill asked his white readers, "Do you know what an apartment in East Harlem is like? . . . Do you know the tone of voice a white cop uses to a Negro?"[7] Unitarians believed in human dignity and reason—but they were coming to doubt whether these things could produce racial harmony. The denomination's fracturing over issues of race illustrated the problem. While many Unitarians were aghast at Black members' desire for an independent caucus, many more came to believe that it was precisely their proclaimed faith in the individual that required them to acknowledge that perhaps not all people saw the world in the same way.

The political and cultural crises of these years soured many more Americans on the notion of consensus. The increasing levels of violence against Black Americans that followed the passage of the Civil Rights Act and Voting Rights Act reached a crescendo with the assassination of Martin Luther King Jr. in April 1968. A month earlier, in March 1968, Lyndon Johnson had announced he would not run for re-election. Only 32 percent of the country approved of his aggressive waging of the Vietnam War, and members of Congress were calling angry attention to Johnson's willingness to mislead them about how well the American forces there were doing. Richard Nixon, the Republican who replaced Johnson, hammered his predecessor for his deceptions while spinning false-hoods of his own, following cheerful assurances of success with secret expansion of the war. And soon Nixon was thoroughly bogged down in a mess of his own making—the metastasizing Watergate scandal, in which journalists and con-gressional investigators seemed every day closer to proving that the president had scrambled to hide the fact that three burglars who broke into the Democratic National Committee offices in the Watergate Hotel were working for his re-election campaign. Nixon resigned in disgrace in August 1974.[8] The damage that Johnson and Nixon did to Americans' confidence that the government could be

trusted reverberated in a widespread suspicion of conventionally paternal figures of white men in suits, be they politicians, scientists, or academics.

Faith in the government was dwindling, then, at the same time the Hills
were growing disenchanted with the traditional sources of authority in which
they once had had such confidence in. Even their denomination was splintering.
At the same time, though, Betty and Barney were learning of other sources of
spiritual authority and ways of finding truth.

The New Age

The term "New Age" may be argued to refer simultaneously to a great deal
and, perhaps, very little. Generally, it is used to refer to a loose network of beliefs
and practices of the sort that fascinated Vallée and that came to prominence in
American culture in the late 1960s and 1970s — psychic power, Tarot and other
forms of divination, channeling, faith healing, mediumship, crystal magic, and
dozens more. It was sustained and spread along networks both personal and
commercial: television producers, journalists, musicians, publishers, book
clubs, yoga classes, workshops. And yet, some scholars have pointed out that in
those heyday years, few participants actually used the term "New Age" to refer
to themselves, and though they often recognized some mutual affinity, did not
necessarily perceive themselves as part of a singular movement. Indeed, many
such beliefs and practices had sometimes disparate roots deep in the American
and European past.[9]

The diffuse nature of the New Age is essential to understanding the Hills'
encounter with it, because they did not understand themselves to be abandon-
ing Unitarianism as they began to explore new beliefs. Indeed, the Hills continued to attend South Church throughout the 1960s and 1970s, even after John
Papandrew was replaced with a minister who seemed less likely to rock the boat.
But at the same time, by the late 1960s they were learning about other ideas that
seemed to give meaning to the world as they now understood it. Their waning
faith in the American establishment sent them on a quest for other sources of
explanation and validation, one they felt took seriously their experiences and
beliefs. By this point, the Hills might be best described as several scholars have

characterized many Americans in the last third of the twentieth century—they became spiritual seekers. They began to take responsibility for finding beliefs and practices that encompassed their thinking about the world, and to question the wisdom of those they had previously taken as authorities, and to drift away from allegiance to their old loyalties.[10]

The word "seeker" should not conjure up images of disconnection or atomization. The Hills did not drift away from the anchors of relationships and congregations and professionals into a world of meaning they fashioned entirely alone. Rather, they found new communities and new mentors, and they followed the links these people offered them from place to place, belief to belief, practice to practice, resting in new places as they found them. By the 1970s, they lived in a quite different world from the one they had entered a decade before. It was a world more characteristic of Jacques Vallée than John Papandrew. Some scholars have suggested that the word "milieu" best captures what the so-called New Age was, because it describes a cultural attitude, an accumulation of practices, and a loose community of explorers rather than a coherent movement. The result was an enthusiastic and wonder-filled blending, exchanging, and linking of a multiplicity of practices, images, and concepts that the scientific and social establishment of the United States considered marginal. But the Hills, feeling rejected by that establishment, found in it a new home.[11]

Three aspects of this seeker-oriented milieu were particularly important to the Hills' story. The first is the notion of bricolage—the shuffling and recombination of a range of ideas from across time, space, and cultures. In this sense, the New Age milieu was born of a genealogy of many ideologies and movements that long predated the 1960s. Among these were the Western esoteric and occult traditions that included the ancient practices of magic, the Jewish mystical practice and theology called Kabbalah, and hermeticism, a system of alchemy, philosophy, astrology, and ritual as paths to unification with God and absolute perfection. Throughout the nineteenth and twentieth centuries, hermetic ideas garnered audiences in the United States and Europe, popping up in movements like Freemasonry, Rosicrucianism, and the Hermetic Order of the Golden Dawn, a secret society that attracted prominent literary figures, among them Arthur Conan Doyle, the creator of Sherlock Holmes, and the Nobel Prize–winning poet William Butler Yeats.[12]

In the United States late in the nineteenth century these traditions were given new life and mingled with an ambitious reinterpretation of Hindu and Buddhist ideas about human nature and reincarnation in the formation of the Theosophical Society, founded in the 1870s by an émigré Russian mystic named Helena Blavatsky. Blavatsky claimed to have traveled through the Near East, Tibet, and India, and she and her circle sought to synthesize hermeticism and Western esotericism with an ambitious reinterpretation of ancient Egyptian practices, Hinduism, and Buddhism. But at the same time, Blavatsky merely made alliances with Americans already pursuing these themes. This conscious bricolage drew in contemporary American practices of spiritualism and mesmerism, integrating them with Blavatsky's conviction that there existed "ascended masters," enlightened beings that wished to aid humanity's spiritual progress. Its followers practiced channeling, speaking in the voices of spirits who promised to aid humanity; they insisted that many religious movements were all fragments of the great story of cosmic progress — a philosophy called perennialism — and they promised that understanding these truths would earn spiritual transcendence.[13]

It was no mistake that many of the combinations of ideas emergent in these movements also appeared in the writings of George Adamski, which helps to explain why Adamski believed himself to be bridging the gaps between science and religion. The old visionary was only the most prominent of the "contactees," a host of people who claimed to have received contact from extraterrestrials who promised them spiritual guidance and messages to aid the progress of humanity. These extraterrestrials were not the strange and sometimes frightening figures Betty and Barney Hill encountered but rather benevolent "Space Brothers," as Adamski called them — in a sense, tangible, materialist, and perhaps even scientific versions of the spiritual beings Helena Blavatsky taught of. Some of Adamski's followers organized their followers into new religious movements. For the contactees, as for Adamski, the language of science was authoritative, and using it would gain them legitimacy and respect.[14] That effort points to the second aspect of the New Age milieu that appealed to Betty and Barney Hill. New Age practitioners did not see themselves in competition with science. Like the Hills, they believed that the practices of science properly understood were harmonious with the practices and philosophies they found elsewhere.

J. B. Rhine, a longtime scientist at Duke University, is a useful figure for understanding this synthesis. Rhine began study of what he called "parapsychology" in the 1930s in a lab he founded at Duke. Throughout the nineteenth century, spiritualists had claimed that their practices of mediumship, extrasensory perception, and seances were indeed scientific, but Rhine's achievement was the integration of spiritualism with the language and practices of contemporary, twentieth-century science. He developed standardized research practices and technical terminology. He coined the term "ESP" and popularized the words "telepathy" and "clairvoyance." He developed systematic methods for testing for such abilities, including a famous card experiment that sought to measure the existence of telepathy. He did his work in laboratories and worked only with properly credentialed colleagues. All of this signaled his awareness of the dangers of the label "pseudoscience." Though Duke University grew increasingly wary of Rhine's conclusions, his scientific practices marked an effort to present his work, on the one hand, as compatible with the rigor of modern professionals but, on the other, as open to accommodating the experiences of those interested in the esoteric world of the New Age milieu.[15] Jacques Vallée said that establishment science in the Cold War era, swaddled in a maze of bureaucracies and state power and largely inaccessible to laypeople, had "shut itself off from the common man." For his part, Rhine tried to democratize it, giving words and offering validation to experiences many people were having. In Rhine's work, New Age believers saw the sort of science they hoped for. They never stopped believing that "science," whatever it might be, was significant and powerful. What changed was the people they were willing to call "scientists."[16]

In their draft of the open letter later printed in *The Interrupted Journey*, the Hills had expressed the third concept present in the New Age milieu that would be meaningful to them. They called their encounter "the greatest event in the history of mankind since Columbus discovered America," ascribing to it world-historical importance. Adamski had said the same of his encounters with Orthon, and so did the founders of many other UFO movements in the 1950s. Like Blavatsky, they promised a transformation in human consciousness — one to which Alice Bailey, one of Blavatsky's disciples, gave the name the "New Age." Steven Sutcliffe has argued that over time focus on such a wide social transfor-

mation gave way to a tighter focus on personal spiritual practice and inner transformation. But still, Betty and Barney's hope for a new society in the United
States had not been accomplished through the conventional liberal politics they
had been raised with. They began seeking it in other ways.[17]

Under the influence of Donald Keyhoe, Betty and Barney had understood
their experience as a visit from a spacecraft from another world. The path that
led to Benjamin Simon taught them to see it also as a source of trauma. By the
late 1960s they began to see it in yet another way. It was one part of a grand,
coming transformation of humanity, one link in a great chain that connected
their lives to deeper and revolutionary realities. The Hills' introduction to the
New Age came through their associations with other UFO believers and shows
how their experience opened them to a variety of connections and communities
that provided them new ways of understanding their experience. From these
connections they came to understand their story in spiritual and eventually conspiratorial ways, layering new meanings upon it and drawing away from the
liberal politics in which they had once believed.

By the time they met Jacques Vallée, in other words, they were ready for him.

Herbert and Helen Knowles's Bricolage

Soon after their sessions with Dr. Simon came to an end, the Hills and their
friend, a NICAP member named Lorraine D'Allessandro attended a luncheon at
the home of Herbert and Helen Knowles, a prominent Portsmouth couple interested in UFOs. At one point during the meal the widow of a deceased UFO investigator produced a chunk of metal her husband told her had come from a
large flaming object that had fallen from the sky near the St. Lawrence River.
D'Allessandro donned a blindfold and took the object in her hand and began
describing its extraterrestrial origins.

Betty was astounded. D'Allessandro explained that she was performing remote viewing, in which a psychic (who may or may not be handling an object)
can visualize events and objects distant in time or location. She told Betty she had
studied with J. B. Rhine, who called remote viewing "psychometry." It turned out
the Knowleses were interested in all sorts of phenomena: UFOs, certainly, but

also psychic powers like remote viewing, telepathy, and the practice of unconscious or automatic writing, in which a medium writes messages under the control of another mind. Herbert Knowles told the Hills about a woman named Frances Swan who lived near Portsmouth. "She is in contact with the occupants of UFOs through automatic writing. Almost daily she sits and receives messages," Betty wrote in her journal. The Knowleses warned her that "Barney and I met the wrong ones – the evil ones, the ones of wrong vibrations." Betty remembered being stunned by the entire luncheon; it was a world she had not glimpsed before. "In those days," she wrote, "we had never heard of George Adamski."[18]

And yet, the Knowleses seemed hardly like Adamski at all to the Hills. They were entirely conventional and respected citizens. Herbert Knowles had spent years commanding a submarine for the U.S. Navy before teaching electrical engineering at the Naval Submarine School in Connecticut. When he and his wife Helen retired to a historic farmhouse across the Piscataqua River from downtown Portsmouth, Knowles was elected to the local school board and Helen became active in the Ladies' Circle at Portsmouth's First Congregational Church. Somehow they managed to both cultivate an active interest in UFOs and psychic phenomena while maintaining public respect. Helen led book groups exploring the work of J. B. Rhine at her church, and her husband brought psychics to lecture at the local American Legion post. They joined NICAP, and their home became a hub for people like D'Allessandro.[19]

The ease with which the Knowleses blended UFO belief with confidence in psychic powers, channeling, and automatic writing illuminated for the Hills alternative routes to the sort of information and validation they craved. They had found mainstream science to be a series of attempts to redirect their understanding of their experience down the pathways of meteorology and psychology, but the bricolage in the Knowleses' dining room undergirded it with a host of new connections that assured the Hills that their experience as they understood it was important. Betty recorded that the aliens who communicated with Frances Swan were "kind, loving, concerned for all; [and] give her messages of brotherhood and the Kingdom of God."[20] They were coming to believe they also had a part to play in such transformations.

The Knowleses' lives also point to two particular aspects of the New Age milieu that appealed to Betty and Barney Hill. The first was their understanding of science as not an arena restricted to experts but a collective project of systematization and correlation of personal experience, something done in conversation with other believers in order to determine patterns and order in a mélange of strange phenomena. This sort of community was what the Hills had been groping for in their confrontations with the Air Force and Benjamin Simon.

Secondly, the Knowleses seemed to the Hills as respectable authorities, people whom they could trust. Throughout the early 1970s Helen Knowles placed advertisements for her book groups in the local newspaper. They promised Helen would offer "a résumé of her own experiences" with psychic phenomena. They also advised the interested public that "appropriate dress will be required" for all attendees.[21] In the juxtaposition of the two propositions sits the lives of people like the Knowleses. Helen's emphasis on the relevance of her own experiences to understanding unexplained phenomena speaks to the way New Age believers thought about science. But just as important, her insistence on appropriate dress revealed her to be committed to an ideal of respectable comportment that liberals for years had leaned on as they sought to fashion an image of a national consensus. It allowed the Hills to understand their new world as one not so different from their old.

This blending had been evident for years in New Hampshire. Throughout the early years of the Cold War many New Hampshire Unitarian congregations treated UFOs with the sort of genteel curiosity the Knowleses shared, little supposing that such inquiries might be disreputable. To select from dozens of such events documented in the state's newspapers, on a cold Sunday in January 1962, the Manchester Unitarian Church invited the Manchester Religious Youth Group to its church for a discussion on UFOs, "exceptionally presented in a talk and colored slides" by a member of the congregation, following which the youth went to the YMCA for basketball and swimming before "a delicious dinner." A few years before, the Women's Fellowship committee at the Nashua First Unitarian Church hosted a talk by the Unitarian Albert Baller, who denounced government secrecy about UFOs as "blasphemy" and insisted the crafts were from outer space. Following Baller's fiery talk, the Women's Fellowship elected its officers for the coming year and served supper to the members. A few years before that, the same church's book group studied the work of Donald Keyhoe.[22]

This mixture of the humdrum and speculative, the respectable and the presumably strange, speaks to the ease with which Americans like the Knowleses edged into the fringes of what became the New Age movement—precisely because they did not perceive these things as forbidden or comical, but rather logical extensions of the science and progress they already celebrated. That the Knowleses were able to conduct these investigations and command respect in the community made them inspiring to the Hills, who wanted to occupy a similar place and find similar meaning in their strange experiences. To the Hills, the Knowleses were a living refutation of George Adamski; they made the couple believe that one could pursue the esoteric and remain respected.

CHAPTER 12

PSYCHOPHYSICS

If the Knowleses introduced the Hills to the possibilities of what some scholars have called "stigmatized knowledge," which was rejected by the cultural establishment, it was Robert Hohmann—who had interviewed them with his partner C. D. Jackson back in 1961—who enlisted them in its fulfillment, and in so doing extended the Hills' networks deeper into the world of the New Age milieu, and introduced them to new ways of comprehending their experience that made them even more suspicious of the political and scientific sources they had once turned to. As their faith in the establishments that had undergirded their liberal politics waned, they grew increasingly attracted to the logic of conspiracy.

In the summer of 1965, Betty Hill and Hohmann exchanged letters for the first time in several years.[1] Hohmann wanted a copy of the Hills' tapes with Simon, and after some cordialities, he told Betty that in November he had a professional visit to make in Plymouth, about halfway between Portsmouth and Franconia Notch. He asked the Hills if they would show him the site of their encounter after his meetings were done. They were amenable. Around three in the afternoon on November 6, the Hills found Hohmann in the parking lot of his hotel, Tobey's Motor Lodge, and they began the drive up Route 3 to Franconia Notch. On the way, they told each other stories of the years since they had last met.[2]

In 1961 Robert Hohmann had been interested in radio waves and rocketry, the sort of conventional science an IBM employee might have been expected to favor. But now he had come to believe that UFOs affected reality in ways that sort of science could not recognize. He proposed to the Hills that their true communion had not been simply physical and visual: rather, it took place in spaces mental and spiritual. He asked Barney if he was sure he had seen creatures dressed in jackets, scarves, and caps. Hohmann suspected Barney's mind had touched that of the aliens and "clothe[d] the appearance of the visitors in some conventional image in order to minimize the shock." Even more, Hohmann believed this connection had continued. He said he felt it. "During our conversation we were four in number. I was, however, distinctly aware of a fifth presence," he wrote to Betty after returning home. This "monitoring, I felt, was both visual and audial."[3]

It did not surprise Hohmann. He explained that the Hills' experience was no single encounter but one episode of a long-gestating phenomenon encompassing the whole human race. "If [my] theory is correct you are part of the communications-media for the Northeastern U.S.," he somberly explained. He had determined this "by deductive reasoning, the ecological interrelationship of the UFO and the geophysical configurations of the U.S., Argentina, Australia, and Mexico." He had studied "the role of the Argentine native, the Australian aborigine, and the Mexican/Indian strain" in facilitating human-UFO contact, and his calculations revealed that the Hills had also been given such responsibilities.[4]

Like J. B. Rhine, Hohmann thought of himself as a scientist. He worked hard to position himself in a space similar to that of the Duke researcher — between what he saw as dull mainstream professors, on the one hand, and wild-eyed UFO worshipers, on the other. The former lacked imagination, the latter rigor. He denounced "lurid journalism — which I abhor, or the curiosity-seeker, which I am not." Instead, he told Betty that he was engaged in "study, data assembly, literature search; all lead upward to the point where correlation begins, then to theory, and eventually to test or to proof."[5] For Hohmann UFO encounters like the Hills' could be rendered comprehensible, reproducible, and exact. His attempt to systematize and technologize the cultures of indigenous peoples was another expression of this impulse, one common among New Age believers.[6]

———

To this point Hohmann's beliefs were not so distinct from those of the Knowleses. What he brought that was new to the Hills was conviction that all this strangeness was pointing to an imminent transformation in the social order. He told Betty that "we have entered into some new phase of the UFO phenomenon."[7] She and Barney had a role to play.

It was all the prompting that Betty Hill needed. She had wanted to be told that her experience was important from the beginning, when she felt Major Paul Henderson had not taken her and her husband seriously enough. Once Hohmann had drawn these connections she was terribly relieved. She told Hohmann that since their experience, "We go around looking over our shoulder." Strange things had been happening. At her sister Janet's home the front door opened and shut on its own, with no human nearby (although once "the cat walked in"). Disembodied footsteps came up the stairs of the Hill home at night, and in the apartment they maintained in their home the faucets turned on and off with no one near. Objects vanished and reappeared in new places. One day Betty and Barney came home to find a large oval chunk of ice unaccountably sitting on the kitchen table. Dark cars drove up to their house. Once, Janet watched a car park in her yard and a "man get out, stand on the front steps, and light a cigarette." When she threw the front door open, nobody was there. But a large ball of light was drifting across the wide-open New Hampshire lawn toward the barn across the street.[8]

Before their interactions with Hohmann, Betty and Barney were not sure what to make of these events. Betty insisted that "we do not believe in ghosts" and claimed they were a family of "practical realists." She was sincere; she and Barney still saw themselves as hard-headed, faithful to respectable rationality and science. But now, in the light of the threads Hohmann drew, she and Barney could understand how all this strangeness fit together. "At first we thought all these were coincidence, but I am changing my mind," she explained. They were "in preparation of another direct contact."[9] Hohmann encouraged the idea. "The experiences come under the heading of 'prods,' or unpleasant goadings," he suggested. The travelers were planning something, and suddenly Betty's life made sense to her. Her sense of reason was sustained — even though the world was coming to seem a more complicated place than it had ever been before.[10]

181

When Hohmann proposed that they try to contact a UFO, the Hills were willing to listen. Hohmann asked them what they thought would be needed to establish contact and began formulating his own plans.[11] Betty's first suggestion – of an attempt on August 20 – was too soon for him. So that night Betty and Barney went to her parents' house by themselves. At midnight a "bright, traveling light" swooped over her parents' backyard. The music on Betty's portable radio stopped, and a slow series of five to seven single notes played, with short pauses between each. The dog began "jumping around and howling." Betty wrote Hohmann, plaintively, "Would you have any ideas about all of this?"[12]

Hohmann willingly stepped into the role of guide. He told the Hills that they should not blame themselves for their inability to interpret these signs. They had a "minimum of working data." In short, they needed him. "When and if the time comes that you need technical assistance," he promised in his next letter, "I will do what is possible to help." He told them he had met with Allen Hynek in order to explain to the great astronomer how the "science of psychophysics" applied to the Hills' experience. Hohmann thought Betty Hill was a "transducer." The word describes a device that converts energy from one form into another (microphones, for instance, are transducers, converting sound into electric signals). For Hohmann Betty was capable of translating between two worlds.[13]

Hohmann's use of the term "psychophysics" is a good example of the New Age's engagement with science. Early pioneers of psychology in nineteenth-century Germany used the term to refer to the study of the interaction between physical stimulus and subjective response: the relationship, for instance, between the scent of a flower and the emotion of pleasure.[14] But almost from the beginning a number of mystics and esoteric thinkers began to theorize beyond the response to physical stimuli to the very interaction between the mind and the body, thoughts and the environment, the nature of causality itself. Could the mind, as Robert Hohmann suggested, influence the external world? Could Betty Hill summon a UFO with her thoughts?

Nineteenth-century advocates of what was called "New Thought" began to invoke the language of psychophysics to make the case. New Thought derived from the work of Phineas Quimby, an antebellum clockmaker who believed physical illness was rooted in disordered thinking. For Quimby, the mind affected physical reality in tangible and measurable ways. One of his followers, Horatio Dresser, linked Quimby's ideas to psychophysics. Dresser studied at Harvard under William James, the famed psychologist and philosopher who was also a patient of Horatio's mother, Amelia, whose New Thought methods cured his insomnia. Dresser and James had a cordial relationship, and from James, Dresser took the principle that "we are conscious beings living in a psychophysical world." Dresser concluded that "the mind affects the body and the body affects the mind."[15]

By the mid-twentieth century such ideas were popular. More than anyone, the famous minister Norman Vincent Peale spread the mantra that thoughts create reality in his explosively popular 1952 book *The Power of Positive Thinking.* As Peale put it, "If you shift your mind from fear to faith you will stop creating the object of your fear and will instead actualize the object of your faith." But others took the principle beyond the business deals and happy marriages Peale touted to far more transformative possibilities. These were progenitors and participants in the New Age movement. The followers of the Russian mystic George Gurdjieff established a center in New York City in the 1950s. "The Work" the Gurdjieff Foundation taught promised to teach full integration of mind, body, and emotion to unlock a transcendent experience of reality. Robert Masters and Jean Houston, co-authors of the books *The Varieties of Psychedelic Experience* (1966) and *Mind Games* (1972) and founders of the Human Potential Movement, instructed that not only human thoughts but human "ways of experiencing the physical external world, are also subject to countless modifications."[16]

These were the ideas that Robert Hohmann urged upon Betty Hill. In May of 1967, he reported that "the discussion of psychophysics with Dr. Hynek has stimulated the interest of the scientific community."[17] This community was what Hynek called the "invisible college," an informal, or as Hynek put it, "subterranean," alliance of American scholars interested in the problem of UFOs but unwilling to state so publicly. The term "invisible college," Vallée explained in his diary, referenced "the early 1660s in England, at a time when it was very dangerous to be interested in natural philosophy," what would eventually become science.[18]

In *The Edge of Reality,* a collection of conversations between Vallée and Hynek, Valleé observes that in the contemporary United States science was defined in terms of what could draw institutional support. "Just get some funds for this UFO subject and everybody will want it," Hynek agrees wryly, and mourns how many institutions were "passing the UFO buck." In his mind the battles over science had left the state-sponsored, institutional researchers Hynek had been working with lethargic and overly cautious. And in such a way did J. Allen Hynek, who ten years prior had warned Walter Webb to avoid public association with UFO investigation, find himself sympathetic to psychophysics. It was not necessarily that Hynek had renounced conventional science; it was rather that its own boundary maintenance had left it seeming irrelevant to him. As Hynek told Vallée, "Science may have to be torn apart at the seams."[19]

In late May 1967, Hohmann reported that both Hynek and John Fuller were interested enough to spend a weekend in New Hampshire discovering if Betty Hill could summon a flying saucer to the wilderness abutting the backyard of her mother's home in Kingston. A photographer would come too, as would a few other of Hohmann's friends. And then, wonder of wonders, Hohmann managed to persuade Benjamin Simon to join them. Hohmann hoped to get funding from the Condon committee, but Hynek, knowing the lay of the land, discouraged him from trying. Instead, all agreed to pay their own way.[20]

There would be a total of nine people. They would gather the afternoon of Saturday, June 10, at the Kingston campsite. That night, Hohmann would draw a white circle on the ground. Inside they would erect scientific equipment, and outside they would set up distance markers to easily judge how far away any phenomenon that appeared might be. On June 6, Hohmann sent Betty a letter. He wanted her to go to her back porch at nine every evening and attempt to communicate mentally with the occupants of the craft. The effort was not new, but Hohmann now provided her with a script. It ran: "Today is [blank], the [blank] day of the year. In [blank] more days, go to [blank; Betty filled this in with "my parents' farm"] in New Hampshire. Best science men are there. Show lights to science men. Come close to science men. All is safe."[21]

Betty did it.

On May 31, Hynek concluded he would not be able to make it and asked Jacques Vallée to fill in for him. Vallée and his wife Janine went, though he was skeptical of the Hills and Hohmann alike. His conclusions about what happened in Kingston reveal the struggles over science, respectability, and power, which Americans sympathetic to the New Age milieu had to navigate.

——

Betty and Barney Hill pose in Betty's mother's field for *Look* magazine in spring 1966. *Look* Magazine Collection, Prints and Photographs Division, Library of Congress, LC-L9 66–2889–02800–02814u.

As did many men, Vallée found Betty's personality suspiciously strong and used that observation to downplay her beliefs. "Clearly Betty is the dominant mind here," he wrote. He thought she was easily influenced and charismatic enough to persuade others — a dangerous combination. Vallée did not put much stock in Hohmann either, calling him "melodramatic" in his journal when Hohmann described what he hoped Vallée would do during "phase two." That was, as Vallée put it wryly, "when I am supposed to take command of the interaction with the aliens when they land." His incredulity was no less real for its dryness. Upon arriving in Kingston, he met Benjamin Simon and judged him a "sly old practitioner, an empiricist of vast experience" who "doesn't really care whether or not they have been abducted." Vallée thought Simon simply wanted to watch.[22]

One reason Vallée was wary of the whole affair was that he was growing increasingly certain that whatever these objects were, they were most likely not spacecraft from another planet. A few months later he would publish *Passport to Magonia,* a groundbreaking book that stands as a representative work of the New Age. The book combined Valleé's reading in European history, folklore, esoterica, and contemporary UFOs, and in his diary he said that it suggested "a formal parallel between the UFO phenomenon of today and the medieval tradition about elementals, elves, and fairies." He hypothesized all these things were the same phenomenon manifested according to the expectations of the age in which they appeared.[23] Valleé's melding of Renaissance grimoires with the technical work of the Condon committee was right at home in the 1960s. But such an explosion of creativity meant that agreement was hard to come by, even among advocates of the New Age. Vallée's theories did not mesh well with Hohmann's anticipation of the arrival of spacecraft from another planet.

By the time Vallée, Janine, and John Fuller (who had carpooled to New Hampshire with them) reached Hohmann's campsite in Kingston on the afternoon of June 10, it was oppressively hot. "The sweltering heat moistened everything," Vallée wrote. Fuller morosely confirmed that night would not ease the humidity. Hohmann and his colleagues had already pitched the tents and drawn the circle. Vallée set up his Geiger counter and began measuring temperatures. He chatted with Simon. They all settled in to wait. Hohmann delivered an impromptu lecture on the psychic powers of Australian aborigines. Every so often, as night fell, a meteor or satellite would cross overhead or a swarm of fireflies would flash in the woods. Vallée wrote in his journal that each time Betty Hill "jumped up excitedly," only to settle back down in disappointment. Nothing happened. Finally, around three in the morning, everybody drifted off to sleep.[24]

The next morning Vallée and Janine spent some time with Betty and Barney. Valleé wrote that "they were nice and warm people once they didn't have to play Transducers in front of a bunch of crazy scientists anymore." The Hills took the Valleés to a lake and then back to Portsmouth, where they listened to the tapes of the hypnosis sessions. Vallée judged Hohmann's theories about psychic contact with aliens "childish" and the Hills' story of a "ludicrous (or symbolic) medical examination . . . straight out of a bad movie." But his conclusion was less about the Hills' experience than their interpretation of it. He thought something strange did happen to the two, and he noted that the problem inspired his work in *Passport to Magonia.* "We learned nothing useful about extraterrestrial life" in

Kingston, he wrote. "But we learned that our current concepts of space and time were wrong; that a larger reality, other dimensions existed."[25]

If Vallée and Hohmann disagreed on many things, they did agree on that. Shortly after returning home Hohmann wrote to the Hills to assure them that "no one was disappointed that the expected phenomenon did not appear." He arranged another gathering in Kingston in early September; this time, Vallée, Fuller, and Simon declined to join. Again, little occurred.[26] But again, Hohmann was undeterred. He told the Hills, "I think that such prior notice will be extremely subtle." He told them of one example. He followed a strangely marked map to Lake Desolation, New York, and having arrived there, fastened a card in a magnetic clip holder to his dashboard, and then camped out to wait. On the card he had written, "Huntsville, Alabama, East to West." At 12:15 in the morning, he saw the car door open, the dome light come on, and when he reached the car, the card tipped face down. "We can expect at some future (unspecified) date there will be an East to West UFO phenomenon over Huntsville, Alabama," he predicted. A year later he delightedly told them that C. D. Jackson's son — living in Huntsville, Alabama — indeed had seen a light in the sky.[27]

The Hills' correspondence with Hohmann grew increasingly sensitive to such subtleties. Hohmann seemed convinced that the failure of his psychophysics experiments was not a sign that their assumptions were incorrect, but only a failure of interpretation. These conclusions reflected another trend growing common within the New Age: conspiracy belief. Conspiracy belief was suspicious of conventional accounts of cause and effect. It doubted the faith in institutions that liberal politics was premised on. Independent of the conventional American political spectrum, it questioned the value of traditional forms of authority — science, democracy, academia — in the first place. The New Age, with its openness to multiple ways of finding truth and its suspicion of tradition, was fertile ground for conspiracy. Because of their ordeal of the last few years, the Hills were open to Hohmann's worries that the forces at work in the federal government were not necessarily benign. By January 1969 they were discussing "where the Condon committee went wrong," and Hohmann was decrying the "intrigue" at work in the government that enabled such a "terrible injustice to science."[28]

And then Barney died.

CHAPTER 13

MAPS

It was sudden, and devastating. February 25, 1969, was a snowy day, as Betty remembered it to Allen Hynek a few years later. The weather meant that Barney had the day off. The Hills enjoyed a leisurely breakfast and then played a few rounds of pool downstairs near the fireplace. Partway through the game Barney felt a sudden sharp pain in the back of the neck, like a hornet sting. He headed back up to the main floor of the house but fell to his knees halfway and began to crawl up the stairs. He made his way to the couch to rest but couldn't hold himself upright and slipped to the floor. He cried out to Betty that something was wrong. She called an ambulance. At the hospital Barney grew confused and then slipped into unconsciousness. The doctor told Betty he had suffered a cerebral hemorrhage and that he almost certainly would not survive. He advised her to go home to wait. "The only thing that he could suggest was that I pray, or knock on wood, or whatever I used to obtain my own wishes that he die quickly," she wrote later. That night she wrote in her diary with the New England stoicism she must not have been feeling at the time: "The hospital would call me when he died. I kissed Barney goodbye and left." She went home and began the work of notifying friends and family. Her sister Janet. Benjamin Simon. John Fuller promised to drive up from Connecticut. "The wind blew the snow against the house and I sat alone in my living room," she remembered, wrapped in a blanket but still cold, "a candle on the table beside me in case the electricity went off." Her minister—John MacPhee, John Papandrew's replacement—arrived at her door just as the hospital called. It was 7:20 p.m. Barney was forty-six.[1]

On March 1, the NAACP and South Church joined forces to organize the funeral, filling the vestibule with mourners and Betty's freezer with casseroles. The service was attended by the mayor of Portsmouth. Thomas McIntyre, one of New Hampshire's US senators, sent his condolences. A week later Betty ventured out for the first time to visit her mother in Kingston. Around 9:00 p.m. she headed home. Above the powerlines on the cold and lonely Route 125 she noticed two red lights approaching. Then she saw the lights were on either side of a craft, a craft with shadowy windows that looked quite similar to what she and Barney had seen in Franconia Notch so many years ago.

She stopped the car and got out. She was thinking, "What do they want? What is different? Barney, maybe they are looking for him."

She rushed around the car and threw open the passenger door, so the occupants could see there was nobody there. Then she began shouting at the sky. "Do you want to know where Barney is? Barney died. He is no longer alive." She started to cry. She went back to the driver's door and clambered back into the car. "We bury our dead," she yelled. She told them Barney was in the cemetery and pointed the way. She told them they could find him "by the flowers on his grave." As she spoke, the craft "rocked back and forth three or four times, crossed the highway, and headed the direction I had pointed."[2]

And thus began a new era for Betty Hill. She couldn't bear to put Barney's motorcycle up for sale until June.[3] Throughout her life sympathetic friends asked if she thought the experience might have somehow led to Barney's death. In 1976, for instance, the UFO researcher and University of Wyoming psychologist Leo Sprinkle reached out to Betty. He had known her for years, which is why he felt he could ask if there were "unusual symptoms associated with [Barney's] death." A heart rate that broke 200 beats per second. Leaking cerebrospinal fluid. Sprinkle expressed regret for being so blunt but said he felt it was imperative to learn more about "UFO witnesses through psychic exploration."[4]

Betty never conceded that the experience might have caused Barney's death. She denied the possibility to Sprinkle and told another friend who asked if the abduction had weakened Barney's health that "this was not the case."[5]

189

But by 1969, she was ready to believe that Barney's death did mean something, that in some mysterious way the occupants were aware of it, and witnesses to it, even if they were not its cause. She remembered that winter there was "a bright flashing light outside of my home at night." She saw it the night before Barney's death and again just before he felt the hornet sting on the back of his neck the next day.[6] The mysteries of her strange experiences now seemed to Betty bound into the equal mysteries of life and death, the cycles that governed the universe in total.

Consonant with her new networks and spiritual guides, she grew less and less interested in proving her experience in the sort of conventional ways that would have satisfied Paul Henderson and the Air Force. Rather, she began to think of its meaning resting in its cosmological, spiritual, and transformational potential. Following the new relationships she was cultivating, she began to link her experiences to other esoteric systems. And she moved toward a world darker and more dangerous than the sunny, harmonious society her Unitarianism had promised because it was one that she could understand, and in a sense, control.

Marjorie Fish Maps the Cosmos

One of Betty's guides was Marjorie Fish. A schoolteacher from Lakeside, a small town on the banks of Lake Erie in northern Ohio, Fish had read *The Interrupted Journey,* and she felt a connection to Betty. They were both Unitarians; they graduated from college the same year. Marjorie reached out in June 1969 in a long letter. She outlined some of these commonalities and confessed that she was particularly intrigued with the star map Betty described in her dreams and in her interviews with Benjamin Simon. Prompted under hypnosis by Simon, Betty had drawn the map, and Fuller published her sketch in *The Interrupted Journey.* She had long believed the constellation Pegasus was a good match, having seen a diagram of it in the newspaper.[7]

"I've been working on the map you drew for almost four years now," Fish wrote to Betty. It contained approximately two dozen dots or circles of varying sizes, twelve connected by lines of differing thickness, some straight, some broken. Fish believed it should be possible to chart Betty's map onto the sky and

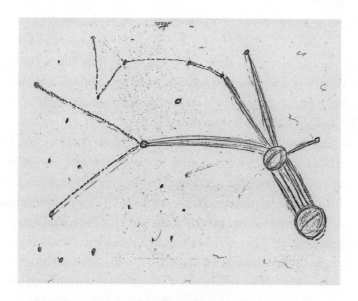

Betty Hill's sketch of the star map she saw on the alien craft. She reported while under hypnosis that the "leader" of the creatures showed her a map that indicated their home planet. She drew this sketch while under hypnotic suggestion from Benjamin Simon. Box 6, Folder 1, BBHP, University of New Hampshire. Used with permission.

locate its pattern. Pegasus was an unlikely match, Fish explained, for a number of reasons. Chief among them was the fact that Betty's sketch was two-dimensional, and Pegasus was not. The challenge was to formulate a three-dimensional model of space and locate similarities to Betty's map within it. This Fish did: she spent years researching the positions of stars within a reasonable distance from Earth, and in her living room she painstakingly constructed a model of the nearby universe. She was writing to Betty to inquire about a few odds and ends. It would be of great use, Fish wrote, if Betty could clarify if the map was in color or not, or if there was a grid on it. She offered to send Betty a copy of her report if it was of interest.[8]

It was. Betty responded enthusiastically, promising to "do all I can to help you." She told Fish that the map was three-dimensional, "like looking out a window." She believed it was done from the perspective of the occupants' home planet, and that the earth was on it somewhere. There was no grid, but the size of each star in Betty's drawing was intended to represent how close the stars were to the viewer. Fish was delighted to get this information and proposed a meeting; the two women's relationship was warm from the beginning. Fish went to Portsmouth on August 4, staying overnight, and she and Betty sat up late talking. Betty confirmed some details; the map was approximately two by three feet, and she had seen it from the side.[9]

By the time Fish left Portsmouth, she and Betty were dear friends. Within a month of their meeting, Fish was signing letters "your friend, always," and after a few letters their correspondence ranged beyond the technicalities of the star map to, in almost equal proportion, the world of UFO and paranormal belief and the stuff of being a woman in early 1970s America. Fish could relate to many of Betty's experiences. The two commiserated about loneliness — Betty, the recent widow, and Fish, who was unmarried. They shared their equal frustration with men not taking them seriously because of their forceful and outspoken personalities. Fish told Betty that she had bristled when her school board critiqued her classroom dress, and Betty shared her own exasperation with government officials believing they could push her around. To this, Fish confessed something she was "rather ashamed of." When a UFO organization to which she had sent her work refused to take the ideas of a single, female, elementary school teacher seriously, she forwarded to them her scores on the entrance exam for Mensa, the society for people who score in the top 2 percent on standardized IQ tests. The organization has "looked the material over now," she reported. They talked about organizing classes in "auto mechanics for women" to "give a little security" to their other female friends. Eventually, Marjorie Fish made a present to Betty of a sculpted bust based on the alien heads David Baker had sketched. Betty christened it "Junior."[10]

In their own way, Fish and Betty were engaged in work similar to many other women in the era. Another Betty, Betty Friedan, had published her book *The Feminine Mystique* nearly a decade earlier, giving voice and name to the inchoate frustrations that Betty Hill and Marjorie Fish shared, and in the intervening years many women were engaged in "consciousness-raising" exercises that transformed their perception of their private struggles into something shared and structural in modern society. In so doing, they created the second-wave feminism — and Betty and Marjorie Fish found in these shared frustrations a source of bonding that propelled Marjorie's work to the spotlight of media coverage of the Hill case.[11]

After her return to Ohio Fish threw herself back into the model, tirelessly mapping the roughly thousand stars within a plausible distance of the earth. She visited the libraries of nearby universities, consulted with astronomers, and painstakingly copied out by hand the coordinates of nearby stars from astronomer Wilhelm Gliese's regularly published *Catalogue of Nearby Stars*. In 1969 Gliese greatly expanded his earlier 1957 edition, and Fish found it helped her work immeasurably. It had taken her two years to identify what she believed were the first five stars, but after her visit with Betty and with Gliese's updated edition, she identified four more by the end of 1969. She used different colored beads to represent types of stars in her living room model, looking for stars the right size and age to support life. She believed that the lines on Betty's map "represented a logical travel pattern to investigate all the best stars for life." Finally, in fall 1972, she had a breakthrough. The star Zeta Tucanae sat awkwardly in the middle of her model; it was certainly at that point in space but it did not fit Betty's pattern. But if Fish tipped her viewing angle forty-five degrees, Zeta Tucanae was occulated by Zeta 1 Reticuli and Zeta 2 Reticuli, a binary star system Fish believed to be at the center of the model. Suddenly, the very pattern of the sixteen primary stars Betty had drawn leapt out at her. She had found it.[12]

Fish concluded that the two large stars at the bottom right corner of Betty's map were the Zeta Reticuli binary system. The sun was directly above that system on the chart, reasonably close but a bit out of the way in the system the map depicted. This meant the creatures might be native to the Zeta Reticuli system.[13] She sat back, triumphant.

Marjorie Fish already knew Stanton Friedman, a physicist and UFO lecturer. He agreed to check her math and became her loudest advocate. Friedman firmly believed in Donald Keyhoe's vision of UFOs: they were mechanical craft from other worlds. He took Fish's work to be validation of interstellar travel and joined her on visits to scientists at Ohio State University and the University of Colorado. The scientists used computer analyses to test Fish's numbers, and largely confirmed her work. Friedman tried to interest the National Science Foundation in the map (suggesting that, UFOs aside, such a map of the nearby

Marjorie Fish's star model. Fish saw an image of Betty's star map in John Fuller's book *The Interrupted Journey* and spent several years in the late 1960s building a model of the universe near the earth with beads and thread in her living room. Eventually she believed she found a match to Betty Hill's map.
Box 6, Folder 1, BBHP, University of New Hampshire. Used with permission.

cosmos would invariably be useful) and arranged a meeting with Allen Hynek himself in December 1972.[14]

Friedman persuaded some people. Walter Webb, for one, was thoroughly convinced. He wrote to Hynek that Fish "believes her work has ruled out hoax or coincidence, and I must agree the reasons she cites are compelling."[15] In July 1973 Friedman published a magazine article describing Fish's map, and he sent a copy to a thirty-year-old science writer — Terence Dickinson — he had met while delivering a lecture about UFOs. Dickinson had just become editor of the brand-new magazine *Astronomy,* whose glossy photos and provocative headlines aimed squarely at a popular audience, and he thought the Fish map would be a good fit.[16] In December 1974 Dickinson wrote and published an article titled "The Zeta Reticuli Incident." He had read *The Interrupted Journey* and interviewed both Fish and Friedman, as well as several scientists who had reviewed Fish's work. The article was lavishly decorated with charts comparing the map and the night sky. "Coincidence, possibly; hoax, improbable," Dickinson concluded.[17]

After Dickinson's article appeared, the publishers of *Astronomy* were deluged with aggravated letters and complaints, but there was also demand for the issue, which sold quickly. The young editor may not have anticipated the firestorm the story would cause — one that demonstrated how far the scientific establishment had pushed UFO research from its own borders. In October 1976 the magazine published a special issue titled *The Zeta Reticuli Incident,* compiling Dickinson's article with critiques from the young but famous astronomer Carl Sagan, Steven Soter (a researcher under Sagan at Cornell University), and Robert Sheaffer, a computer programmer at NASA. Dickinson also solicited responses from David Saunders of the University of Colorado, one of Hynek's students named Jeffrey Kretsch, and Marjorie Fish herself. The critics hit a common note: as Sagan and Soter put it, "We can always pick and choose from a large random data set some subset that resembles a preconceived pattern." There were thousands of stars visible to the naked eye and they were in three-dimensional space. It was unsurprising that Fish found a match. For her part Fish and her allies pointed out that her dataset was not random. She restricted her stars "according to their probability of having planets and also on the logic of the apparent travel paths" depicted in Betty's map.[18]

And there the argument remained for years. A few months later, *Astronomy* fired Terence Dickinson, quite possibly because of the flap. It sold magazines, but many on the magazine's staff found the controversy embarrassing. As a later editor wrote, "Even in 1982, when I joined the staff as an assistant editor, the magazine crew still jokingly referred to this legendarily awful story as The Zeta Ridiculi Incident."[19] Some believers in UFOs had begun following Jacques Vallée's lead. Instead of conceiving of UFOs as objects physically flown from another star system, they had begun emphasizing the metaphysical meanings of the Hills' experience. Thus, they set aside the sort of hard science that Fish and Stanton Friedman trafficked in. Vallée doubted the star map showed any real location. "Betty's drawing is a map to nowhere," he wrote. If it was not simply the product of Betty's mind, it showed a metaphysical symbol, not an interstellar location. Fish told Betty that Vallée never responded to her letters.[20]

Even Hynek seemed uncomfortable with the map. He met with Fish in 1972 but had not responded to her correspondence before that date. Webb prodded him to support Fish for a five-thousand-dollar award the tabloid *National Enquirer* had offered for proof of extraterrestrial life. Hynek had agreed to sit on the award committee. After Webb put him on the spot, Hynek told Fish (who needed the money) that the committee was unwilling to put "their scientific reputation on the line" for the sake of her map. Eventually Stanton Friedman began to berate Hynek in his characteristic boisterous style. "Are you rejecting Marjorie Fish's work as irrelevant or not substantial or none of the above??" Friedman asked. "As I understand it you and Jacques Vallée are leaning toward a parapsychological explanation for UFOs with things popping in and out of time warps or whatever," he wrote in bafflement. "I have a semantic problem here." And Hynek confirmed it. In a letter to Sagan about the map fight, he confessed, "I do not subscribe to Stan Friedman's cliché 'UFOS are someone else's spacecraft.' "[21]

Hynek and Vallée did not view their position as a retreat or a concession. Rather, they understood themselves to be moving past Friedman's naïve scientism and the lack of imagination of UFO debunkers. That choice was one small point in the growing lack of faith in establishment science that was overtaking the United States in the late 1960s, fueled most powerfully by discontent with the Cold War and the American government in total. In some ways, UFO believers had beaten the rest of the country there.[22]

The Rise of Conspiracy

As with other experts the Hills had encountered, Marjorie Fish offered Betty new ways to understand her experience. First, she tried gently to guide Betty Hill past reliance on the sort of conventional science the Hills had long sought validation from. She recommended Betty read *Intelligent Life in the Universe,* a 1966 book Carl Sagan had co-written. He had a graceful and accessible writing style and an energetic public manner; he would soon become the most famous scientist in America. The book maintained that intelligent life elsewhere in the universe was a near certainty, albeit in all likelihood tremendously remote from humanity in both distance and time. Sagan also offered some speculation about the ancient Sumerian mythic figure Oannes, a fishlike being who taught humanity writing and sciences. As a thought experiment Sagan mused about possible contact "between human beings and a non-human civilization of immense powers on the shores of the Persian Gulf." Such contact might have spurred the rise of the Sumerian civilization thousands of years ago. This earned Sagan raised eyebrows from his colleagues but the admiration of Marjorie Fish, who recommended Betty read the book to learn "which stars could have potential life and why."[23]

Fish also pushed Betty to stop thinking about the creatures on the craft in the sort of evolutionary and scientific terms she had borrowed from Carleton Coon. When Betty described her evolutionary theories regarding "similarities between the humanoids and a group of Indians," Fish asked "how Betty actually saw them." Like Robert Hohmann, she thought the Hills' perception of the creatures was probably psychically generated and gently suggested that evolution was not the way to think about their origins. Though Betty told Fish that she drew the map under posthypnotic suggestion, insisting that Simon's expertise enhanced her memory, Fish repeatedly described the process as "automatic drawing," citing "automatic writing" of the sort the Knowleses' psychic friend had done, and implying that the creatures existed on a different psychic plane than did the human race.[24]

Marjorie Fish was a New Age nexus. She showed Betty how belief in extraterrestrial intelligences might be linked to other pieces of forbidden knowledge, generating a new vision of how the universe worked far from the brightly lit clear paths of conventional science. The world that emerged in Marjorie Fish's letters was deep and ancient, governed by strange powers like psychic communion and alien visitors that not all people could access or replicate. Shadowy figures lurked in its corners. It ranged from places as far as Zeta Reticuli to as intimate as the psychic receptors in the human mind, from the ancient builders of Stonehenge to secret agencies monitoring UFOs in the contemporary United States. But Betty, perhaps remembering the dark man on her sister's doorstep, recognized it. Unlike Benjamin Simon, who Betty thought dismissed her memories, unlike Carl Sagan, who dismissed her education, Marjorie Fish took Betty seriously. She showed Betty how her experience might help her understand the seemingly baffling currents of the world around her. If it was a lonelier place than the optimistic democracy she grew up in, that was a small price to pay.

As with many of her contemporaries Fish was not an undiscriminating consumer. She sought to position herself as scientific. Like Robert Hohmann, she wanted to "stay halfway between the objective groups and the far out ones" who "would butcher the map."[25] So it was with no small amount of disappointment that she wrote to Betty, "There was a poltergeist case up the road with flying lights, water turning on (I think) etc. I tried to get permission to go to investigate but no luck."[26] As she said, "I'm always looking for logical explanations for the parapsychological." By that she meant that like many New Age believers she wanted to stand between conventional establishment scientists and the enthusiasts she thought undisciplined. She explained that her use of the term "parapsychological" derived from J. B. Rhine's work. She thought psychic powers derived from "sensors every bit as understandable in a mechanical-chemical-electrical way as the ear."[27]

Despite her dabbling in ghosts and psychics, Marjorie Fish's real passion was history. In 1968 a Swiss hotel manager named Erich von Däniken published a book, titled in its English translation as *Chariots of the Gods: Unsolved Mysteries of the Past*. It was a bestseller in the United States, perhaps because its everything-and-the-kitchen-sink style mirrored that of the New Age itself. In a rambling, conversational style, assiduously punctuated with astonished exclamation points and baffled question marks, von Däniken synthesized a secret human history. He proposed that civilization was in fact the work of extraterrestrials guiding human beings for purposes of their own. The existence of pyramids in Egypt, Babylon, and ancient Mesoamerica showed that all these societies were inspired by a single intelligence. The mysterious Nazca Lines, gargantuan images sketched into the earth in Peru, were designed to be viewed from high in the atmosphere. The *vimanas*, "flying machines" described in the Hindu Ramayana, were saucers. "What are the Eskimos doing talking about metal birds? Why do the Red Indians mention a Thunderbird? How are the ancestors of the Maya supposed to have known that the earth is round?" von Däniken demanded.[28]

Fish was willing to criticize von Däniken when she found him overly credulous. In August of 1972 she wrote to Betty about his discussion of the Palenque stone, a dense bas relief on the tomb of the Mayan ruler Pakal. According to von Däniken it depicted Pakal in a spaceship, dressed as an astronaut. Fish thought that "Däniken went on for pages about the Maya . . . without (apparently) recognizing the typically Mayan garb the figure wore."[29]

But regardless, von Däniken's premise seized Fish, because for all his faults he painted a comprehensive vision that explained so much about human existence. She was convinced that ancient humans possessed technology beyond the reach of modern scientists; she told a fascinated Betty that "ancient Crete had modern plumbing."[30] Such insights, Marjorie thought, cast human history into new light. She recommended Betty study the Piri Reis map, a 1513 chart of the Atlantic drawn by Reis, an Ottoman cartographer, and discussed in *Maps of the Ancient Sea Kings* by Charles Hapgood, one of Marjorie's favorite books. The map appears to show Antarctica and the Andes Mountains, years before Europeans were aware of these geographic features. Hapgood argued that some unknown ancient civilization capable of designing maps with startling accuracy had left fragments for Reis's use.[31] Fish also heartily recommended Betty read the work of Charles Berlitz, who argued that the civilization Hapgood described was in fact Atlantis and that the Atlanteans were in touch with extraterrestrials.[32]

Of course, like Hohmann's theories about Australian aborigines, von Däniken's ideas created a caricature of ancient and indigenous peoples, apparently helpless without the aid of extraterrestrial creatures, in the service of New Age visions. Betty picked up these ideas from Marjorie Fish and passed them along. In letters to her friend Vera de Gill, an eccentric globetrotter, Betty asked about temple builders among the Inca and Aztec and told de Gill about similar architectural features "along the Mississipy [*sic*]." De Gill assured Betty that "neither Zapoteks, Mayas, or any of the other nations who flourished in what today is Mexico, arrived and started to build pyramids and large god-figures out of thin air." She believed that these civilizations "communicated telepathically" with extraterrestrials and urged Betty to pay attention; who knew how they might use her?[33]

This way of understanding the world was conspiratorial in a particularly modern sense. "Conspiracy" and "conspiracy theory" refer to the belief that a relatively small and secretive clique has sought control over society or the nation or the world for opaque ends. Many scholars have argued that conspiracy theory underwent a fundamental shift in the mid-twentieth century, impacted by a number of factors: the exposure of genuine conspiracies at work in the national security state in the 1960s and the 1970s, for example, the lies surrounding the Vietnam War and the activities of the Central Intelligence Agency; the increasing diversity of the American media in both medium and aim; the growing diversity in American culture, characterized in part by the rise of the New Age milieu; the increasing interconnectedness of politics, economics, and the media through processes of globalization and corporatization. Condemnations of conspiracy theories as simply "paranoid" or "pathological," then, miss the ways in which conspiracy belief has been nurtured by modernity. In particular, Betty Hill's embrace of conspiratorial belief is comprehensible when viewed in the totality of her experience.[34]

The conspiratorial world scholars observe emerging in the years after the assassination of President John F. Kennedy was increasingly capacious. Michael Barkun has used the term "superconspiracy" to describe how modern conspiracy believers began to link together smaller, seemingly discreet, conspiratorial ideas into broader networks, chains of belief that stretched across entire swaths of modern life, seeming to absorb and even supplant traditional sorts of authority.[35] Political liberals who subscribed to older ways of conceiving of American life, people like John Papandrew or Donald Keyhoe, were confident that transparency and human ingenuity could solve the problems of American life. Keyhoe popularized the notion that the federal government was concealing information about UFOs, but in his books conspiracy was bland concealment, beige doors swung shut and polite dismissals over telephone. He was fully confident that scientists would be able to unravel the mystery of UFOs if given a chance. In contrast, Fish's sense of the forces at work in human life made scientists seem paltry and confused, and Keyhoe recoiled. In 1973 Keyhoe wrote that while he thought the Hills had indeed seen an alien spacecraft, he found their story of abduction too fanciful, "imaginary pictures created by their subconscious minds." But by then Betty Hill had shifted her allegiances to Marjorie Fish.[36]

This sort of conspiracy thought was fueled by the suspicion that ran like a dark river through American culture during the Cold War. In 1949 and 1950, the journalist Frank Scully published two magazine articles and then a book claiming government agents were concealing the wreckage of UFO crashes in New Mexico. But beyond simply the claim—nothing Keyhoe would have disputed—

loomed Scully's dire warning about what such concealment really meant. It was not, as Keyhoe argued, simply because the government feared panic. Rather, secrecy about UFOs was one part of a deeper threat. Scully's book invoked what he called the "loyalty hysteria" of the 1940s and 1950s: the deathly fear of communism that pervaded American politics and culture and gave rise to the fear-mongering career of Senator Joe McCarthy, who built a national reputation on insinuation and accusation of communist sympathy against dozens of figures in the government. And then several actual spies were captured. President Harry Truman signed an executive order creating loyalty review boards to monitor federal employees. Congress required American communist organizations to register with the government. Hollywood produced films with titles like *I Married a Communist* and *I Lead Three Lives,* showing a world in which neighbor could not trust neighbor and anyone might be a potential communist subversive.[37]

For Scully, concealment of UFOs was part and parcel with this drift toward authoritarianism. "Between the people and the government today lies a double standard of morality," he wrote. "Our sons in uniform do not report to us but to Central Intelligence (which as far as we can make out reports to nobody and is answerable to nobody)." Keyhoe worried the government was hiding evidence, but Scully declared that democracy was already a facade. "The worst feature of our present predicament is that the military has first crack at everything," he said, describing UFO case after case in which the military apparently usurped local governments, shunted aside journalists, and ignored Congress.[38]

Scully's was not the only voice. In 1956 a West Virginian named Gray Barker wrote a book on the story of his friend Albert Bender, a UFO investigator who abruptly shut down his work upon receiving a visit from three "rough" men in "dark clothes and black hats." They threatened him. "Another word out of your office, you're in trouble," one said. Barker begged his friend to reveal who had sent them, but Bender, haggard and tense, had but one answer. "I can't answer that." Barker, though, thought he could. "Could the saucers," he wondered, "have already landed, and have infiltrated even the government, either secretly or by force?" He predicted that "martial law . . . might not be far in the future."[39] By the late 1960s the ominous figures of Barker's fears, now called the "Men in Black," had come to symbolize the conspiratorial subversion of the American state.

———

Such fears would not have seemed entirely outlandish in the increasingly cynical 1970s. Throughout the years that Fish and Betty were exchanging letters, Lyndon Johnson and Richard Nixon were mired in their lies about the Vietnam War, and Betty, at least, was frustrated with politics. In 1974, things seemed to take an even darker turn, one that seemed to validate the message of the Men in Black stories. Richard Nixon resigned the presidency that year, but there was even more troubling news. The Idaho senator Frank Church began holding heavily covered hearings that proved the Central Intelligence Agency had plotted assassinations of at least five foreign leaders (from Fidel Castro of Cuba to Patrice Lumumba of Zaire) and that the National Security Agency tracked Americans' mail and phone calls.[40]

Many Americans were horrified by such revelations. White evangelical Christians, already worried at the social tumult of the 1960s, were galvanized by Hal Lindsey's 1970 bestseller *The Late Great Planet Earth*. This book, which sold more copies than any other in the 1970s, warned that the world was being dragged toward the battle of Armageddon by a satanic conspiracy bent on overturning God, and it promised that apocalyptic nuclear war was inevitable. Gray Barker's last meditation on alien conspiracy, written as he was dying of AIDS in the late 1970s, did not sound so different. He warned that the American government had succumbed to a plot driven not by Satan but by aliens equally bent on violence and subjugation. "This theory is even more attractive today, in light of recent exposés of excesses on the part of the intelligence community. We have had the murders of the Kennedys and King," he wrote.[41]

This was the 1970s that both Betty Hill and Marjorie Fish experienced, and UFO investigators were among many groups of Americans who grew correspondingly suspicious of authority, wary of the federal government, and ready to believe in ever more complex conspiracy. In November 1969 a young man who lived near Fish saw a UFO and recovered a strange chunk of metal from the site of the encounter. Fish told Betty about the strange visitors who appeared in the neighborhood after the fragment. They were "threatening men who wanted it. Their car had an unissued number — probably CIA. This is one of the few MIB cases that seem authentic."[42] She suspected that she herself was being watched. Frustrated that her star chart material had not made it through the mail to a UFO research group, she told Betty, "It's being sidetracked. I don't think the FBI would keep it but who knows what the CIA would do." She recommended Betty read William Turner's *Hoover's FBI: The Men and the Myth,* a juicy exposé of the FBI director's freewheeling monitoring of American citizens.[43]

From Marjorie Fish, Robert Hohmann, and Herbert and Helen Knowles, Betty Hill learned a new way of viewing the world, one that helped her understand the long years of grief after Barney's death. The recriminations she shared with Marjorie as they discussed the frustrations of being scorned by the media, the federal government, and even Marjorie's school board helped generate a feeling of alienation from those institutions. All of it meant that other scorned figures (like von Däniken) seemed to them increasingly sympathetic. By late in her life Betty was listing the tremendous events she had seen — from world wars to the Kennedy assassination — and wondering, "Were ufos coming here because of these changes?"[44]

CHAPTER 14

OBSERVERS

By the mid-1970s Betty was working out what it meant to live without Barney, and more, in retirement, as ill health forced her to step down from her position at the New Hampshire Division of Welfare in 1975 at age fifty-six.[1] The experience in Franconia Notch more and more structured her life, and she came to see it as her window into a deep pattern that connected the abduction, Barney's death, and her life in Portsmouth to the forces that governed the universe.

"The period between 1970 and 1976 I call the *Period of Exploration*," Betty wrote in a 1985 essay she titled "Observations of UFOs." She and Barney had occasionally reported sighting a UFO to Walter Webb in the 1960s, but now Betty began seeing them multiple times a week. She discovered a special place just east of her parents' home in Kingston. There, she said, "ufos were coming in almost nightly." She wrote to Raymond Fowler, an investigator for NICAP, that she went there three nights a week beginning in 1971. East Kingston was a farming community—quite rural, Betty's niece remembered, "spotted with dairy, horse, chicken and turkey farms." A railroad passed through near large quartz deposits to the south. "Nightly," Betty said, "a ufo landed on the railroad tracks while others flew up to this one," referring to a particular spot she would watch from. She said that the UFO numbers "varied from a few to more than a hundred" each night. "Sometimes they used colored beams of light. . . .

Sometimes when they were leaving several would attach themselves together so they looked like a huge craft."[2]

She did not visit the field simply to marvel. She called it a "control area" and told Fowler she wanted to "learn as much about ufos, from direct observation, as possible." She was attempting to replicate the psychophysics experiments, and she organized a community of "observers," as she called them, who met regularly at a small restaurant to share their sightings and develop hypotheses. "Scientists, pilots, military, police, media, doctors, ministers, teachers, fishermen," she claimed. They took photographs and film, kept careful notes, and Betty logged it all. She wrote to one UFO skeptic, "If you lived in this area you would be convinced that ufos are extraterrestrial craft." Recalling Hohmann's theories about her, she promised she would "try to think positively about a ufo going your way." Sometimes she would bring reporters along. One observed that she would abruptly stop conversation in the middle of sentences as lights drifted through the sky. He reported a "reddish-looking object with a bright white light" that appeared then abruptly vanished, as he and his fellow reporters blinked in confusion. "They do that all the time," said Betty. The night ended when Betty pointed out a "beam light," which the reporters thought "was a bright light at a nearby farm house." They all returned home with the dispute unresolved.[3]

One encounter was particularly meaningful to her. On September 19, 1978, in the field in East Kingston, Betty saw a "ufo travel behind some trees" and heard sounds — what seemed like a woman screaming and the deep resonant chords of an organ, playing what seemed to her to be the Christian hymn "Rock of Ages." Betty was struck. "Since this is the anniversary of our capture," she wondered, "did it mean they recognized Barney's death?"[4]

The question revealed that Betty's research was not simply academic. She was in mourning. The meaning she sought to discern might further human progress, but it was also quite personal, about whether her relationship with her husband mattered, whether Barney's life remained marked upon the universe somehow. Two forces — her burgeoning belief in the spiritual interconnectedness of the universe, her growing skepticism of the establishment powers that Marjorie Fish warned her against — wound together to express her mourning and to make Barney's death something sensical.

Psychics

Her interactions with psychic phenomena are a case in point. "I was constantly being asked about psychic experiences since my capture," she wrote. As the Knowleses' luncheons had shown, by the 1970s "it was assumed that anyone who had close contact with ufos must be psychic." Grappling with the question she enrolled in a "psychic development class." She and other students sat in different rooms or even different cities and attempted to project images back and forth. Betty couldn't do it. "I tried, but nothing happened with me—all wrong," she wrote in confusion.[5]

The saving grace of the course was the one exercise that did work for her, a meditation sequence called "the Cottage of Peace." It revealed to Betty that she had lived a past life as "an English girl, herding geese." It was 1754, she learned, and she was "dirty, unkempt [with] long straggly brown hair. Barefooted." She found the experience "very relaxing." She began to guide others in this exercise and saw many people who "could go backward and forward in time." Even though Betty did not learn she was psychic, she took comfort in learning that life did not end with death, that Barney might still be out there somewhere.[6]

In June 1974 Hans Holzer, a New Age writer, visited Betty. He was in New Hampshire investigating the mystical properties of Mystery Hill, a strange collection of stone huts, platforms, and megaliths in nearby Salem, which he believed to be an ancient locus of spiritual power. That Holzer transitioned from his investigation of the site to an interview with Betty Hill marked the porous boundaries of New Age culture, and so did Betty's next request. After discussing UFOs, Betty asked if she could meet Ethel Meyers, a medium whom Holzer had written about in his earlier book on ghosts.

In November Holzer brought Meyers to meet Betty and tactfully withdrew. When Betty emerged she pronounced herself "satisfied." Meyers told Holzer later she had indeed contacted Barney's spirit and that the couple had a tearful reunion. Barney had brought up the encounter and explained that "they had gotten off easy, for he now knew the fate of many others who had been carried off." According to Holzer, Barney's spirit explained that the extraterrestrials were kidnapping humans for breeding experiments—a notion growing popular among those who believed in a UFO conspiracy. Holzer offered to hypnotize her

---

and interrogate her anew about the experience in light of this new information, but Betty turned him down.[7]

What mattered to her was that she had reached her husband again. A few years later she wrote to P. M. H. Edwards, a British ghost researcher. She told him some of the same stories she had once told Robert Hohmann: mysterious sounds, the movement of objects; a clock that seemed to stop and start and to wind itself. Hohmann had told her these things were evidence of aliens trying to communicate with her. But now she had a different theory. Could it be, she asked Edwards, a ghost? A particular ghost? The business with the clock, perhaps. "This could be to show the interval between physical death and spiritual reawakening," Edwards mused. "The time, to them, of course, doesn't appear long, at all; but it does so appear, to us. Cases of ghosts appearing long after death, are rare; but they do occur."[8]

The Cosmic Watergate

The connections Betty built between personal trauma, strange experiences, and conspiracy belief were perhaps best illustrated in her friendship with Marianne Cascio. Marianne saw a UFO in June 1952, when she was eleven years old. She was playing with her brother in a wooded area near her home in Agawam, Massachusetts, when a sudden flash of light in the sky struck her deep with terror, fear that even at the time seemed to her confusing. She fled home and buried herself in her bedroom. Soon afterward, she began to lose her vision. Her doctors blamed deteriorated retinas.[9]

As with many blind people she could see shadows, light and dark, shapes and outline – enough to negotiate her way through the world. But in 1974 she began seeing what Betty called "the outline of things and people in bright changing colors." Over time she came to understand that these lights had meanings. She seemed to be seeing people's auras. She stopped sleeping much, underwent hypnosis, and gained memories of being taken aboard the strange light she had seen in the sky. Overwhelmed and exhausted, she sought out the most famous person who had made contact with UFOs. In mid-1975 she called Betty Hill.[10]

Betty Hill was at her best in situations like this. Her social worker instincts, her sense of justice, and her concern for the vulnerable were on display as she took Marianne under her wing. She found not simply a protégé but someone in her own way as vulnerable as Betty herself was. As with Marjorie Fish, the two could comfort and protect each other. At a UFO convention in 1977, Betty was introduced as her "mentor and advisor."[11]

Betty guided Marianne in a series of experiments designed to assure the younger woman that she was not losing her mind. She installed a model of Marjorie Fish's star map on plywood, painting the star systems, and inserting Christmas lights for the stars. She wrote she was tempted to paint the words "You Are Here" in the appropriate place but did not—for that was the test. She placed the model in the field outside her mother's home and asked Marianne to send a UFO to it. On December 7, 1975, Betty was at her mother's home, and at 9:00 p.m. she looked outside and "saw a bright white star which gave the appearance of rising from the ground . . . it rose up and then dropped back down." By the next summer Marianne herself saw UFOs from time to time.[12]

The experiment was designed to show Marianne that her seemingly random traumas were part of a larger networked universe, deeply connected along routes unknown to most Americans. It carried a dark side, though. In November 1975, following Betty's advice, Marianne and some friends were attempting to track down a UFO she had seen in the sky. They found a circular imprint in a field near her home. But then, Betty wrote, as they stood gazing at the mark, a helicopter "appeared from behind a cloud and was circling them, each time coming down to a lower altitude." It was black, with no identifying sounds or symbols, and seemed to make no sound.[13]

By December such craft were following Betty as well. "Most people assume the helicopters are of the military and do not question their presence," Betty reported. But she knew better. She turned to her network of observers. Three women in western Pennsylvania reported they visited a UFO landing site and a helicopter "circled around them. It was a small craft, with two figures, one of whom put his head out the window." A friend of Betty's in southern Maine saw two helicopters hovering over a snowy road late one night, "a connection going from one to the other." All of her pregnant rabbits vanished that night. Betty called Pease Air Force Base—just as she had fifteen years earlier to report her own strange sighting. But this time the Air Force flatly denied that Betty saw what she

---

208

claimed. There were no helicopters at the base. This time Betty took the rejection with far more suspicion than she had her conversation with Paul Henderson.[14]

In the mid-1970s, stories of black helicopters were circulating among UFO conspiracy theorists like Gray Barker; they represented the malign fusion between the military on the one hand and UFOs on the other. Betty's use of the trope illustrated her growing suspicion of the state. In 1972 she wrote to a NICAP official, using language that echoed her experiences with psychophysics. She had come to loathe the Vietnam War, believing it to be the result of profound government corruption. "I am sending thought waves for them [extraterrestrials] to go to Washington DC, find the Pentagon, and disintegrate it," she wrote her correspondent, half in jest, half in frustration. "Don't repeat this—people will think I have flipped out." After a few days she sent a second letter admitting that these were "silly stupid statements . . . so out of character for me," and that she regretted them almost as soon as she dropped the letter in the mailbox.[15]

The statements might have been out of character, but they reflected where Betty Hill's mind was in the mid-1970s. Even though she disavowed her half-baked plot about the Pentagon, she reported to the same official that a few weeks earlier she had predicted that J. Edgar Hoover, director of the FBI, "will probably die in bed—two days later he did; then I said that I was surprised that someone had not killed [George] Wallace [governor of Alabama and a notorious advocate for segregation]—and the same day he was shot." She told him that "the trends of the times seem to be going in these directions," and she wondered if a government that seemed no longer trustworthy but a force for destruction and chaos was interfering in her life.[16]

She began to notice people following her. Once a neighbor saw two men entering her home in the middle of the day. When Betty arrived home her tax records were gone. Once she picked her phone up to make a call and noticed her lines were open. "I said 'Hello.' Someone answered, 'Federal Agency,' " she told an interviewer. Later on, Barney's cousin Marge called several times, could not get through, and was stunned when a strange voice came on the line and said, "The Hills are not home. They've gone to a meeting." Betty speculated that whoever was monitoring her calls "got tired of listening to Marge dialing."[17]

Her friends and family were followed too. Barney's son, Barney III, was in the military and stationed in Panama. Late one night, while serving guard duty, he was approached by a strange man calling himself "Mr. Geist." Mr. Geist dressed all in white, spoke with a strange accent, and asked about the Franconia Notch experience. This was alarming enough, but Betty was even more distressed when her stepson told her that his military superiors interrogated him about Mr. Geist and seemed to be hiding something. This seemed confirmed when Lauri D'Allessandro told Betty that a strange, "nasty" man came to her home to berate her for helping Betty. He claimed to be a federal official and said that he could have the military imprison D'Allessandro. The two called the Air Force, as they had several times by then, and the Air Force denied, as it had several times, that it had anything to do with Betty's experiences.[18]

As revelations of government corruption poured out of Washington, D.C., political cynicism gave Betty a language for her suspicions. In 1976 she told an interviewer that a few years earlier she had confronted a strange man who followed her to work and home again. He called himself "Donald Simmons." Months later while watching news coverage of the Watergate investigations, she saw that one of Nixon's men, Donald Segretti, was convicted of forgery. "I learned that Donald Segretti used the name Donald Simons [sic] when he was in N.H. and closely resembled the man who came to my home," she said. In linking Nixon's story so closely to her own, Betty was finding a way to legitimate her experience, ascribing relevance to it in the language contemporary Americans were attuned to.[19] It was no mistake that at the same time, Stanton Friedman, one of her most vocal defenders, began labeling the whole state of affairs the "cosmic Watergate."[20]

A Common Sense Approach to UFOs

Donald Keyhoe was not the only one of Betty's old allies growing ambivalent about the course of her journey. As early as 1967, Walter Webb expressed his feelings in a letter to her. He noted they had not spoken in "a long time," but he felt it necessary to reach out because James Moseley, publisher of the newsletter *Saucer News,* had invited the Hills to speak at his annual UFO convention. Webb was worried. "I would strongly urge you not to attend that convention," he wrote. "It could do you more harm than good to become linked to the fanatics and cultists you undoubtedly will meet there."[21]

In January 1979, some of Betty's other friends visited her. She took them to the field in Kingston to watch the UFOs. After the visit they offered her another warning. John Fuller wrote the letter. He sent a copy to Allen Hynek with a note: "She'll probably be irate, but it's got to be done." Fuller reminded Betty that he found her original story compelling "because of the cautious approach of you and Barney to the subject, and your careful analysis of your own experience." By contrast, he said, in the Kingston field he saw "nothing that appeared that could not be identified as planes on a normal traffic pattern." He pleaded with her to relearn how to see the world the way she had before.[22]

But Betty seemed committed to her new path. The very next year, 1980, she attended James Moseley's convention in New York City, and stood with Moseley, Stanton Friedman, and Charles Berlitz (author of the books on Atlantis that Marjorie Fish had recommended to Betty) at a press conference calling on Jimmy Carter and Ronald Reagan, the two major candidates for president, to "make flying saucers a down to earth campaign issue." Betty signed the statement and wrote a short biography to introduce herself. "Since her retirement she has been involved in ufo research," as well as "related areas such as animal mutilations, mystery helicopters, big foot and other strange creatures, the Men in Black."[23] Her world was, at least to her, a unified whole.

She spent the last years of her life before her death in 2004 composing a book laying out that comprehensive vision. *A Common Sense Approach to UFOs* was part memoir, part theory, and it bore a title that showed Betty's fusion of her longstanding faith in her own rationality with the New Age. She explained her work: "In a three year period of time, I filmed more than 200 different kinds of ufos."[24] As Fuller predicted, she was frustrated with those who would not see what she saw. Once she spent two nights showing an investigator the UFOs of East Kingston only to have him sputter that he "could not go back and tell his organization what he had seen here, because it was contrary to all his beliefs." Betty left him with, "Don't let your beliefs be upset by the facts."[25]

If she ascribed the difficulties of some critics to mulishness, she had a darker vision of others. In the book she described a world pulsing with dark and invisible energy. Strange crafts intervened in the electrical grid. Animals were found dead and mutilated. "Big Foots" roamed rural forests, and every now and then people were abducted by extraterrestrials. And more, all of these things slid together into a shadowy pattern Betty had come to believe the government and scientists were cooperating to hide. When she asked electric companies about strange power surges, "their answer was confidential, top secret." Over and over again, she was given denial and warnings. She met with astronauts and was "given confidential information many times, with the warning that if I quoted the person he would deny it." She showed an object she had discovered in Kingston to government officials, and "they all gasped. They asked in puzzlement, 'Where in hell did you get this? It is top secret.' " Over the years, she concluded, "I learned to distrust anyone who offers to analyze anything I find."[26]

And yet, at long last, her optimism won out. She wove conspiracy and high strangeness together and made of them a story meaningful to her. What did we know about the pilots of the UFOs, she asked? They seemed as though they were visiting Earth for the long term. They traveled in groups. They did not seem dangerous unless threatened. And finally, most important to Betty, "They must have extremely long lives or they have abolished death."[27]

The last point was why she believed these creatures were benevolent, as she had instinctively believed since her moment of fascination at the sight of the star that fell upward in September 1961. "A very long lifespan is the greatest threat to governments today," she wrote. "Death is our biggest business. No death results in no wars, rebellions, violence, disease." The government, Betty suspected, did not want human beings to learn the secrets of those ships.[28]

But they were here anyway. Great possibility hovered within humanity's reach. All of Betty's confusion and pain came down to this. She closed her book with a story of a friend of hers, an "elderly Black woman" who was with Betty when Betty's television showed a report on Kenneth Arnold's 1947 sighting of strange crafts in the sky. As Betty remembered it, this old woman began clapping her hands. "You white folks are going to learn," she said. She told Betty that her great-grandparents, enslaved in North Carolina, used to see "messengers from God" that "came down from the heavens and flew around the fields" at night. Her ancestors believed these lights "were here to free them from slavery." Betty asked, "Are they here to free us from slavery? The first freedom we need is freedom from disease and death."[29]

She must have, could only have, been thinking of Barney.

COSMOS

John Fuller's *The Interrupted Journey* was published in 1966 and sold nearly 300,000 copies in the United States and more in eight other countries over the next decades. But by the mid-1980s, it had gone out of print. By then, the way most Americans came to learn about the story of Betty and Barney Hill was television. In 1975 and again in 1980, the Hills' story was depicted twice — first on NBC in *The UFO Incident,* a made-for-television movie based on Fuller's book, and second on PBS as a segment in Carl Sagan's wildly popular miniseries *Cosmos.* The medium that Betty and Barney had sought to mobilize on their behalf had slipped from their control; the Hills' story was more and more used by others, adapted for new purposes that Betty found distant from her own.

In late spring of 1972, James Earl Jones called Betty Hill at her home. At that point Jones was a well-known actor transitioning from the stage to film; he had won a Tony Award in 1969 and had received an Academy Award nomination in 1971 but was still several years away from providing the voice to Darth Vader in *Star Wars.* As his Hollywood star was ascending, Jones found that he had the finances and influence to make projects he was interested in. And he remembered reading the condensed version of Fuller's *The Interrupted Journey* in *Look* magazine. He called Fuller first, and then Betty Hill.[1]

Betty was initially resistant to making a film. "It is too much responsibility to give to somebody else, without any control," she wrote to Stuart Nixon of NICAP after Jones spoke with Fuller and Fuller with her. "If someone said he would produce it exactly as it happened, I would agree. And that is the only way, I would agree."[2] But after speaking with Jones, she was comforted. "James Earle [*sic*] Jones called me and we talked for an hour about the way it would be produced," she wrote to Nixon later. She had asked Jones to "leave the ending open, or slanted toward UFOs a little. He is a believer," she assured Nixon. After her conversation with the actor, she agreed to allow Jones to buy the movie rights. Jones went to New Hampshire, met with Betty, and drove the route the Hills had taken that night, through Franconia Notch and past the Indian Head resort.[3]

Betty hoped that the film would bolster her long quest for public respectability; she thought, as she had always thought, that if people heard the whole story they could not but accept its truth. Television seemed an ideal medium. Other UFO supporters were eager for the film for the same reason. After hearing from Betty, Stuart Nixon eagerly wrote to Jones. They had never met, but Nixon wanted to, on behalf of NICAP, "offer whatever assistance we can in the film's research and production." The two eventually spoke on the telephone and had breakfast together, and over the next year and a half Nixon followed up repeatedly, asking about the status of the film's script and production and even offering to help raise money for the production. Like Betty, Nixon was enthusiastic about the film's possibilities to validate UFO belief. "I am hopeful they will agree to do it your way," he wrote to her. "I think it could be very effective if handled that way."[4]

James Earl Jones seemed amenable. "I am convinced that something of the sort really happened," he told the *Boston Globe*. He cited Betty's map and insisted that not only did he find the story believable but he also felt it was a compelling narrative. But he selected this story out of many he could have produced for a specific reason. He told the *Los Angeles Times* he wanted to keep it "from falling into the science fiction or horror movie area."[5] Instead, the movie Jones eventually shepherded into production is, as one critic put it, "more a study of the trauma and the way it preyed on the insecurities of an interracial marriage than [it is] an account of an abduction by spacecraft invaders."[6] It aired on NBC the week before Halloween 1975.

———

The film, eventually named *The UFO Incident,* holds closely to the details of *The Interrupted Journey,* but it is at its strongest as an actors' showcase. For long, long stretches Jones and Estelle Parsons, the Academy Award–winning actress who plays Betty Hill, sit in the office of Benjamin Simon (played by Barnard Hughes) and deliver excerpts from the hypnosis transcripts printed in Fuller's book. It is often riveting. But these monologues are interwoven with fictionalized scenes of the Hills' daily life that dramatize the social tension the two feel around them, and their marriage grows tense. "Here in Portsmouth it's an all-white society!" Barney cries out at one point. They argue about the 1964 presidential election, Barney denouncing Republican candidate Barry Goldwater, who opposed the Civil Rights Act. In a moment of vulnerability Betty confesses, "I was afraid you thought you loved me, you thought I was pretty, because I was white." Worrying about the anxiety and stress he feels, and struggling with the memories coming back to him, a worried Barney tells Betty, "With you I can look like a fool, but with my friends I can't afford to look like a fool." The film's tension derives from the actors' performances and the social pressures that increasingly burden their characters. The alien creatures appear only briefly, and not until the film is two-thirds over.

It was not quite the story that Betty Hill wanted to tell. "The original had much more of the ufo in it," she wrote to Walter Webb. "I was disappointed that so much was left out." She had read the script and approved it because she thought it introduced "ufos to the general public who had no knowledge of them in a way that they would be believable." But the version that appeared on TV was the story that James Earl Jones wanted to tell. The UFO incident was a trigger for the Hills' deeper anxiety about the pressure of being an interracial couple in 1960s America. In the closing voiceover of the film, Simon declares that whether the abduction was real or fantasized "remains a question." But Betty's last lines are significant: "Do you remember when we were in the middle of all that mess," she asks, while the two are happily barbecuing in their yard after Simon's treatment is complete. "We were fighting all the time, about everything." But now, she tells her husband, "You've given me so much love." The real triumph of the film is not the Hills' recovered memory; it is the preservation of their marriage across the racial divide.[7]

Five years later, the Hills' story was again told on television – but this time by their old nemesis Carl Sagan. His PBS miniseries *Cosmos* was an

Carl Sagan in 1980, at the founding of the
Planetary Society, a nonprofit designed to
encourage astronomical research.
The Seth MacFarlane Collection of the
Carl Sagan and Ann Druyan Archive,
Library of Congress.

extraordinary success, a thirteen-episode exploration of the universe, the history of science, the origins of human life, and the structure of the galaxy. More than 500 million people in sixty countries have seen it; the book by the same title that Sagan published alongside the series was on the *New York Times* bestseller list for seventy weeks from 1980 to 1981.[8]

The final two episodes of the miniseries deal in part with the possibility of extraterrestrial intelligence. Episode 12, "Encyclopaedia Galactica," opens with a nine-minute segment exploring the Hills' experience. Like *The UFO Incident,* it dramatizes their encounter with the spacecraft and its occupants, but unlike the film, the episode does not give much care to matching the details of the story as the Hills told it. As the actors playing the Hills drive through the woods in the dark, rain is crashing down. The radio buzzes with strange static, the Hills' dog, Delsey, panics in the back seat for no apparent reason, and when the craft lands on the road in front of their car the Hills clamber out of the front seats and stagger toward it Frankenstein-like, presumably in some sort of trance. Smoke and light throw them into dramatic silhouette.

—

These are for the most part minor details, though none derives from any account of the experience told to that point. They do, however, evince how Sagan conceived of their account. His voiceover introducing the Hills states that their story has more to do with "superstition than with science," and the segment portrays the incident as a horror movie, a heightened narrative that has little to do with reality. It was the sort of genre storytelling James Earl Jones wanted to avoid, but for Sagan it fits the dramatic, theatrical, and therefore to his mind fictional nature of the account. After the reenactment Sagan holds up to the camera a version of Betty's star map, repeating the argument he made in *Astronomy* magazine: with an entire galaxy full of stars that might be viewed from any perspective it would be surprising if the Hills' supporters did not find a match. He does not credit Marjorie Fish for her work. Instead, Sagan insists famously, "Extraordinary claims require extraordinary evidence."[9]

Betty and her advocates were furious. "In the dramatization which was shown, the experience was false from what actually happened," Betty complained, "a Saganized fantasy but using our names."[10] But the complaints of other UFO advocates revealed how her supporters had begun to fragment among themselves, as interpretations of UFOs had become increasingly diffuse. Stanton Friedman, characteristically, erupted. The day after the episode aired he called William Lamb, a senior vice president at the PBS station that produced *Cosmos,* and followed up with a three-page letter. "I do not believe that any reasonable person watching the segment and reading the book [*The Interrupted Journey*] could say that it was anything other than a hatchet job," he declared, before listing the many errors he believed the segment contained. Friedman challenged Sagan's "total lack of scientific methodology" and declared that, in fact, the weight of scientific research was in favor of the Hills' experience. "Note the many references in my papers," he said. "There have been more than 10 volumes of papers by scientists about UFOs — more than 5 of collections of data about sightings — PhD theses have been done about UFOs," he railed. "Superstition??" He closed with a challenge to Sagan to a televised debate.[11]

But if Friedman was convinced that Sagan's problem was a failure to do proper scientific research, other of Betty's defenders attributed darker motives to the astronomer. Jim Lorenzen, one of the founders of the Aerial Phenomena Research Organization, a civilian UFO research group, wrote to Betty offering his sympathy on her misrepresentation. He was less convinced than Friedman that Sagan was merely a lackadaisical researcher. Rather, said Lorenzen, Sagan was of "those elements of the establishment who would discredit your initial experience." To Lorenzen, Sagan was not persuadable no matter how many tons of published peer-reviewed papers Stanton Friedman might drop with a thud on his desk. Sagan was part of a national conspiracy dedicated to deflating UFO belief. "It seems to be very important to Sagan and his ilk to debunk you," Lorenzen warned, urging Betty to speak out and "fight back!"[12]

John Fuller, for his part, threatened to sue. He wrote to the beleaguered William Lamb, informing him that "Sagan's shoddy and unscientific appraisal of the UFO subject is one thing, but his dramatization of a portion of my book THE INTERRUPTED JOURNEY without permission is another." He mourned that such a "public-spirited" organization as PBS would put such a lurid dramatization on air and warned Lamb that his attorneys would be in touch. Despite his irritable protests, a PBS attorney shrugged off the complaints, stating that *Cosmos* "used sources which in no way infringed upon your rights as author." Ultimately Fuller's case went nowhere.[13]

The distinctions between Sagan's presentation of the Hill story and Jones's — not to mention among those people who weighed in on each — show how many things UFOs had come to mean in the years after the Hills' experience. To Jones and his production team, they were a signifier of the strain that Black men in the United States still felt; to Jim Lorenzen, they signaled the secretive conspiracies of the American elite; to Sagan, the alarming fuzziness of many Americans' understanding of science. And though John Fuller staunchly backed up Stanton Friedman's continuing crusade to defend the old-fashioned notion that there was at least something scientifically interesting about UFOs, his primary argument pointed to something new about the Hill case: that it had become show business.[14]

The Hills had instinctively realized that years before, when they were appearing on television in the late 1960s. They were trying to appropriate some of television's authoritative aura, trying to prove themselves respectable and believable. But the stream of adaptations that followed them did the opposite, drawing their story into the dramatic forms and tropes of television fiction and away from the reality they believed the experience's singularity implied. Jones downplayed the abduction itself in favor of his invented dramatic arc about the Hills' marriage; Sagan, quite consciously, treated the story as a fantasy or fairy tale. Fuller's dispute with Lamb was about the details and presentation of the narrative as a story more than its veracity. More and more, the arguments surrounding Betty Hill and her story were about how it functioned as a story; more and more, they were about its adaptations.

Betty Hill was conscious of the strengths and weaknesses that the notion of adaptation might bring to her story. Reducing UFO experiences to narrative tropes was a way to delegitimate them that both Betty and those who found her story improbable would use. By the early 1980s, Betty was growing frustrated with the increasing numbers of people coming forward with abduction stories that sounded like her own.

In the mid-1970s the artist Budd Hopkins, having read about the Hill case, grew intrigued. He solicited the help of psychologists to hypnotize volunteers; soon he began hypnotizing them himself. In 1981 he published a book, *Missing Time,* covering nineteen abduction cases he had studied in the previous few years. He cited the Hill experience as an archetype, "a control in weighing the validity" of later abduction accounts. Rendering the abduction narrative into literary form, he developed a typology: often the sighting of a light in the sky and then, critically, what Hopkins called "missing time" — a gap in people's memories. "People are being picked up, examined — sometimes marked for life — and released, their memories conveniently blocked," he wrote. Hopkins believed these experiences were traumatic and that his work was advocacy and care for victims. "It is better to ventilate a traumatic experience that might otherwise, if it is kept buried, cause difficulties," he wrote.[15]

Betty Hill found this intolerable. She viewed these people with a wariness that seemed to mix her own desire to be taken seriously with her certainty that her experiences were unique. Betty insisted that "real abductions do exist, but they are extremely rare." She knew Budd Hopkins; they had been on television together and she had been a guest in his home. But she was worried that reducing her experience to archetype and turning its features into trope would make it seem less and less reliable — particularly as Hopkins's subjects recalled elements that Betty found unbelievable. Creatures from Venus; visits to other planets; people floating out of their beds. "Good old common sense works," she pleaded, hearing these stories. "Have they ever seen or heard of anyone who could walk through walls, without damage to the walls or themselves? Or float out windows?"[16]

It seemed to Betty that Hopkins was simply repeating what so many others starting with Benjamin Simon had said about her and Barney; that they suffered from psychological pathology. She found in Hopkins, therefore, not support, but another way to undermine her respectability. "Real abductions do not result in therapy," she insisted. "The person has very little stress or fears." Against Hopkins's amateur hypnosis, she insisted that Benjamin Simon had laid out "criteria for separating real abductions from the psychological ones" and that too many investigators were botching hypnotic treatment. Simon's hypnosis of the Hills had elicited from them the truth; Hopkins's subjects were confabulating. "It can be very upsetting to find a real abduction, and then to learn its value has been totally destroyed by the wrong type of investigation," she wrote.[17]

But just as Betty feared that others were adapting her story in ways that made it seem less reliable, so did others describe her as an unreliable adaptor. In 2013, the family of Marjorie Fish claimed in her obituary that near the end of her life, having seen updated data about star positions in the nearby universe, Fish changed her mind about her findings. By the time she died, Fish thought "the correlation" between her model and Betty's map "was unlikely." Similarly, in 1990 and 1994, the UFO skeptic Martin Kottmeyer published two articles proposing that the story of the Hills' experience was itself an adaptation of various science fiction stories. The 1953 movie *Invaders from Mars* featured a woman abducted by Martians, placed on a rectangular table, and penetrated with a needle. More triumphantly, Kottmeyer pointed out that "The Bellero Shield," an episode of the science fiction television series *The Outer Limits,* first aired on February 10, 1964. That was twelve days before Barney described the slanting, curving eyes of the terrifying leader on the craft to Benjamin Simon. Kottmeyer claimed that the alien creature in "The Bellero Shield" had eyes that were "unusually long and wrapped around the side of the face." More, the alien tells a human character that it can read her eyes, for "all who have eyes have eyes that speak." Twelve days later, of course, Barney would cry out to Simon that the leader's eyes "are talking to me."[18] Years after the fact Betty Hill insisted that neither she nor Barney had seen the show, and other rebuttals pointed out that the alien in "The Bellero Shield" does not actually have large slanting eyes; instead, bony ridges around its eyes extend along the side of its head.[19]

From the beginning, the Hills' project was one of adaptation, of explaining the inexplicable in a language already understood, and Kottmeyer's interpretation was no different. What happened to them the night of September 19, 1961, was, and remains, undocumentable. Some have suggested that the light was the planet Jupiter or, more recently, the signal light on the top of Cannon Mountain, one of the preeminent peaks in Franconia Notch that has hosted a ski resort since the 1930s. If the light Betty said was "falling upward" and then pointed out to Barney was indeed the planet or the signal, it may have seemed to move as the Hills themselves passed along the winding Route 3. But the distant glow of a star or planet or a signal light does not match the behavior that Betty and Barney described in the light they remembered. It is possible that they were confused, that Benjamin Simon's suggestion that stress and anxiety overwhelmed their faculties is correct. But, to paraphrase what Simon said, he did not know what it was they had seen, and he believed neither did the Hills themselves.[20] Such strangeness, seemingly irresolvable, was intolerable to the Hills, to their supporters, to their critics. If they could agree on anything, it was that such strange objects in the sky must be identifiable. The suggestion that they might not be ran counter to the confident ethos of the age, and until Jacques Vallée came on the scene, nobody seemed to think the task impossible. (And of course, for all his doubts, Vallée himself eventually proposed a solution.)

And so the Hills began to grope for explanations. The notion that the strange light and all the anomalies that surrounded it was an extraterrestrial spaceship would have been incomprehensible two hundred years earlier, but it was immediately at hand for Betty Hill. The proximate reason was the interest of her sister Janet in such things; the deeper reason was that she lived in a nation saturated with Cold War pride and fears, a nation consumed with the promise and terror of technology — and especially technology of the sky. That Donald Keyhoe, the pilot, became one of the nation's leading interpreters of these strange sights is evidence for that, and that Betty chose to seek him out. Donald Keyhoe's works, blending military language with stories of bizarre lights, further makes the point. Keyhoe and his emissaries, Walter Webb, C. D. Jackson, and Robert

Hohmann, of course, only reinforced the idea. The light was a spacecraft. The figures were pilots, of a kind. It was, however strange, within the world that Americans accustomed to stories about air warfare and the missile gap understood.

When a host of debunkers—ranging from Simon to Sagan—began to assail that conclusion, it frustrated the Hills because it implied to them that their own reason and perceptions could not be trusted. It seemed catastrophic to them, not only because of their experience but because it implied that the nation was run not by its citizens but by a dominant and trained elite. Benjamin Simon telling the Hills their story was simply an adaptation of their inner anxiety and turmoil added insult to injury. That this explanation became so popular strengthened the insult. And then Carl Sagan insisted that the Hills' minds and memory did not comport with science, comparing, as did Martin Kottmeyer, what they remembered to a B-grade science fiction movie.

It is no wonder that Betty Hill turned to new ways of understanding American life that, at the least, affirmed her own perceptions.

The condescension and frustrations the Hills experienced should not, though, be taken as validation of their recovered memories. Rather those experiences should point us toward Americans' fascination with science, their loathing of communism, their sense of providential mission. These things led Americans into overconfidence that national problems might easily be solved. Donald Keyhoe's assertions about UFOs were born of that faith.

But of course, such problems were not easily solved. The challenge of American racism, the complex workings of the human psyche, the intractable persistence of American economic inequity, the daunting problems of foreign policy: none of these could be tamed with a simple answer. In that sense, the Hills' conundrums were only those of the nation writ large, and its failure— their failure—to answer the light above Franconia Notch was emblematic of the pains of the entire postwar era.

And finally, of course, this text is an adaptation as well. As did other interpreters, I am using the story Betty and Barney told in ways that they might not have appreciated. I largely concur with Benjamin Simon's conclusions, if not his reasoning. I believe the Hills saw a strange object in the sky that was not readily

---

Clinton Meister's Hill tarot card "The Lovers" depicts Betty and Barney Hill. Courtesy of the artist.

identifiable, and I am skeptical of explanations that posit the elaborate and strange appearance of the sighting was simply a planet. At the same time, the story of the abduction seems to me to lack proof beyond the Hills' own hypnotically recovered memories, a genre well known to be fraught and malleable. And a story of medical examination and interstellar travel seems too simple for the realities the Hills claimed to glimpse.

And so, like Simon, I am taking the Hills' story and making something new with it, translating it into the language of the historian, making it a story of the American Cold War period, and directing it toward American concerns in the early twenty-first century, a time when conspiracy and distrust roam freely. That I am skeptical of such impulses but sympathetic to their causes might be evident to the reader, but, again, it would not have satisfied Betty and Barney Hill, who remained to their deaths convinced that, in fact, they had made contact with life from another star.

NOTES

ABBREVIATIONS

BBHF   Betty and Barney Hill File. International UFO Museum and Research Center, Roswell, New Mexico.

BBHHT   "Betty and Barney Hill Hypnosis Transcripts," copyright John Fuller, 1966; annotations by Betty Hill and Kathleen Marden, 1995. Betty and Barney Hill Papers, Box 5, Folders 8–9, Milne Special Collections and Archives, Dimond Library, University of New Hampshire.

BBHP   Betty and Barney Hill Papers. Milne Special Collections and Archives, Dimond Library, University of New Hampshire.

BHF   Betty Hill File 18–1. Center for UFO Studies, Chicago, Illinois.

BSBS   "Barney Summary – Betty Summary, 3/5/66." Transcript of John Fuller's interview with Betty and Barney Hill, March 5, 1966. John G. Fuller Collection, Box 3, Folder 7, Howard Gotlieb Archival Research Center, Boston University.

DSC   "Dr. Simon Chronology Interview, 3/7/66." Transcript of John Fuller's interview with Benjamin Simon, March 7, 1966. John G. Fuller Collection, Box 3, Folder 7, Howard Gotlieb Archival Research Center, Boston University.

JGFC   John G. Fuller Collection. Howard Gotlieb Archival Research Center, Boston University.

JPF   John Papandrew Files. Unitarian Universalist Association Minister Files, 1825–2010, Harvard Divinity School Library.

UA1   Betty Hill, untitled autobiographical sketch beginning "New Hampshire is my home." Box 3, Folder 1, Betty and Barney Hill Papers, Milne Special Collections and Archives, Dimond Library, University of New Hampshire.

UA2   Betty Hill, untitled autobiographical sketch beginning "I was born on June 28, 1919, in Newton, New Hampshire." Box 3, Folder 1, Betty and Barney Hill Papers, Milne Special Collections and Archives, Dimond Library, University of New Hampshire.

Webb1   Walter N. Webb, "A Dramatic UFO Encounter in the White Mountains, N.H." (October 26, 1961). Box 5, Folder 14, BBHP. This is Walter Webb's first report on the Hill case. It covers what Webb called their "first encounter," the sighting of the craft.

Webb2   Walter N. Webb, "A Dramatic UFO Encounter in the White Mountains, New Hampshire, Sept. 19–20, 1961" (August 30, 1965). Box 5, Folder 14, BBHP. This report is of what Webb called the Hills' "second encounter," their sighting of the craft and their memories of the abduction recovered after the hypnosis. Written four years after Webb1, it greatly expanded on the earlier report.

INTRODUCTION

1. BSBS, 76.

2. The politics of the New Deal coalition are explored most famously in the essays in Steve Fraser and Gary Gerstle, eds., *The Rise and Fall of the New Deal Order, 1930–1980* (Princeton: Princeton University Press, 1989), particularly Alan Brinkley, "The New Deal and the Idea of the State," 85–122, and Jonathan Rieder, "The Rise of the Silent Majority," 243–269, and in Gary Gerstle, Nelson Lichtenstein, and Alice O'Connor, eds., *Beyond the New Deal Order: US Politics from the Great Depression to the Great Recession* (Philadelphia: University of Pennsylvania Press, 2019), particularly 1–17. On growing suspicion of the military-industrial complex throughout the 1960s, see James Ledbetter, *Unwarranted Influence: Dwight D. Eisenhower and the Military-Industrial Complex* (New Haven: Yale University Press, 2011), 188–211; Rebecca Klatch, *A Generation Divided: The New Left, the New Right, and the 1960s* (Berkeley: University of California Press, 1999), 27–30; Kelly Moore, *Disrupting Science: Social Movements, American Scientists, and the Politics of the Military, 1945–1975* (Princeton: Princeton University Press, 2008), 158–190.

3. Moore, *Disrupting Science*, 96–130.

4. Betty Hill, *A Common Sense Approach to UFOs* (Greenland, NH: The Author, 1995), 129, 172.

5. Carl Jung, *Flying Saucers: A Modern Myth of Things Seen in the Sky*, trans. R. F. C. Hull (Princeton: Princeton University Press, 1978), 112–131; Jung's current most prominent disciple when it comes to UFOs is David J. Halperin, *Intimate Alien: The Hidden Story of the UFO* (Berkeley: University of California Press, 2020), 31–65.

6. The term "resonance" is Lepselter's, from Susan Lepselter, *The Resonance of Unseen Things: Poetics, Power, Captivity and UFOs in the American Uncanny* (Ann Arbor: University of Michigan Press, 2016), 3–5; Jodi Dean, *Aliens in America: Conspiracy Cultures from Outerspace to Cyberspace* (Ithaca: Cornell University Press, 1998), 5–8, 25–55; Bridget Brown, *They Know Us Better Than We Know Ourselves: The History and Politics of Alien Abduction* (New York: New York University Press, 2007), 6–7. Dean argues that the UFO is an engine and an example of

the fragmentation of truth in the postmodern American media landscape. Lepselter and Brown are interested in how stories of aliens and UFOs give narrative voice to disempowerment of all sorts.

7. John Mack, *Abduction: Human Encounters with Aliens* (New York: Scribner, 1994), 36; Brown also advances this argument in *They Know Us Better Than We Know Ourselves*, 6–7. D. W. Pasulka, *American Cosmic: UFOs, Religion, Technology* (New York: Oxford University Press, 2019), 10–17, sees in UFO belief the generation of an entire system of meaning-making, comparable to religion.

8. I draw here to some extent on Robert Orsi's work on what he calls the power of "presence" in the lives of religious believers. Orsi, *History and Presence* (Cambridge: Harvard University Press, 2016), 1–12. See also Brenda Denzler, *The Lure of the Edge: Scientific Passions, Religious Beliefs, and the Pursuit of UFOs* (Berkeley: University of California Press, 2003), 155–161. Denzler explores how UFO belief and the technological solutions that many Americans have offered to resolve its conundrums have begun to take on functions of belief, salvation, and transcendence that are often ascribed to religion. As Debbora Battaglia has it, UFO experiences "destabilize prior knowledge" and in so doing "constructively reveal gaps and inefficiencies." Battaglia, ed., *ET Culture: Anthropology in Outerspaces* (Durham: Duke University Press, 2005), 6; see also her "For Those Who Are Not Afraid of the Future: Raelian Clonehood in the Public Sphere," in that volume, 149–179.

9. John G. Fuller, *The Interrupted Journey: Two Lost Hours Aboard a Flying Saucer* (New York: Dial Press, 1966).

10. Budd Hopkins, *Missing Time: A Documented Study of UFO Abductions* (New York: Richard Marek Publishers, 1981), 154, see also 26–28. See also Terry Matheson, *Alien Abductions: Creating a Modern Phenomenon* (New York: Prometheus Books, 1998), 64–74, and Mack, *Abduction*, 10–37. Thomas Bullard, "UFO Abduction Reports: The Supernatural Kidnap Narrative Returns in Technological Guise," *Journal of American Folklore* 102:404 (June 1989), 148–149; Jerome Clark, "The Extraterrestrial Hypothesis in the Early UFO Age," in David M. Jacobs, ed., *UFOs and Abductions: Challenging the Borders of Knowledge* (Lawrence: University of Kansas Press, 2000), 122–140.

11. On the limits of the politics of consensus, Gary Gerstle, "The Reach and Limits of the Liberal Consensus," in Robert Mason and Iwan Morgan, eds., *The Liberal Consensus Reconsidered* (Tallahassee: University Press of Florida, 2017), 52–66; Jefferson Cowie, *The Great Exception: The New Deal and the Limits of American Politics* (Princeton: Princeton University Press, 2016), 123–151.

12. Brown, *They Know Us Better Than We Know Ourselves*, 128–133; Stanton T. Friedman and William Moore, *The Roswell Incident: The Beginnings of the Cosmic Watergate* (Cincinnati: MUFON Symposium Proceedings, 1981), 133.

13. Michael Barkun, *A Culture of Conspiracy: Apocalyptic Visions in Contemporary America* (Berkeley: University of California Press, 2003).

14. In retelling this story I have relied on Tim McMillan, "The Witnesses," *Popular Mechanics,* November 12, 2019; Helene Cooper, Leslie Kean, and Ralph Blumenthal, "2 Navy Airmen and an Object That 'Accelerated Like Nothing I've Ever Seen,'" *New York Times,*

December 16, 2017; Helene Cooper, Leslie Kean, and Ralph Blumenthal, "Wow, What Is That? Navy Pilots Report Unidentified Flying Objects," *New York Times,* May 26, 2019; Gideon Lewis-Kraus, "The UFO Papers," *New Yorker,* May 10, 2021, 32–47.

15. Joby Warrick, "Head of Pentagon's Secret UFO Office Sought to Make Evidence Public," *Washington Post,* December 16, 2017; Ralph Blumenthal and Leslie Kean, "No Longer in the Shadows, Pentagon's UFO Unit Will Make Some Findings Public," *New York Times,* July 23, 2020; Reid makes these claims explicit in Harry Reid, "What We Believe about UFOs," *New York Times,* May 21, 2021. Sarah Scoles, *They Are Already Here: UFO Culture and Why We See Saucers* (New York: Pegasus Books, 2020), 56–70, and Ross Coulthart, *In Plain Sight: An Investigation into UFOs and Impossible Science* (New York: HarperCollins, 2021), 129–233, are the best explorations of recent events surrounding UFOs, or what are now called UAPs. There have recently been claims that AATIP was merely a perhaps informal extension of an older and more wide-ranging program, The Advanced Aerospace Weapon System Applications Program, or AAWSAP. James Lacatski, Colm Kelleher, and George Knapp, *Skinwalkers at the Pentagon: An Insiders' Account of the Secret Government UFO Program* (Henderson, NV: RTMA, 2021), 19–30.

16. Warrick, "Head of Pentagon's Secret UFO Office Sought to Make Evidence Public"; Blumenthal and Kean, "No Longer in the Shadows"; Keith Kloor, "The Media Loves This UFO Expert Who Says He Worked for an Obscure Pentagon Program," *The Intercept,* June 1, 2019, https://theintercept.com/2019/06/01/ufo-unidentified-history-channel-luis-elizondo-pentagon/, accessed January 20, 2021. Scoles, *They Are Already Here,* 59–62, 66–70, seeks to unsnarl these relationships.

17. Jose Del Real, "The Lonely Journey of a UFO Conspiracy Theorist," *Washington Post,* September 3, 2021, https://www.washingtonpost.com/nation/interactive/2021/ufo-conspiracy-theorist/, accessed October 15, 2022.

18. Benjamin Simon to Philip Klass, October 28, 1975, Collection of Robert Sheaffer.

CHAPTER 1. BETTY

1. The Hills described that afternoon in BSBS, 78–82, 84.

2. J. Dennis Robinson, "The UFO Romance of Betty and Barney Hill," http://www.seacoastnh.com/History/History-Matters/The-UFO-Romance-of-Betty-and-Barney-Hill/, accessed September 1, 2021; Mark Sammons and Valerie Cunningham, *Black Portsmouth: Three Centuries of African American Heritage* (Durham: University of New Hampshire Press, 2004), 2–12. The Hills' house remains but is now painted yellow. See Clas Svahn, "Revisiting the Hill Abduction Case," *Outer Limits Magazine* 8 (June 2017), 4 and photo P0040_0292, Portsmouth Advocates Collection, Portsmouth Athenaeum, which shows Betty's home in 1975, painted white.

3. William Leutchenberg's *Franklin Roosevelt and the New Deal* (New York: Harper Collins, 2009) is the classic study of the period; I also here rely on Alan Brinkley, *The End of Reform: New Deal Liberalism in Recession and War* (New York: Vintage, 2011) and Gary Gerstle and Steve Fraser, eds., *The Rise and Fall of the New Deal Order* (Princeton: Princeton University Press, 1989), ix–xxiv.

———

4. These arguments are drawn from Lizabeth Cohen's *Making a New Deal: Industrial Workers in Chicago, 1919–1939* (Cambridge: Harvard University Press, 2014), 362–368.

5. UA1, 1, 2.

6. UA1, 2–3; "Massachusetts, Town Clerk, Vital and Town Records," entry for John E. Barrett and Lizzie E. Trafton (July 12, 1887); image 763 of 1559; microfilm 4280497, LDS Family History Library, Salt Lake City, Utah.

7. UA1, 2; UA2, [3].

8. BSBS, 192.

9. UA1, 4–5.

10. UA1, 4; UA2, [11]–[12].

11. UA2, 5–6; *Annual Reports of the Town of Kingston, N.H. for the Year Ending January 31, 1925* (Manchester, NH: John B. Clarke, 1925), 7, 50.

12. *Annual Reports of the Town of Kingston, N.H. for the Year Ending January 31, 1936* (Manchester, NH: John B. Clarke, 1936), 39; *Annual Reports of the Town of Kingston, N.H. for the Year Ending January 31, 1925* (Manchester, NH: John B. Clarke, 1925), 33; *Annual Reports of the Town of Kingston, N.H. for the Year Ending January 31, 1926* (Manchester, NH: John B. Clarke, 1926), 38.

13. Alice Kessler-Harris, *Out to Work: A History of Wage-Earning Women in the United States* (New York: Oxford University Press, 2003), 258–265.

14. UA2, [13]. On women and unionization, Kessler-Harris, *Out to Work*, 268–271; Ruth Milkman, *On Gender, Labor and Inequality* (Urbana: University of Illinois Press, 2003), 172–173.

15. UA2, [10], [13].

16. *Cold War Portsmouth: A Snapshot of Life in the 1950s* (Portsmouth, NH: Preservation Company of the City of Portsmouth, 2020), 2–3.

17. On the unions' strategy of alliance, Douglas Rossinow, "Partners for Progress: Liberals and Radicals in the Long Twentieth Century," in Timothy Stanley and Jonathan Bell, eds., *Making Sense of American Liberalism* (Urbana: University of Illinois Press, 2013), 24–30; Nelson Lichtenstein, *State of the Union: A Century of American Labor* (Princeton: Princeton University Press, 2013), 46–48, 63–65, quotation from 48. Meg Jacobs, *Pocketbook Politics: Economic Citizenship in Twentieth Century America* (Princeton: Princeton University Press, 2007), 137–150. See also Michael Kazin, *The Populist Persuasion: An American History* (New York: Basic Books, 1995), 138–142 on John L. Lewis.

18. UA1, 7.

19. UA2, [10].

20. UA1, 7.

21. On the emergence of ecumenical activism, see Kevin Schultz, *Tri-Faith America: How Catholics and Jews Held Postwar America to its Protestant Promise* (New York: Oxford University Press, 2013), especially 15–43; on the Student Christian Movement in 1940s New Hampshire, see Eugene G. Schwartz, ed., *American Students Organize: Founding the National Student Association after World War II* (Greenwood, CT: Praeger, 2006), 719–743. "Christian Work Inc Makes Future Plans," *New Hampshire* 28:5 (October 12, 1937), 1; "Democracy in Education," *New Hampshire* 31:40 (March 28, 1941), 2; "Special Program at Ballard Tuesday," *New Hampshire*

26:40 (March 31, 1936), 3; "Delegates Attend SCM Conference," *New Hampshire* 31:35 (March 11, 1941), 1. John Fuller describes Betty's work in college in *The Interrupted Journey: Two Lost Hours Aboard a Flying Saucer* (New York: The Dial Press, 1966), 9–10.

22. Dante Scala, *Stormy Weather: The New Hampshire Primary and Presidential Politics* (New York: Palgrave Macmillan, 2003), 12–20; Elizabeth Morrison, *New Hampshire: A History* (New York: W. W. Norton, 1976), 140–141.

23. UA2, [14]; for Betty Hill's breakdown, "Personals," *Portsmouth Herald*, July 15, 1939, 8.

24. Kathleen Marden and Stanton Friedman, *Captured: The Betty and Barney Hill UFO Experience* (Newburyport, MA: New Page Books, 2007), 25; UA2, [14].

25. Stephanie Coontz, *Marriage: A History* (New York: Viking, 2005), 216–228; Stephanie Coontz, *A Strange Stirring: The Feminine Mystique and American Women at the Dawn of the 1960s* (New York: Basic Books, 2011), 35–59.

26. *Cold War Portsmouth*, 12; Betty Hill to The Editor, undated, Box 4, Folder 3, BBHP.

27. Interview transcript in Marden and Friedman, *Captured*, 25; UA2, [13].

28. Kristin Cellelo, *Making Marriage Work: A History of Marriage and Divorce in Twentieth-Century America* (Chapel Hill: University of North Carolina Press, 2009), 76–102; Rebecca L. Davis, *More Perfect Unions: The American Search for Marital Bliss* (Cambridge: Harvard University Press, 2010), 85–99; Elaine Tyler May, *Homeward Bound: American Families in the Cold War Era* (New York: Basic Books, 1988), 16–37; Lizabeth Cohen, *A Consumers' Republic: The Politics of Mass Consumption in Postwar America* (New York: Knopf, 2008), 133–152.

29. Robert Coughlan, "Modern Marriage," *Life* (December 24, 1956), 110.

30. Davis, *More Perfect Unions*, 99–100; Cellelo, *Making Marriage Work*, 83–88.

31. UA2, [14]. Marden and Friedman, *Captured*, 25.

32. "Methodists Elect for Coming Year," *Portsmouth Herald*, March 12, 1957, 7. On the continuity between student Christian activist groups and postwar women finding the churches as a vehicle to continue that work, Janice Allured, *Remapping Second-Wave Feminism: The Long Women's Rights Movement in Louisiana, 1950–1997* (Athens: University of Georgia Press, 2016), 64–66; *Virginia* Lieson Brereton, "United and Slighted: Women as Subordinated Insiders," in William R. Hutchison, ed., *Between the Times: The Travail of the Protestant Establishment in America, 1900–1960* (Cambridge: Cambridge University Press, 1989), 143–169; Lanethea Mathews-Gardner, "From Ladies' Aid to NGO: Transforming in Methodist Women's Organizing in Postwar America," in Kathleen Laughlin and Jacqueline Castledine, eds., *Breaking the Wave: Women, Their Organizations and Feminism* (New York: Routledge, 2011), 99–112.

33. UA2, [16], [15].

34. UA1, 8–9; Marden and Friedman, *Captured*, 25; BSBS, 194–195. Rebecca Lowen, *Creating the Cold War University* (Berkeley: University of California Press, 1997), 67–68; Ethan Schrum, *The Instrumental University: Education in Service of the National Agenda after World War II* (Ithaca: Cornell University Press, 2019), 4–18.

35. Mark J. Sammons and Valerie Cunningham, *Black Portsmouth: Three Centuries of African American Heritage* (Durham: University of New Hampshire Press, 2004), 167–171.

36. UA2, [8], [10], [13].

37. Gunnar Myrdal, *An America Dilemma: The Negro Problem and Modern Democracy* (New York: Harper and Row, 1962), 1:48; see also David Chappell, *A Stone of Hope: Prophetic Religion and the Death of Jim Crow* (Chapel Hill: University of North Carolina Press, 2004), 37–43.

38. *The Intercollegian* 65 (1947), 22.

39. Bayard Rustin, "General Observations on the Journey of Reconciliation," in Bayard Rustin, *Down the Line: The Collected Writings of Bayard Rustin* (Chicago: Quadrangle Books, 1971), 22–23. On the Journey of Reconciliation and Rustin's part in it, Derek Charles Catsam, *Freedom's Main Line: The Journey of Reconciliation and the Freedom Rides* (Lexington: University Press of Kentucky, 2009), 18–28.

40. Homer A. Jack, "Six Activities to Make Brotherhood More Than a Word," *Christian Leader,* February 1948, 28; Fuller, *Interrupted Journey,* 9–10.

CHAPTER 2. BARNEY

1. Bernice Shelton, "Robert Wellington Bagnall," *The Crisis* (October 1943), 334.

2. Richard Newman, *Freedom's Prophet: Bishop Richard Allen, the AME Church, and the Black Founding Fathers* (New York: NYU Press, 2008), 64–65; Gary B. Nash, *Forging Freedom: The Formation of Philadelphia's Black Community, 1720–1840* (Cambridge: Harvard University Press, 1988), 127–129, 210–211.

3. On "civil rights liberalism," Matthew Countryman, *Up South: Civil Rights and Black Power in Philadelphia* (Philadelphia: University of Pennsylvania Press, 2006), 13–48. See also Patricia Sullivan, *Lift Every Voice: The NAACP and the Making of the Civil Rights Movement* (New York: New Press, 2009), 100, 104–105, 224–226, and Gilbert Jonas, *Freedom's Sword: the NAACP and the Struggle against Racism in America, 1909–1969* (New York: Routledge, 2005), 31–67.

4. On the Old Philadelphians and uplift, see Countryman, *Up South,* 14–34, Alexander quoted on 16; Vincent P. Franklin, *The Education of Black Philadelphia* (Philadelphia: University of Pennsylvania Press, 1979), 67–71; James N. Gregory, *The Southern Diaspora: How the Great Migrations of Black and White Southerners Transformed America* (Durham: University of North Carolina Press, 2005), 117–119; Charles Banner-Haley, *To Do Good and To Do Well: Middle-Class Blacks and the Depression: Philadelphia 1929–1941* (New York: Garland Publishing, 1993), 45–62.

5. On the Great Migration generally, Gregory, *Southern Diaspora,* especially 12–19, and Isabel Wilkerson, *The Warmth of Other Suns: The Epic Story of America's Great Migration* (New York: Random House, 2010), especially 8–17, 238–292, 527–538. Rayford Logan, *The Negro in American Life and Thought: The Nadir, 1877–1901* (New York: Dial Press, 1954).

6. Sadie Tanner Mossell, "The Standard of Living Among One Hundred Negro Migrant Families in Philadelphia," *Annals of the American Academy of Political Science,* November 1921, 174–175; James Wolfinger, *Philadelphia Divided: Race and Politics in the City of Brotherly Love* (Chapel Hill: University of North Carolina Press, 2007), 12–16.

7. Enumeration District 51–461, sheet 12B, "United States Census, 1930." Database with images. *FamilySearch,* http://FamilySearch.org, accessed June 14, 2018. Citing NARA microfilm publication T626 (Washington, DC: National Archives and Records Administration, 2002).

8. W. E. B. Du Bois, *The Philadelphia Negro* (Philadelphia: University of Pennsylvania Press, 1899), 296–297, 305–306; Robert Gregg, *Sparks from the Anvil of Oppression: Philadelphia's African Methodists and Southern Migrants, 1890–1940* (Philadelphia: Temple University Press, 2010), 200–210.

9. Du Bois, *Philadelphia Negro*, 6–7. Emmett J. Scott, *Negro Migration during the War* (New York: Oxford University Press, 1920), 135–136; Countryman, *Up South*, 18–20.

10. Franklin, *Education of Black Philadelphia*, 76–86; Rhodes quoted on 84.

11. John F. Bauman, *Public Housing, Race and Renewal: Urban Planning in Philadelphia, 1920–1974* (Philadelphia: Temple University Press, 1987), 20–33; Marcus Anthony Hunter, *Black Citymakers: How the Philadelphia Negro Changed America* (New York: Oxford University Press, 2013), 69–115; Countryman, *Up South*, 13–47; Franklin, *Education of Black Philadelphia*, 71–86, 135–150.

12. "Laws against Intermarriage," *Philadelphia Tribune*, August 7, 1943, 4; "Police Harassing Innocent West Philadelphia Negroes," *Philadelphia Tribune*, June 29, 1957, 1. On interracial cooperation Stanley Keith Arnold, *Building the Beloved Community: Philadelphia's Interracial Civil Rights Organizations and Race Relations, 1930–1970* (Oxford: University of Mississippi Press, 2014), 36, 8–46.

13. C. Eric Lincoln, *Martin Luther King: A Profile* (New York: Farrar, Straus and Giroux, 1970), 150–151; on the politics of Black respectability generally, Evelyn Higginbotham, *Righteous Discontent: The Women's Movement in the Black Baptist Church, 1880–1920* (Cambridge: Harvard University Press, 1994), 185–230, and Jeanne Theoharis, *The Rebellious Life of Mrs. Rosa Parks* (Boston: Beacon Press, 2013), 83–86.

14. On the transformative potential of the Great Migration, see Wallace D. Best, *Passionately Human, No Less Divine: Religion and Culture in Black Chicago, 1915–1952* (Princeton: Princeton University Press, 2005), 13–35. Enumeration District 51-461, sheet 12B, "United States Census, 1930." Database with images. *FamilySearch*, http://FamilySearch.org, accessed June 14, 2018. Citing NARA microfilm publication T626 (Washington, DC: National Archives and Records Administration, 2002). Barney Hill Sr., death certificate, "Pennsylvania, Death Certificates, 1906–1966," database with images, *Ancestry.com;* Barney Ross Hill (October 8, 1961); certificate 096798–61; Commonwealth of Pennsylvania Department of Health Vital Statistics. Mossell concludes that two-thirds of migrant families were successful in supporting themselves. "Standard of Living," 214–215.

15. Harvey Cohen, *Duke Ellington's America* (Chicago: University of Chicago Press, 2010), 13–14; Horace Roscoe Clayton, *Black Metropolis: A Study of Negro Life in the Modern City* (New York: Harcourt, Brace, 1970), 2:606–608; E. Franklin Frazier, *The Negro Family in the United States* (Chicago: University of Chicago Press, 1940), 396, 484–485.

16. See, for instance, "Rosebud Club," *Philadelphia Tribune*, July 10, 1943, 8; "Cornish Post," *Philadelphia Tribune*, March 31, 1938, 17; "May Prom," *Philadelphia Tribune*, July 4, 1931, 4; "The Week in Clubdom," *Philadelphia Tribune*, September 20, 1934, 8; "The Club World of

Philadelphia," *Philadelphia Tribune*, April 28, 1832, 6; "The Week in Clubdom," *Philadelphia Tribune*, October 5, 1933, 8; "The Club World," *Philadelphia Tribune*, February 18, 1932, 6.

17. Fuller, *Interrupted Journey*, 55–56; "Small Parties," *Philadelphia Tribune*, February 11, 1934, 6.

18. *Report of the Survey of the Public Schools of Philadelphia* (Philadelphia: Public Education and Child Labor Association, 1921), 1:62, 269; Lucy L. W. Wilson, "Evolution of the Dalton Plan in the South Philadelphia High School," *High School Clearing House* 4:10 (June 1930), 582–587; Alan Keiler, *Marian Anderson: A Singer's Journey* (Urbana: University of Illinois Press, 2002), 40–41. Barney's school career in "Ruby Horne Hill," *Philadelphia Tribune*, July 1, 2015, 22 and Richard Newman, "Barney Hill," *Africana: The Encyclopedia of The African and African American Experience* (New York: Oxford University Press, 2005), 205.

19. "WPA To Feature Role of Negro in National Defense," *Philadelphia Tribune*, February 6, 1941, 3; "Solution," *Philadelphia Tribune*, December 7, 1939, 4; "Students Rap Race Bias in Visit to DC," *Philadelphia Tribune*, June 12, 1941, 1.

20. Betty Hill to George Fawcett, January 6, [1986?], BBHF; "Ruby Horne Hill," *Philadelphia Tribune*, June 16, 2015.

21. Marden and Friedman, Captured, 26; BSBS, 191; "Constitution Subordinates Human Rights to Property Rights," *Philadelphia Tribune*, September 16, 1937, 3.

22. For this "contributionist history," see Stephen G. Hall, *A Faithful Account of the Race: African American Historical Writing in Nineteenth Century America* (Chapel Hill: University of North Carolina Press, 2009), especially 123–151; Megan Ming Francis, *Civil Rights and the Making of the Modern American State* (New York: Cambridge University Press, 2014), 123–129.

23. "Constitution Subordinates Human Rights," 3; Robert W. Bagnall, "Taken in Stride," *Philadelphia Tribune*, November 3, 1938, 4; "Local NRA Administrators Accused of Discrimination," *Philadelphia Tribune*, December 14, 1933, 2.

24. "CFC's New $40,000 Office Building Visited by 1000 in 3 Weeks," *Philadelphia Tribune*, January 10, 1959, 3. Wolfinger, *Philadelphia Divided*, 212–235.

25. Betty Hill, "Our Marriage," 2, Box 3, Folder 1, BBHP.

CHAPTER 3. THE UNITARIANS

1. Marden and Friedman, *Captured*, 23–24; Betty Hill, "Our Marriage," 2, Box 3, Folder 1, BBHP.

2. Myrdal, *American Dilemma*, 54–55; Paul Spickard, *Mixed Blood: Intermarriage and Ethnic Identity in Twentieth Century America* (Madison: University of Wisconsin Press, 1989), 374–375.

3. Du Bois, *Philadelphia Negro*, 360–367, 366; Spickard, *Mixed Blood*, 274–278; Randall Kennedy, *Interracial Intimacies: Sex, Marriage, Identity, and Adoption* (New York: Pantheon, 2003), 98–100.

4. Betty Hill, "Our Marriage," 1; Renee Romano, *Race Mixing: Black-White Marriage in Postwar America* (Cambridge: Harvard University Press, 2003), 91–93; Kennedy, *Interracial Intimacies*, 99.

5. Peter Wallenstein, *Tell the Court I Love My Wife: Race, Marriage, and Law: An American History* (New York: Palgrave Macmillan, 2002), 200–214.

6. Betty Hill, "Our Marriage," 1–2; Betty Hill to George Fawcett, January 6, [1986?], BBHF.

7. Marden and Friedman, *Captured*, 27–29; BSBS, 194–195.

8. "John Papandrew Biography," Box 333, Folder 1, JPF; "Rev. John Papandrew," *Boston Globe*, June 18, 2003, 88; Joseph Barth to Maxine Thurston, August 25, 1967, Box 333, Folder 5, JPF; on the Tuskegee Airmen, see J. Todd Moye, *Freedom Flyers: The Tuskegee Airmen of World War II* (New York: Oxford University Press, 2010), 98–123.

9. On Holmes, see his autobiography *I Speak for Myself: The Autobiography of John Haynes Holmes* (New York: Harper and Row, 1959); and Joseph Kip Kosek, *Acts of Conscience: Christian Nonviolence and Modern American Democracy* (New York: Columbia University Press, 2009), 82–84.

10. W. E. B. Du Bois, "John Haynes Holmes, The Community Church, and World Brotherhood," in *The Community Church of New York: Commemorative Book* (New York: The Community Church, 1948), 36–37.

11. John Papandrew, "What's with This God Is Dead Business?," Sermon, February 20, 1966, 5, 13, Box 333, Folder 6, JPF. On the neo-orthodox movement in the United States, see Andrew Finstuen, *Original Sin and Everyday Protestants: The Theology of Reinhold Niebuhr, Billy Graham, and Paul Tillich in an Age of Anxiety* (Chapel Hill: University of North Carolina Press, 2009), especially 69–93.

12. John Papandrew, "A Letter to My Congregation," Sermon, November 17, 1963, Box 333, Folder 7, JPF; John Papandrew to Leon Fay, March 24, 1961, Box 333, Folder 7, JPF. John Papandrew, "Ministerial Record Sheet," Box 333, Folder 1, JPF.

13. "The Role of the Negro in American Unitarianism," *Christian Register*, September 1956, 12–13. On these demographics, see also Mark D. Morrison-Reed, *The Selma Awakening: How the Civil Rights Movement Tested and Changed Unitarian Universalism* (Boston: Skinner House Books, 2004), 39–44.

14. Patrick Allitt, *Religion in America since 1945: A History* (New York: Columbia University Press, 2003), 8–16; Robert S. Ellwood, *The Fifties Spiritual Marketplace: American Religion in a Decade of Conflict* (New Brunswick: Rutgers University Press, 1997), 1–10.

15. William Roger Greeley, "30 Million Religious Liberals?," *Christian Register*, February 1955, 22–23, John Buehrens, *Unitarians and Universalists in America* (Boston: Skinner House, 2011), 167–181."

16. James Luther Adams, "The Impact of Modern Thought on Unitarianism," *Christian Register*, May 1948, 21–23.

17. Andrea Greenwood and Mark Harris, *An Introduction to the Unitarian and Universalist Traditions* (Cambridge: Cambridge University Press, 2011), 214–234, and David Robinson, *The Unitarians and the Universalists* (Westport, CT: Greenwood Press, 1987), 123–143; "Liberal Line for Kennedy/Johnson," *Rochester Democrat*, October 27, 1960, 12; *The Free Church in a Changing World* (Boston: Unitarian Universalist Association, 1962), 47, 51, 52.

---

18. "Protest in Portsmouth May Bar African Student," *Boston Globe*, August 13, 1961, 48; "No Problem Here," *Nashua Telegraph*, August 15, 1961, 4. The student's name is spelled differently in different sources. I have chosen "Karagol."

19. "Portsmouth, NH Facing Suit over Free Tuition for African," *New York Times*, August 20, 1961, 47; "Student from Kenya Upsets Portsmouth," *Nashua Telegraph*, August 12, 1961, 1.

20. "Student from Kenya Upsets Portsmouth," 1.

21. BSBS, 191, 194. "Canvassers," [1966?], South Church [Unitarian] Records, Portsmouth Athenaeum, Portsmouth, NH.

22. UA1, 9.

23. BSBS, 95, 96.

CHAPTER 4. THINGS SEEN IN THE SKY

1. John Luttrell, "UFO Chiller—Did THEY Seize Couple?," *Boston Traveller*, October 25–29, 1965, A1. Webb's two reports are Webb1 and Webb2. Webb1 was paraphrased in the *A.P.R.O. Bulletin* (March 1963), 7; the editor received a copy of the report from the Hills. It was also summarized in *UFO Investigator* (January–February 1962), 2.

2. BSBS, 96–97; Fuller, *Interrupted Journey*, 10; Marden and Friedman, *Captured*, 95–97, 165–166. In *The Interrupted Journey* Fuller alters the material from his interviews with the Hills several times; for instance, he omits any mention of the pistol, instead referring to it as a "tire wrench," 87.

3. BBHHT, Hypnosis Session 3, March 7, 1964, 2–3; Hypnosis Session 1, February 22, 1964, 2.

4. BBHHT, Hypnosis Session 1, February 22, 1964, 7; Hypnosis Session 3, March 7, 1964, 2. See also Marden and Friedman, 89–99, for an exhaustive discussion of the Montreal-Colebrook trip. Betty Hill also recalls no trouble other than the language barrier in her late-in-life autobiography, *A Common Sense Approach to UFOs* (Greenland, NH: n.p., 1995), 16–17.

5. There has been much discussion concerning the timeline of the Hills' drive. Both Hills recalled leaving just after 10:00 p.m., and that recollection is widely accepted, but there remains dispute over how long the drive south would have taken, depending on how fast Barney, who had the wheel, might have driven. See, for instance, Peter Brookesmith, "Of Time and the River," and Karl Pflock, "A Singular Visitation," in Pflock and Brookesmith, eds., *Encounters at Indian Head: The Betty and Barney Hill UFO Abduction Revisited* (New York: Anomalist Books, 2007), 152–186, 209–239.

6. BBHHT, Hypnosis Session 4, March 14, 1964, 16.

7. Marden and Friedman, *Captured*, 34, 33–35; BSBS, 79; Webb1, 12; BBHHT, Hypnosis Session 4, March 16, 1964, 16–18.

8. BBHHT, Hypnosis Session 4, March 14, 1964, 18.

9. "Foo-Fighter," *Time*, January 15, 1945, 72; Donald Keyhoe, "The Flying Saucer Story," *UFO Investigator*, July 1957, 15; Hubert Griffith, "The Gremlin Question," *Royal Air Force Journal* 13 (April 18, 1942), 67; Jerome Clark, "The Extraterrestrial Hypothesis in the Early UFO Age," in David M. Jacobs, ed., *UFOs and Abductions: Challenging the Boundaries of Knowledge* (Lawrence: University of Kansas Press, 2000), 122–141.

10. Donald E. Keyhoe, *Flying with Lindbergh* (New York: Grossett and Dunlap, 1929), 34–36; David M. Jacobs, The UFO Controversy in America (Bloomington: Indiana University Press, 1975), 36–47; Peebles, *Watch the Skies,* 22–24.

11. Edward Ruppelt, *The Report on Unidentified Flying Objects* (Garden City: Doubleday, 1956), 40.

12. On the history of federal reliance of expertise I have used Brian Balogh, "Meeting the State Halfway: Governing America, 1930–1950," in Balogh, ed., *The Associational State: American Governance in the Twentieth Century* (Philadelphia: University of Pennsylvania Press, 2015), 139–171, who describes the emergence of a "prominstrative state," as well as Alan Brinkley, *The End of Reform: New Deal Liberalism in Recession and War* (New York: Random House, 1995), 48–65. On the development of the atomic bomb, I have used Neil Sullivan, *The Prometheus Bomb: The Manhattan Project and Government in the Dark* (Lincoln: University of Nebraska Press, 2016), 50–52.

13. Brian Balogh, *Chain Reaction: Expert Debate and Public Participation in American Commercial Nuclear Power, 1945–1975* (New York: Cambridge University Press, 1991), 5–14, 21–26; funding discussed on 24. Daniel Kevles, *The Physicists: The History of a Scientific Community in Modern America* (New York: Vintage Books, 1979), 340–343; Audra Wolfe, *Competing with the Soviets: Science, Technology, and the State in Cold War America* (Baltimore: Johns Hopkins University Press, 2013), 24–30.

14. John Earl Haynes and Harvey Klehr, *Venona: Decoding Soviet Espionage in America* (New Haven: Yale University Press, 2000), 322–330.

15. On the ghost rockets, Michael D. Swords, *UFOs and Government: A Historical Inquiry* (San Antonio: Anomalist Press, 2012), 12–25; Truman memorandum reprinted on 22–23; George Gallup, *The Gallup Poll: Public Opinion, 1935–1948* (New York: Random House, 1972), 666; Clark, "Extraterrestrial Hypothesis in the Early UFO Age," 123.

16. Kenneth Arnold, "I Did See the Flying Disks," *Fate* 1:1 (Spring 1948), 9–10; Kate Dorsch, "Reliable Witnesses, Crackpot Science: UFO Investigations in Cold War America, 1947–1977" (PhD diss., University of Pennsylvania, 2019), 20–22.

17. Nathan F. Twining to Commanding General, Army Air Force, September 23, 1947, photograph of memo reprinted in Swords, *UFOs and Government,* 476–478; "Unidentified Aerial Objects: Project Sign," February 1949, Report Number F-TR-2274–1A, v–vi, 9; Swords, *UFOs and Government,* 32–44; Jacobs, *UFO Controversy in America,* 36, 35–41; Keyhoe, *Flying Saucers Are Real,* 24–29. There are reports that Project Sign produced an earlier document, often called the "Estimate of the Situation," which defended the hypothesis that UFOs were extraterrestrial craft but which was rejected by Hoyt Vandenberg, Air Force chief of staff. See Ruppelt, *Report on Unidentified Flying Objects,* 55–56.

18. James Bryant Conant, *Modern Science and Modern Man* (New York: Columbia University Press, 1952), 21; Christopher Hamlin, "The Pedagogical Roots of the History of Science: Revisiting the Vision of James Bryant Conant," *Isis* 107:2 (2016), 282–308; Justin Biddle, "Putting Pragmatism to Work in the Cold War: Science, Technology and Politics in the Writings of James B. Conant," *Studies in History and Philosophy of Science* 42:4 (2011), 552–561; John Rudolph, *How We Teach Science: What's Changed and Why It Matters* (Cambridge: Harvard University Press, 2019), 130–137.

---

19. Vannevar Bush, *Science – The Endless Frontier* (Washington, DC: Government Printing Office, 1945), 12; See also Ethan Schrum, *The Instrumental University: Education in the Service of the National Agenda after World War II* (Ithaca: Cornell University Press, 2019), 6–14.

20. Joseph Turner, "An Academic Question," *Science* 125:3245 (March 8, 1957), 425.

21. "New Bombs Make Real Peacemakers," *New York Times,* May 19, 1950, 21; Kelly Moore, *Disrupting Science: Social Movements, American Scientists, and the Politics of the Military, 1945–1975* (Princeton: Princeton University Press, 2008), 31–34; Bruce Lewenstein, "The Meaning of 'Public Understanding of Science' in the United States after World War II," *Public Understanding of Science* 1 (1992), 45–68.

22. "Knowledge Is Power," *Time,* November 18, 1957, 22, 23; Robert A. Devine, *The Sputnik Challenge: Eisenhower's Response to the Soviet Satellite* (New York: Oxford University Press, 1993), 157–166.

23. "Science and Life in the World: George Westinghouse Educational Foundation Forum, 16–18 May," *Science* 103:2683 (May 31, 1946), 664; Rudolph, *How We Teach Science,* 119–127.

24. Michael Gordin, *The Pseudoscience Wars: Immanuel Velikovsky and the Birth of the Modern Fringe* (Chicago: University of Chicago Press, 2012), 1–18; Michael Gordin, *On the Fringe: Where Science Meets Pseudoscience* (New York: Oxford University Press, 2021), 100–101; Daniel Patrick Thurs applies the notion of pseudoscience to the UFO debate in *Science Talk: Changing Notions of Science in American Culture* (New Brunswick: Rutgers University Press, 2007), 152–156; Daniel Thurs and Ronald Numbers, "Science, Pseudoscience, and Science Falsely So-Called," in Peter Harrison, ed., *Wrestling with Nature: From Omens to Science* (Chicago: University of Chicago Press, 2011), 296; Thomas Gieryn, "Boundary-Work and the Demarcation of Science from Non-Science: Strains and Interests in Professional Ideologies of Science," *American Sociological Review* 48:6 (December 1983), 781–795; Dorsch, "Reliable Witnesses, Crackpot Science," 11–13; Greg Eighigan, "Making UFOs Make Sense: Ufology, Science and the History of Their Mutual Mistrust," *Public Understanding of Science* 26:5 (2017), 612–626.

25. Immanuel Velikovsky, *Worlds in Collision* (New York: Macmillan, 1950); Gordin, *Pseudoscience Wars,* particularly 19–49.

26. Larrabee's letter is reprinted in Immanuel Velikovsky, *Stargazers and Gravediggers: Memoirs to Worlds in Collision* (New York: William Morrow, 1983), 314.

27. Velikovsky, *Worlds in Collision,* 32; Velikovsky, *Stargazers and Gravediggers,* 304.

28. Martin Gardner, *Fads and Fallacies in the Name of Science,* 2nd ed. (New York: Dover Publications, 1957), 7, 32, 30–33; Martin Gardner, *Did Adam and Eve Have Navels? Debunking Pseudoscience* (New York: W. W. Norton, 2001), 1.

29. Gardner, *Fads and Fallacies in the Name of Science,* 6, 150; Gordin, *Pseudoscience Wars,* 32.

30. Project Blue Book, *Special Report Number 14: Analysis of Reports of Unidentified Aerial Objects* (1955), vii–viii, 2–3, 94; see also Dorsch, "Reliable Witnesses, Crackpot Science," 77–85. Many historians have observed that in the Cold War advocates for the social sciences argued that they were just as "scientific" as the natural sciences and leaned on claims of rationality and empiricism to do so. Mark Solovey, *Shaky Foundations: The Politics-Patronage-Social Science Nexus in Cold War America* (New Brunswick: Rutgers University Press, 2013), 1–20; Paul Erickson, Judy L. Klein, Lorraine Daston, Rebecca Lemov, Thomas Sturm, and Michael D. Gordin, *How Reason Almost Lost Its Mind: The Strange Career of Cold War Rationality* (Princeton: Princeton University Press, 2013), 107–133; Andrew Jewett, *Science, Democracy, and the American University from the Civil War to the Cold War* (Cambridge: Cambridge University Press, 2014), 312–315.

31. H. W. Smith and G. W. Towles, *Unidentified Flying Objects: Project Grudge: Project No. XS-30L* (Dayton, OH: Air Materiel Command, 1949), 10; Dorsch, "Reliable Witnesses, Crackpot Science," 44–46.

32. Sidney Shallett, "What You Can Believe about Flying Saucers," *Saturday Evening Post*, May 7, 1949, 36–37.

33. Frederick Durant, "Report of Meetings of Scientific Advisory Panel on Unidentified Flying Objects," reprinted in Edward U. Condon, *Final Report on the Scientific Study of Unidentified Flying Objects* (Boulder: University of Colorado Press, 1969), 916. On the panel, see Jacobs, *UFO Controversy in America*, 50–51, 90–94; Swords, *UFOs and Government*, 184–193. The Robertson Panel was first publicly described in Ruppelt, *Report on Unidentified Flying Objects*, 59–61.

34. Department of the Air Force, Air Force Regulation No. 200–2, "Intelligence: Unidentified Flying Objects Reporting," August 26, 1953.

35. Alex Wallerstein, *Restricted Data: The History of Nuclear Secrecy in the United States.* (Chicago: University of Chicago Press, 2021), 6–7, 179–231; see also Joseph P. Masco, "The Secrecy/Threat Matrix," in Mark Maguire, Ursula Rao, and Nils Zurowski, eds., *Bodies as Evidence: Security, Knowledge and Power* (Durham: Duke University Press, 2018), 175–201.

CHAPTER 5. NICAP AND ITS CRITICS

1. BSBS, 85–86; "Air Form 112, Air Intelligence Information Report 100–1-61," September 21, 1961, BBHP, Box 5, Folder 14.

2. All quotations in the preceding paragraphs from "Air Form 112, Air Intelligence Information Report 100–1-61," September 21, 1961, BBHP, Box 5, Folder 14.

3. "Extract of Daily Report of Controller, AACS Form 96 For the Date 20 Sept 1961," attached to "Air Form 112, Air Intelligence Information Report 100–1-61," September 21, 1961, BBHP, Box 5, Folder 14.

4. "Extract of Daily Report of Controller, AACS Form 96 For the Date 20 Sept 1961," attached to "Air Form 112, Air Intelligence Information Report 100–1-61," September 21, 1961, BBHP, Box 5, Folder 14.

5. "Project 10073 Record Card," BBHP, Box 5, Folder 14.

6. "Air Form 112, Air Intelligence Information Report 100–1-61" BBHP, Box 5, Folder 14; Betty remembers Barney's resistance to calling the base in BSBS, 87, 84–86, and under hypnosis in BBHHT, Hypnosis Session 4, March 14, 1964, 19.

7. BSBS, 87; BBHHT, Hypnosis Session 4, March 14, 1964, 20.

8. BSBS, 79–80.

9. BBHHT, Hypnosis Session 4, March 14, 1964, 19–20.

10. I draw here on Dean's work on the space race in the early 1960s in *Aliens in America*, 62–97; Alton Blakeslee, "Cosmic Rays and Gravity," *Philadelphia Inquirer*, August 6, 1957, 1.

11. "U.S.-Japanese Pact under Fire," *New York Times*, March 30, 1954, 8; "Long-Deadly Particle Found in Atom Ash," *New York Times*, March 26, 1954, 5; Steven Spencer, "Fallout: The Silent Killer," *Saturday Evening Post*, August 29, 1959, 27, 88; Paul Boyer, *By the Bomb's Early Light: American Thought and Culture at the Dawn of the Atomic Age* (Chapel Hill: University of North Carolina Press, 1994), 352–354.

12. Glenn Seaborg, *Kennedy, Khrushchev and the Test Ban* (Berkeley: University of California Press, 1983), 81–89. Kennedy would eventually negotiate a successful treaty banning testing anywhere but underground in 1963.

13. Betty Hill to Anthony Brooke, January 14, 1966, BBHP, Box 1, Folder 4.

14. *Bulletin of the Atomic Scientists* (September 1957), 264. Kelly Moore, *Disrupting Science: Social Movements, American Scientists, and the Politics of the Military, 1945–1975* (Princeton: Princeton University Press, 2008), 96–130; Jessica Wang, *American Scientists in an Age of Anxiety: Scientists, Anticommunism, and the Cold War* (Chapel Hill: University of North Carolina Press, 2000), 44–85.

15. Jack Mendelsohn, *Being Liberal in an Illiberal Age* (Boston: Beacon Press, 1985), 6–7; on "scientism" more broadly, Andrew Jewett, *Science under Fire: Challenges to Scientific Authority in Modern America* (Cambridge: Harvard University Press, 2020), 109–118. Many Unitarians were influenced by John Dewey's worries that Americans were passive about democratic participation. John Dewey, *The Public and Its Problems* (Chicago: Crossway Books, 1926), 123; Jessica Wang, "Scientists and the Problem of the Public in Cold War America, 1945–1960," *Osiris* 17 (2002), 323–347; Andrew Jewett, *Science, Democracy and the American University from the Civil War to the Cold War* (Cambridge: Harvard University Press, 2012), 172–173; James Kloppenburg, "Pragmatism: An Old Name for Some New Ways of Thinking," *Journal of American History* 83:1 (June 1996), 100–138.

16. Stephen Fritchman, "On Being a Unitarian," in Stephen Fritchman, ed., *Together We Advance* (Boston: Beacon Press, 1946), 9.

17. John Papandrew, "Statement on Your Current Concept of the Liberal Ministry," Box 333, Folder 1, JPF; "Passover Sunday at Community," *New York Amsterdam News*, April 9, 1960, 23.

18. Charles Coughlen, "Atom Scientists in the Bible Belt," *Christian Register*, January 1951, 18.

19. Cited in Wang, *American Scientists in an Age of Anxiety*, 303. On science imaging itself as apolitical, see Audra J. Wolfe, *Freedom's Laboratory: The Cold War Struggle for the Soul of Science* (Baltimore: Johns Hopkins University Press, 2018), 1–17.

20. "Post-War Culture Asked by Shapley," *New York Times*, June 3, 1944, 14; "Scientists Needed to Build World Peace," *Boston Globe*, December 12, 1947, 35.

21. Harlow Shapley, "Long Range Foresight," *Christian Register*, June 1957, 10–11.

22. Harlow Shapley, *The View from a Distant Star* (New York: Basic Books, 1963), 99.

23. Betty tells Benjamin Simon about her familiarity with Shapley in BBHHT, Hypnosis Session 4, March 14, 1964, 7.

24. BSBS, 5.

25. The Levelland case was examined by Project Blue Book and by the National Investigation Committee on Aerial Phenomena; J. Allen Hynek consulted with both and wrote about the case in J. Allen Hynek, *The UFO Experience: A Scientific Inquiry* (New York: Ballantine Books, 1977), 159–165; see also Jacobs, *UFO Controversy in America,* 134–139, and Antonio Rullan, *The Levelland Sightings of 1957* (El Paso, TX: Privately Printed, 1999).

26. George Dolan, "This Is Texas," *El Paso Times,* November 5, 1957, 1; "Flying Egg Reported over Texas Highway," *New York Times,* November 4, 1957, 9.

27. Donald Menzel and Lyle Boyd, *The World of Flying Saucers: A Scientific Examination of a Major Myth of the Space Age* (New York: Doubleday, 1963), 175-176, 146–147; Swords, *UFOs and Government,* 254–255.

28. "Did the Air Force Deceive the Public about the November Sightings?," *UFO Investigator* 1:3 (January 1958), 1, 2.

29. This biographical sketch is derived from Donald E. Keyhoe, *Flying with Lindbergh* (New York: Grossett and Dunlap, 1929), 2–5; Curtis Peebles, *Watch the Skies: A Chronicle of the Flying Saucer Myth* (New York: Berkley Books, 1995), 44–53. On the romanticization of flying aces, see Linda Robertson, *The Dream of Civilized Warfare: World War I Flying Aces and the American Imagination* (Minneapolis: University of Minnesota Press, 2003), 361–402.

30. Donald E. Keyhoe, *The Flying Saucers Are Real* (New York: Fawcett Publications, 1950), 7.

31. Keyhoe, *Flying Saucers Are Real,* 30. Punctuation original.

32. Keyhoe, *Flying Saucers Are Real,* 173–174.

33. Keyhoe, *Flying Saucers Are Real,* 38, 151.

34. Keyhoe, *Flying Saucers Are Real,* 151; "Rear Adm. Herbert B. Knowles, Ret.," *UFO Investigator,* July 1957, 17; "Albert H. Baller," *UFO Investigator,* July 1957, 16; Donald E. Keyhoe, "Questions and Answers," *UFO Investigator,* October 1961, 8.

35. Donald Keyhoe, *The Flying Saucer Conspiracy* (New York: Henry Holt, 1955), 13, 279.

36. Betty Hill to Donald Keyhoe, September 26, 1961, in BBHF; also transcribed in Webb2, 38-39.

37. Webb2, 39.

38. John G. Fuller interview with Walter Webb, March 8, 1966, 2, Box 3, Folder 7, JGFC; Webb2, 2; Richard Hall, ed., *The UFO Evidence* (Washington, DC: National Investigations Committee on Aerial Phenomena, 1964), 49–50.

39. The best biography of Hynek is Mark O'Connell, *The Close Encounters Man: How One Man Made the World Believe in UFOs* (New York: HarperCollins, 2017); Hynek's interaction with the Hills is discussed most fully in Marden and Friedman, *Captured,* 100–102; he discusses their case, and the spectrum of encounters, in Hynek, *UFO Experience,* 115–205, 197–205.

40. Hynek describes his work in J. Allen Hynek, *The Hynek UFO Report* (New York: Dell Books, 1977), 11–25, 46, and Hynek, *UFO Experience,* 15–16.

41. Walter Webb, "Allen Hynek as I Knew Him," *International UFO Reporter* (January–February 1993), 5. On Hynek's uneasy position, Dorsch, "Reliable Witnesses, Crackpot Scientists," 111–121.

———

42. George Adamski and Desmond Leslie, *Flying Saucers Have Landed* (New York: British Book Group, 1953), 4, 9–10.

43. Adamski and Leslie, *Flying Saucers Have Landed*, 129, 126, 133–143.

44. Ruppelt, *Report on Unidentified Flying Objects*, 23.

45. "UFO Witnesses Reliable, Says AF Expert," *UFO Investigator* 2:9 (June–September 1963), 3; "False Claims by Self-Styled NICAP Agents," *UFO Investigator* 1:10 (July–August 1960), 8; "Adamski's Latest Claim Blasted by NICAP Affiliate," *UFO Investigator* 1:8 (June 1959), 1, 4; "Resignations," *UFO Investigator* 1:5 (August–September 1958), 2.

46. George Adamski, *Inside the Flying Saucers* (London: Arco Publishers, 1956), 89; George Adamski, *Flying Saucers Farewell* (London: Abelard-Schuman, 1961), 119. On Adamski's Theosophical inheritance and his "physicalist" translation of it, Christopher Partridge, "Understanding UFO Religions and Abduction Spirituality," in Partridge, ed., *UFO Religions* (London: Routledge, 2003), 3–45; Christopher Partridge, *The Reenchantment of the West: Alternative Spiritualities, Sacralization, Popular Culture and Occulture* (London: Bloomsbury, 2006), 183–189.

47. Webb1, 1.

48. Walter Webb to Richard Hall, October 19, 1961, BHF; Webb1, 1, 5–6.

49. Walter Webb, "Reflections on the Hill Case," in Karl Pflock and Peter Brooksmith, eds., *Encounters at Indian Head: The Betty and Barney Hill Case Revisited* (San Antonio: Anomalist Books, 2007), 239–272; Webb1, 5. Barney's doubts are recorded in BBHHT, Hypnosis Session 5, March 21, 1964, 18.

50. All quotations in this paragraph and the next three are from Webb1, 2, 3, 4.

51. BBHHT, Hypnosis Session 1, February 22, 1964, 12. BSBS, 90.

52. Fuller interview with Webb, March 8, 1966, 8.

53. James Cortada, *IBM: The Rise and Fall and Reinvention of a Global Icon* (Cambridge: MIT Press, 2019), 99–101, 149–177; Michael Swords, "Radio Signals from Space, Alien Probes, and Betty Hill," *International UFO Reporter* 29:4 (Fall 2002), 10–15. Robert Hohmann to Donald Keyhoe, October 9, 1961, BHF. Walter Webb claims Jackson lived in Rhinebeck, New York; Webb2, 13; Betty remembered him in Alabama; Betty Hill to Barbara Becker, undated, BHF.

54. The letter is reproduced in Fuller, *Interrupted Journey*, 43.

55. Hill to Becker, undated; BSBS, 92. Marden and Friedman confirm the assumption in *Captured*, 54.

56. BSBS, 93–95.

57. BSBS, 94. Barney and Betty assert that the suggestion came from Jackson and Hohmann on page 108. Marden and Friedman claim that it was MacDonald's suggestion in *Captured*, 56–57, as does Fuller in *Interrupted Journey*, 47. In Betty Hill to Walter Webb, November 27, 1961, BBHF, Betty states "Mr. Hohmann is going to send us the names of competent psychiatrists who use hypnosis." Webb notes MacDonald's presence at the meeting in "Addenda to A Dramatic UFO Encounter in the White Mountains, N.H., 8/25/1962," in BHF.

CHAPTER 6. THE INTERPRETATION OF DREAMS

1. H. W. Smith and G. W. Towles, *Unidentified Flying Objects: Project Grudge: Project No. XS-30L* (Dayton, OH: Air Materiel Command, 1949), 10.

2. Ellen Herman, *The Romance of American Psychology: Political Culture in the Age of Experts* (Berkeley: University of California Press, 1995), 52, 29–50, 124–153; Jonathan Herzog, *The Spiritual Industrial Complex: America's Religious Battle against Communism in the Early Cold War* (New York: Oxford University Press, 2011), 124–127; Jonathan Engel, *American Therapy: The Rise of Psychotherapy in the United States* (New York: Penguin Books, 2008), 43–76.

3. Herman, *Romance of American Psychology*, 2–3.

4. "Are You Always Worrying?, *Time*, October 25, 1948, 69." 69; "Human Nature and Peace," *Society for the Psychological Study of Social Issues Newsletter* (March 1945), 1; Herman, *Romance of American Psychology*, 54, 77–78.

5. Julia Garbus, ed., *The Brown v. Board of Education Trial* (Farmington Hills, MI: Greenhaven Press, 2015), 37; see also James Patterson, *Brown v. Board of Education: A Civil Rights Milestone and Its Troubled Legacy* (New York: Oxford University Press, 2002), 61–68 and John P. Jackson, *Social Scientists for Social Justice* (New York: New York University Press, 2001), 131–147.

6. Barney Hill, "Speech to Be Given at the Portsmouth Naval Yard," Oversized Box 3, Folder 5, BBHP.

7. Betty Hill, "Our Marriage," 1, Box 3, Folder 1, BBHP; Betty connects her profession to her familiarity with psychology in Betty Hill to Mark Rodeghier, March 10, 1994, BHF. John Ehrenreich, *The Altruistic Imagination: A History of Social Work and Social Policy in the United States* (Ithaca: Cornell University Press, 1985), 119–137; Barbara Simon, *The Empowerment Tradition in American Social Work* (New York: Columbia University Press, 1994), 88–90.

8. UA2, [5]; Betty Hill to George Fawcett, January 6, [1986?], BBHF. Davis, *More Perfect Unions*, 2–5.

9. Betty Hill to Donald Keyhoe, September 26, 1961, 38–39.

10. Carl Wennerstrom, *Pastoral Care in the Liberal Churches.* James Luther Adams and Seward Hiltner, eds. (Nashville: Abington Press, 1970), 10, 15, 21–22, 37–38.

11. "The Reverend Carl Wennerstrom," *Chicago Tribune*, August 21, 1963, 34; Wennerstrom, *Pastoral Counseling in the Liberal Churches*, 27.

12. Rudolph Druikers, "Don't Sell Your Emotions Short," *Christian Register*, March 1961, 11.

13. Molly Harrower, "Psychological Tests in the Unitarian Universalist Ministry," *Journal of Religion and Health* 2:2 (January 1963), 129–142; Molly Harrower, "Mental Health Potential and Success in the Ministry," *Journal of Religion and Health* 4:1 (October 1964), 35, 34; Jack Mendelsohn, *Why I Am a Unitarian* (New York: Thomas Nelson and Sons, 1960), 99; Jack Mendelsohn, *Being Liberal in an Illiberal Age* (Boston: Skinner House Books, 1970), 95–96.

14. Betty Hill, "Dreams or Recall?," [1]. BBHP, Box 4, Folder 2. Betty claims to have written this document in November 1961 in BSBS, 99, following her conversations with Jackson and Hohmann; she describes timing and initial note making on 87–88 and her conversations with Barney and with Jane McLoughlin on 133. Marden and Friedman, *Captured*, 84, transcribes a later interview with Betty describing her encounter with McLaughlin.

15. Betty Hill, "Dreams or Recall?," [1].

16. Betty Hill, "Dreams or Recall?," [1], [2].

17. Betty Hill, "Dreams or Recall?," [2], [3].

18. Betty Hill, "Dreams or Recall?," [4], [5].

19. Betty Hill, "Dreams or Recall?," [4].

20. Albert Gilgen, *American Psychology since World War II: A Profile of the Discipline* (Westport, CT: Greenwood Press, 1982), 81–84; Herman, *Romance of American Psychology,* 112–118.

21. BSBS, 126–127.

22. BSBS, 123–124; Benjamin Simon disagreed with the diagnosis of teratoma and describes discussing Barney's drinking with Duncan Stephens in DSC, 3, 67, and in Benjamin Simon to Charles Holmes, August 6, 1964, Box 3, Folder 10, JGFC. Betty describes Barney's hospitalization in Betty Hill to Walter Webb, June 1, 1965, BBHF; copy also in Box 2, Folder 5, BBHP.

23. Betty Hill to Walter Webb, November 27, 1961, 2, BBHF.

24. Betty Hill to Walter Webb, November 27, 1961, 2–3; BSBS, 101–106; 103, 105, 106, 101.

25. Eunice and Barney Hill to Dr. Patrick Quirke, March 12, 1962, BBHP, Box 5, Folder 7. Fuller mistranscribes the letter in *Interrupted Journey,* 53; BSBS, 109.

26. BSBS, 107–108; Betty Hill to Walter Webb, April 24, 1962, BBHF.

27. BSBS, 109, 110, 111; Betty Hill to Walter Webb, April 24, 1962, BBHF. The notion of two people having "the same hallucination at the same time" is known as "folie à deux." Benjamin Simon, the Hills' later hypnotist, also dismissed the possibility, telling journalist John Fuller that such phenomena were rare and generally generated over long periods of time — "hardly a thing you would expect to find in a single overnight experience." DSC, 44.

28. BSBS, 111.

29. BSBS, 124–127; Betty Hill to Walter Webb, April 24, 1962, BBHF. The NICAP member was named C. Wesley Fitch; C. W. Fitch to Betty and Barney Hill, March 29, 1962; April 9, 1962; May 24, 1962, Box 1, Folder 11, BBHP. Stephens had moved from Connecticut to New Hampshire in February 1962. "Exeter Clinic," *Portsmouth Herald,* February 23, 1962, 23; "Psychiatrists Seat Slate," *Portsmouth Herald,* May 4, 1961, 10.

30. Betty Hill to Walter Webb, January 22, 1962, and September 18, 1962, BBHF; Walter Webb, "Reflections on the Hill Case," in Brookesmith and Pflock, eds., *Encounters at Indian Head,* 248.

31. Howard Roy, "The Off Beat," Box 5, Folder 14, BBHP.

32. Kathleen Marden, Betty and Barney's niece, possesses Betty's diary. She declined to share it with me but has included excerpts in Marden and Friedman, *Captured;* this quotation from 69.

33. Webb describes the meetings in his September 9, 1995, memo "Early Public Discussions by Barney and Betty Hill," BBHF. The three primary sources for the November meeting (offering somewhat contradictory recounting of it) are BSBS, 128–130; Betty Hill to Walter Webb, November 25, 1962, BBHF; copy also in Box 2, Folder 5, BBHP; "Ben H. Swett Testimony, November 29, 2005," Box 5, Folder 11, BBHP. On the March meeting see Betty Hill to

Walter Webb, March 18, 1963, BBHF; copy also in Box 2, Folder 5, BBHP. Fuller wrongly puts this meeting in September 1963; Fuller, *Interrupted Journey*, 57–58.

34. In BSBS, 129 Barney states that after Swett was finished reading his poetry, "we were asked to tell about our sighting." "Ben H. Swett Testimony, November 29, 2005" describes the Hills and Swett talking privately after the main meeting; Betty Hill to Walter Webb, November 25, 1962, BBHF, echoes Barney's claim.

35. "Ben H. Swett Testimony, November 29, 2005"; Betty Hill to Walter Webb, November 25, 1962.

CHAPTER 7. THE PROBLEM OF HYPNOSIS

1. Jessie Jean Marsh, "Santa Monica League Will Revive Charity Ball," *Los Angeles Times*, January 19, 1947, 37; Jessie Jean Marsh, "Santa Monica Assistance League Schedules Bridey Murphy Ball," *Los Angeles Times*, May 6, 1956, C5.

2. Herbert Brean, "Bridey Murphy Puts Nation in a Hypnotizzy," *Life*, March 16, 1956, 29–30; Marsh, "Santa Monica Assistance League Schedules Bridey Murphy Ball," *Los Angeles Times*, May 6, 1956, C5; Carolyn Hughes, "Here's a Bridey Murphy Ball," *Washington Post*, August 6, 1956, 22.

3. Morey Bernstein, *The Search for Bridey Murphy* (New York: Doubleday, 1956), 7–10, 21, 25; Bernstein refers to Tighe as "Ruth Simmons" in the book. Paul Edwards, *Reincarnation: A Critical Examination* (Amherst, NY: Prometheus Books, 2002), 60–68; Courtney Bender, "American Reincarnations: What the Many Lives of Past Lives Tell Us about Contemporary Spiritual Practice," *Journal of the American Academy of Religion* 75:3 (September 2007), 589–614; Robert Genter, "Hypnotizzy in the Cold War: The American Fascination with Hypnosis in the 1950s," *Journal of American Culture* 29:2 (June 2006), 154–169; Brean, "Hypnotizzy," *Life*, March 16, 1956, 29–30.

4. Brean, "Hypnotizzy," 30, 33; see also Alison Winter's discussion of the confrontation between historical and psychological investigations of Bridey Murphy in *Memory: Fragments of a Modern History* (Chicago: University of Chicago Press, 2012), 114–121.

5. Brean, "Hypnotizzy," 31–32. Emily Ogden's *Credulity: A Cultural History of US Mesmerism* (Chicago: University of Chicago Press, 2019), 17–24, argues that the question of mesmerism, a nineteenth-century precursor of hypnosis, was fundamentally the question of the relationship between the credulous and the self-identified rational who used mesmerism to manipulate the credulous and hence confirm their own rationality. Wolberg's defense of the boundaries of science repeats this effort.

6. Stanley Jackson, *Care of the Psyche: A History of Psychological Healing* (New Haven: Yale University Press, 1999), 258–260; Judith Pintar and Steven Jay Lynn, *Hypnosis: A Brief History* (Malden, MA: Wiley-Blackwell, 2008), 98–120; Robin Waterfield, *Hidden Depths: The Story of Hypnosis* (New York: Macmillan, 2002), 304–330; for views on hypnosis contemporary to the Hills I have used John G. Watkins, "Hypnosis in the United States," in F. L. Marcuse, ed., *Hypnosis Throughout the World* (Springfield, IL: Charles C. Thomas, 1964), 265–301, and Milton V. Kline, ed., *The Nature of Hypnosis: Transactions of the 1961 International Congress on Hypnosis* (Baltimore: Waverly Press, 1962), particularly vi–x, and Milton V. Kline,

"Hypnotherapy," in Benjamin Wolman, ed., *Handbook of Clinical Psychology* (New York: McGraw-Hill, 1965), 1276, 1275–1290.

7. Edward Hunter, *Brain-Washing in Red China* (New York: Vanguard Press, 1951), 10–11. See also John Driscoll, "Airmen Who Confessed to Germ Warfare Were Captives," *Troy Record*, October 30, 1952, 14; "Peping Confirms Charge: Broadcasts Purported Findings of Scientists on Germ Warfare," *New York Times*, September 15, 1952, 3; Matthew Dunne, *A Cold War State of Mind: Brainwashing and Postwar American Society* (Amherst: University of Massachusetts Press, 2013), 14–23; Ron Robin, *The Making of the Cold War Enemy: Culture and Politics in the Military-Intellectual Complex* (Princeton: Princeton University Press, 2001), 162–164.

8. William J. Bryan, *Legal Aspects of Hypnosis* (Springfield, IL: Charles C. Thomas, 1962), ix, 20, 179; Winter, *Memory*, 129–136.

9. Josef Breuer and Sigmund Freud, *Studies on Hysteria,* trans. James Strachey (New York: Basic Books, 1955), 9; Bernstein, *Search for Bridey Murphy,* 133.

10. BSBS, 6.

11. Betty Hill to Donald Keyhoe, September 26, 1961.

12. Robert Jay Lifton, *Thought Reform and the Psychology of Totalism: A Study of 'Brainwashing' in China* (New York: W. W. Norton, 1961), 3–4; Milton V. Kline, ed., *A Scientific Report on the Search for Bridey Murphy* (New York: Julian Press, 1956), ix–x, 165; see also Martin Gardner, *Fads and Fallacies in the Name of Science,* 2nd ed. (New York: Dover Publications, 1957), 315–321.

13. Milton Kline, "The Meaning of Hypnotic Behavior," in Kline, ed., *Scientific Report on the Search for Bridey Murphy,* 170; Martin Orne, "The Mechanisms of Hypnotic Age Regression," *Journal of Abnormal and Social Psychology* 46 (1951), 220; Imants Baruss, *Alterations of Consciousness* (Washington, DC: American Psychological Association, 2020), 101–124; Susan Clancy, *Abducted: How People Come to Believe They Were Kidnapped by Aliens* (Cambridge: Harvard University Press, 2005) explores hypnotically recovered memory on 59–80 and the Hill case on 95–98; citing the work of memory researcher Elizabeth Loftus, and discusses the Hills particularly on 95–98.

14. Mark Harris, *Five Came Back: A Story of Hollywood and the Second World War* (New York: Penguin, 2014), 386–400; Ben Shephard, *A War of Nerves: Soldiers and Psychiatrists in the Twentieth Century* (Cambridge: Harvard University Press, 2001), 274–276.

15. "Dr. Benjamin Simon, Retired Neurologist," *Boston Globe,* January 11, 1981, 60; Benjamin Simon, "Hypnosis in the Treatment of Military Neuroses," *Psychiatric Opinion* 4:5 (1960), 24–28; DSC, 1, 50; BSBS, 125. Betty reports the plans for hypnosis to Walter Webb in Betty Hill to Walter Webb, November 23, 1963, Box 2, Folder 5, BBHP. Marden and Friedman, *Captured,* 71, citing only Marden's memory, claim that Barney had a "breakthrough memory" of the September 1961 event. While talking with family in the fall of 1963 he remembered figures in the road gesturing for his car to stop.

16. Milton Kline, "Hypnotherapy," in Benjamin Wolman, ed., *Handbook of Clinical Psychology* (New York: McGraw-Hill, 1965), 1286–1289. The debate about whether hypnosis is a special state of consciousness or not persisted for decades after the 1960s; see Alan Gauld, *A History of Hypnotism* (New York: Cambridge University Press, 1992), 586–602. The social

psychological approach is most fully unpacked in Nicholas Spanos, "Hypnosis and the Modification of Hypnotic Susceptibility: A Social Psychological Perspective," in P. Naish, ed., *What Is Hypnosis?* (Philadelphia: Open University Press, 1986), 85–120; the altered states theory is most associated with E. R. Hilgerd; for instance, *Hypnotic Susceptibility* (New York: Harcourt, Brace, 1965).

17. Benjamin Simon to John G. Fuller, undated, Box 2, Folder 4, JGFC; Simon crossed out Fuller's line "The deep trance would provide details almost tape-recorder perfect," and accused Fuller of a "highly colored sensational style" in Benjamin Simon, notes on manuscript draft of Fuller, "The Interrupted Journey," Box 2, Folder 4, JGFC. Simon makes similar points in "Introduction" to John G. Fuller, *The Interrupted Journey: Two Lost Hours Aboard a Flying Saucer* (New York: Dial Press, 1966), viii–ix. Bowers, "Relationship Between the Hypnotist and His Subject," 94–95; Pintar and Lynn, *Hypnosis*, 126–129.

18. DSC, 12–13, 17–18. On Simon's use of authority, Bridget Brown, *They Know Us Better Than We Know Ourselves: The History and Politics of Alien Abduction* (New York: New York University Press, 2007), 30–32. Brown argues that the Hills read submissiveness to Simon and submissiveness to extraterrestrials as two analogues of the helplessness inherent in modernity; I agree, but extend her argument. After their treatment concluded, the Hills certainly did not feel submissive to Simon.

19. BSBS, 113; DSC, 10. Simon's bills to the Hills are in Box 2, Folder 1, BBHP.

20. DSC, 3, 4, 5.

21. DSC, 6–9.

22. DSC, 41.

23. Fuller, *Interrupted Journey*, 62–63; DSC, 20–21; BSBS, 114–120.

24. BSBS, 116, 117–118, 120–121; DSC, 15–16.

CHAPTER 8. IN DR. SIMON'S OFFICE

1. Benjamin Simon, notes on manuscript draft of Fuller, "The Interrupted Journey," Box 2, Folder 4, JGFC.

2. BBHHT, Hypnosis Session 1, February 22, 1964, 2–3. Spelling original.

3. BBHHT, Hypnosis Session 1, February 22, 1964, 5–6, 7; BBHHT, Hypnosis Session 2, February 29, 1964, 1.

4. BBHHT, Hypnosis Session 1, February 22, 1964, 9, 10, 11, 13; see also BBHHT, Hypnosis Session 3, March 7, 1964, 4, 10.

5. BBHHT, Hypnosis Session 1, February 22, 1964, 13.

6. BBHHT, Hypnosis Session 1, February 22, 1964, 13.

7. BBHHT, Hypnosis Session 1, February 22, 1964, 15, 18; BBHHT, Hypnosis Session 2, February 29, 1964, 7. A number of scholarly studies have drawn parallels between Barney's terror at the craft's inhabitants and his fear of racial persecution; see, for instance, Jodi Dean, *Aliens in America: Conspiracy Cultures from Outerspace to Cyberspace* (Ithaca: Cornell University Press, 1998), 164–166, David Halperin, *Intimate Alien: The Hidden Story of the UFO* (Palo Alto: Stanford University Press, 2020), 74–81, and Christopher Roth, "Ufology as Anthropology:

Race, Extraterrestrials, and the Occult," in Debbora Battaglia, ed., *ET Culture: Anthropology in Outerspaces* (Durham: Duke University Press, 2005), 38–94.

8. BBHHT, Hypnosis Session 1, February 22, 1964, 20; BBHHT, Hypnosis Session 2, February 29, 1964, 8.

9. BBHHT, Hypnosis Session 2, February 29, 1964, 8–9, 12.

10. BBHHT, Hypnosis Session 2, February 29, 1964, 9–10, 13, 14. BBHHT, Hypnosis Session 5, March 14, 1964, 3.

11. BBHHT, Hypnosis Session 1, February 22, 1964, 15, 19–20.

12. Marden and Friedman, *Captured*, 119–154, evaluate these differences in great detail, arguing first that John Fuller's presentation obscured details—particularly sexual details—in Barney's account, and second that the distinctions between Betty's dreams and her hypnotic account make the latter seem more reliable. The primary details they emphasize are (and in all cases with alternatives, the former are from Betty's dream, the latter from hypnosis): (1) the number and behavior of the men in the road; (2) whether the Hills entered the craft via stairs or a ramp; (3) whether the light in the craft was overhead or emanated from the walls (a detail they also find consistent with Barney's account); (4) the vocalizations of the creatures, not described in the dream but by each Hill as a repetitive humming-like sound; (5) the order in which the Hills returned to their car, either simultaneously or sequentially, with Barney first; (6) whether the leader pulled down a hanging map in front of Betty or whether he removed it from the wall; (7) and most striking, the physical appearance of the creatures, which appeared far more human in Betty's dreams than in the Hills' later recollections.

13. BBHHT, Hypnosis Session 3, March 7, 1964, 2–3.

14. BBHHT, Hypnosis Session 3, March 7, 1964, 4, 6–7, 8, 10.

15. B BBHHT, Hypnosis Session 3, March 7, 1964, 14; BHHT, Hypnosis Session 3, March 7, 1964, 17.

16. BBHHT, Hypnosis Session 3, March 7, 1964, 14.

17. BBHHT, Hypnosis Session 3, March 7, 1964, 16, 17.

18. BBHHT, Hypnosis Session 4, March 14, 1964, 7.

19. BBHHT, Hypnosis Session 4, March 14, 1964, 8–9.

20. BBHHT, Hypnosis Session 4, March 14, 1964, 10.

21. Harlow Shapley, "Long Range Foresight," *Christian Register,* June 1957, 10-11.

22. Benjamin Simon to Philip Klass, October 28, 1975, and Benjamin Simon to Philip Klass, March 1, 1976, Collection of Robert Sheaffer.

23. DSC, 38, 40; Walter Webb, Webb2, 14; Benjamin Simon to Philip Klass, October 28, 1975, Collection of Robert Sheaffer.

24. Mark Solovey, *Shaky Foundations: The Politics-Patronage-Social Science Nexus in the Cold War* (New Brunswick: Rutgers University Press, 2013), calls this stance the "scientistic strategy," 4–6; Mark Solovey, *Social Science for What: Battles for Public Funding for the Other Sciences at the National Science Foundation* (Cambridge: MIT Press, 2020), 86–92.

25. Louis Filler, ed., *The President Speaks: From William McKinley to Lyndon Johnson* (New York: G. P. Putnam, 1964), 414–415; Michael Katz, *In the Shadow of the Poorhouse: A Social History of Welfare in America* (New York: Basic Books, 1996), 19–21. Liberal paternalism is

discussed in Michael Freeden, *Liberalism: A Very Short Introduction* (New York: Oxford University Press, 2015), 121–123.

26. Michael Harrington, *The Other America: Poverty in the United States* (New York: Simon and Schuster, 1962), 17. On the emergence of the notion of the culture of poverty, Alice O'Connor, *Poverty Knowledge: Social Science, Social Policy, and the Poor in Twentieth Century U.S. History* (Princeton: Princeton University Press, 2001), 99–123, and Mical Raz, *What's Wrong with the Poor: Psychiatry, Race, and the War on Poverty* (Chapel Hill: University of North Carolina Press, 2013), 76–111.

27. O'Connor, *Poverty Knowledge*, 182; Michael Kazin and Maurice Isserman, *America Divided: The Civil War of the 1960s* (New York: Oxford University Press, 2000), 103–112.

28. Theodore Sarbin, "The Culture of Poverty," in Vernon Allen, ed., *Psychological Factors in Poverty* (Chicago: Markham Publishing, 1970), 34–35; Ellen Herman, *The Romance of American Psychology: Political Culture in the Age of Experts* (Berkeley: University of California Press, 1995), 249–257.

29. BBHHT, Hypnosis Session 6, March 21, 1964, 14-15, 6, 2; Hypnosis Session 7, March 21, 1964, 12.

30. BBHHT, Hypnosis Session 6, March 21, 1964, 2, 4, 5.

31. BBHHT, Hypnosis Session 6, March 21, 1964, 5, 7.

32. BBHHT, Hypnosis Session 6, March 21, 1964, 1; DSC, 7. In his notes on the manuscript of Fuller, "The Interrupted Journey," Box 2, Folder 4, JGFC, Simon confirms that he came to this theory between March 14 and March 21: "Until completion of Betty's second trance and the establishment of the dream resemblance I was baffled. Then it appeared that the reverse of my conjecture had been the case. If it was dream or fantasy and if they were not mutual, it could have been initiated by Betty and absorbed by Barney."

33. Simon to Holmes, August 6, 1964, 2–3; DSC, 37–38; Benjamin Simon to Charles Holmes, August 6, 1964, Box 3, Folder 10, JGFC.

34. DSC, 37–38, 68; see also BBHHT, Hypnosis Session 2, February 29, 1964, 2–3.

35. Walter Webb, "A Dramatic UFO Encounter in the White Mountains, New Hampshire: The Hill Case, Sept. 19–20, 1961," August 30, 1965, 15. Webb describes the meeting in Walter Webb to Kathleen Marden, July 5, 2006, BBHF, and in Walter Webb to Betty and Barney Hill, July 13, 1964, BBHF; copy also in Box 2, Folder 5, BBHP.

36. Sigmund Freud, *Three Contributions to the Theory of Sex,* trans. A. A. Brill (New York: Nervous and Mental Disease Publishing, 1916), 27. Abram Kardiner, "The Flight from Masculinity," in Hendrik M. Ruitenbeek, *The Problem of Homosexuality in Modern Society* (New York: E. P. Dutton, 1963), 27. On latent homosexuality in the Cold War I have used K. A. Courdileone, *Manhood and American Political Culture in the Cold War* (New York: Taylor and Francis, 2006), 145–152, and Barbara Ehrenreich, *The Hearts of Men: American Dreams and the Flight from Commitment* (New York: Doubleday, 1983), 14–29.

37. Walter Webb, "A Dramatic UFO Encounter in the White Mountains, New Hampshire: The Hill Case, Sept. 19–20, 1961," August 30, 1965, 15–16.

38. Walter Webb, "A Dramatic UFO Encounter in the White Mountains, New Hampshire: The Hill Case, Sept. 19–20, 1961," August 30, 1965, 15; Betty Hill to Walter Webb, September 22, 1965; Betty Hill to Walter Webb, June 1, 1965, BBHF; copy also in Box 2, Folder 5, BBHP.

39. Betty Hill to Walter Webb, September 22, 1965, BBHF; copy also in Box 2, Folder 5, BBHP; R. Leo Sprinkle to Betty and Barney Hill, June 6, 1967, Box 2, Folder 2, BBHP; Betty and Barney Hill Profile Sheet, the Adjective Check List, Box 2, Folder 2, BBHP; Betty Hill to Leo Sprinkle, January 22, 1968, Box 2, Folder 2, BBHP.

40. DSC, 10, 44.

41. *Selected Speeches of Dwight David Eisenhower* (Washington, DC: Government Printing Office, 1970), 149. James Ledbetter, *Unwarranted Influence: Dwight D. Eisenhower and the Military-Industrial Complex* (New Haven: Yale University Press, 2011), 41–44. Meg Greenfield, "Science Goes to Washington," *Science,* October 18, 1963, 367; C. Wright Mills, *The Power Elite* (1956; New York: Oxford University Press, 2000), 213, 200. On other critics of the link between science and the survival of democracy, Jewett, *Science under Fire,* 96–103; Kevles, *Physicists,* 393–397.

42. Keyhoe, *Flying Saucers Are Real,* 10, 158; Donald Keyhoe, *Aliens from Space: The Real Story of Unidentified Flying Objects* (New York: Signet, 1973), 70. Aaron Gulyas, *Conspiracy Theories: The Roots, Themes and Propagation of Paranoid Political and Cultural Narratives* (Jefferson, NC: McFarland, 2015), 76–78.

43. Betty Hill to Walter Webb, June 1, 1965 BBHF; copy also in Box 2, Folder 5, BBHP; Betty Hill to Walter Webb, August 23, 1965, BBHF; copy also in Box 2, Folder 5, BBHP; on Spencer's work, see "Maple Season Starts in New Hampshire," *Boston Globe,* March 21, 1948, 106, and *Annual Report of the Officers of the Town of Plymouth, New Hampshire* (Plymouth, NH: Record Press, 1955), 4; for his UFO sighting, *NICAP Special Bulletin,* May 1960, 4. Betty Hill, "Hypnosis," BBHP, Box 5, Folder 7.

44. Barney Hill to James MacDonald, n.d. (but likely October 1967), Box 1, Folder 1, BBHP. Spelling corrected. See also Walter Webb to Betty Hill, July 13, 1964, BBHF; copy also in Box 2, Folder 5, BBHP.

45. BSBS, 10; Betty Hill, "My Blue Dress," Box 5, Folder 4, BBHP; Harry Mark to Leonard Stringfield, May 11, 1978, Box 5, Folder 4, BBHP. Twenty years later, in 2002, Phyllis Budinger, a member of the Mutual UFO Network and an analytical chemist performed another analysis of the dress. She argued that the stains (1) were from a "natural oil and protein substance," and (2) came from the outside in, not the reverse, thus ruling out "any natural substances originating from Betty, such as urine, perspiration and vomit." P. A. Budinger, "Analysis of the Dress Worn by Betty Hill during the September 19, 1961, Abduction in New Hampshire," 6, Box 5, Folder 4, BBHP. The dress is in Oversize Box 1, BBHP.

46. "Ben H. Swett Testimony, November 29, 2005," Box 5, Folder 11, BBHP.

47. BSBS, 9.

48. "Ben H. Swett Testimony, November 29, 2005," Box 5, Folder 11, BBHP; Fuller, *Interrupted Journey,* 287–288; Marden and Friedman, *Captured,* 191–192. Fuller and Swett have the date of the Dover meeting as November 8; Marden and Friedman as November 7.

49. "John Fuller, Playwright, Author of UFO Books," *Chicago Tribune,* November 18, 1990, 18; "Trade Winds," *Saturday Review,* April 14, 1962, 12; see also July 19, 1958, 6; June 10, 1961, 12.

50. "Trade Winds," *Saturday Review,* October 2, 1965, 10, 16.

———

51. John G. Fuller, "Outer-Space Ghost Story," *Look* 30:4 (February 22, 1966), 36, 38; John G. Fuller, *Incident at Exeter: The Story of Unidentified Flying Objects over America Today* (New York: G. P. Putnam, 1966); Fuller, *Interrupted Journey,* ix. Betty describes her early contact with Fuller in Betty Hill to Walter Webb, October 5, 1965, BBHF.

52. John O. Parker to John G. Fuller, February 24, 1966; Dial Press to John G. Fuller, March 11, 1966, both in Box 3 Folder 7, JGFC. An earlier letter from Betty Hill to Simon dated December 27, 1965, proposed an equal three-way split of the advance and royalties; it is reproduced in Marden and Friedman, *Captured,* 192–193.

53. Fuller, *Interrupted Journey,* xii–xiv; the draft letter is in Box 3, Folder 1, JGFC.

54. Fuller, *Interrupted Journey,* 67, 293–296. See also Brown, *They Know Us Better Than We Know Ourselves,* 25–32; " '61 Close Encounter Untrue—Psychiatrist," *Pittsburgh Post-Gazette,* February 21, 1978, 2.

CHAPTER 9. THE NATIONAL ASSOCIATION FOR THE ADVANCEMENT OF COLORED PEOPLE

1. UUA General Assembly statement cited in Mark D. Morrison-Reed, *Revisiting the Empowerment Controversy: Black Power and Unitarian Universalism* (Boston: Skinner House Books, 2018), 12; see also 11–18; Mark D. Morrison-Reed, *The Selma Awakening: How the Civil Rights Movement Tested and Changed Unitarian Universalism* (Boston: Skinner House Books, 2014), 187–223. Homer Jack, "A Flaw Within: Toward Integrating our Liberal Churches," *Register-Leader,* May 1967, 9–10.

2. Cited in Aram Goudsouzian, *Down to the Crossroads: Civil Rights, Black Power, and the Meredith March against Fear* (New York: Farrar, Strauss, and Giroux, 2014), 142–143.

3. Morrison-Reed, *Revisiting the Empowerment Controversy,* 46–54.

4. Henry Hampton, "An Insider's View of the Black Caucus," *Register Leader,* December 1967, 4; Joseph Ulman, "Shattered Dream," *Register Leader,* December 1967, 2.

5. Morrison-Reed, *Revisiting the Empowerment Controversy,* especially 308–318.

6. *Census of Population, 1960: New Hampshire* (Washington, DC: Government Printing Office, 1961), 17, 29. See also Mark Sammons and Valerie Cunningham, *Black Portsmouth: Three Centuries of African American Heritage* (Durham: University of New Hampshire Press, 2004), 5–12, 180–181.

7. "NAACP Appoints Executive Board," *Portsmouth Herald,* February 11, 1963, 2; "Toastmasters Hold Meeting," *Portsmouth Herald,* February 28, 1964, 25; National Association for the Advancement of Colored People Portsmouth Branch Minutes, May 12, 1964, October 6, 1964, June 1, 1964; National Association for the Advancement of Colored People, Portsmouth Branch Records, Box 1, Folder 8, Special Collections and University Archives, UMass Amherst, Amherst, MA. Barney and Betty's lifetime membership plaques are in Oversized Box 3, BBHP.

8. On the politics of Black respectability, Evelyn Higginbotham, *Righteous Discontent: The Women's Movement in the Black Baptist Church, 1880–1920* (Cambridge: Harvard University Press, 1994); on respectability and the Old Philadelphians, Willard Gatewood, *Aristocrats of Color: The Black Elite, 1880–1920* (Fayetteville: University of Arkansas Press, 2000), 98–104.

9. *Laws of the State of New Hampshire, 1961* (Concord: Evans Printing Company, 1961), 272; "Vote against Discrimination," *Portsmouth Herald*, May 10, 1961, 4; "Anti-Bias Bill Action," *Nashua Telegraph*, June 21, 1961, 16; "Barber Shop Report," Oversized Box 3, Folder 3, BBHP; "Barber's Case Going to High Court," *Portsmouth Herald*, July 26, 1963, 3.

10. "Group to Battle Discrimination," *Portsmouth Herald*, January 17, 1963, 1, 3. Similar committees had been organized in other cities in the area in the years prior; "Fair Practices Committee," *Portsmouth Herald*, December 13, 1962, 4.

11. "April 16 Date Set for Hearing on Discrimination," *Portsmouth Herald*, February 27, 1963, 1.

12. Robert Shaines to Barney Hill, May 13, 1963, Oversized Box 3, Folder 3, BBHP.

13. "Barber's Case Going to High Court," *Portsmouth Herald*, July 26, 1963, 3; "Local Barber Loses Plea in High Court," *Portsmouth Herald*, April 30, 1964, 1; "State Bias Law Tested," *Nashua Telegraph*, February 5, 1964, 10. National Association for the Advancement of Colored People Portsmouth Branch Minutes, July 14, 1964, National Association for the Advancement of Colored People, Portsmouth Branch Records, Box 1, Folder 8, Special Collections and University Archives, UMass Amherst, Amherst, MA.

14. Ethelred Brown, "I Have Two Dreams," *Christian Register*, December 1947, 471.

15. Donald Harrington, "Community Church Continues to Pioneer in Promotion of Race Equality," *Christian Register*, February 1949, 33; Holland Emerson Wolfe, "Are You a Lip Service Liberal?," *Christian Register*, January 1953, 17.

16. Carl Seaward, "Beyond Tolerance to Good Will," *Christian Register*, February 1948, 28–29.

17. UA2, [6].

18. Betty Hill, "Our Marriage," Box 3, Folder 1, BBHP.

19. Fuller, *Interrupted Journey*, 10, 4; quotation on 10. This quotation does not appear in BSBS.

20. John Papandrew, *What Is Evil? A Deepavali Sermon* (New York City: The Community Church, 1960), 3. Spelling original.

21. Lynn Walters, "King Found Spiritual Ally in NH," *Boston Globe*, January 18, 2004, 2–3.

22. "Human Rights for Minorities: Sunday, June 9, 7:30 PM," Oversized Box 3, Folder 2, BBHP; "Three Marchers to Speak Sunday at South Church," *Portsmouth Herald*, September 6, 1963, 6; "Off to Washington," *Portsmouth Herald*, August 27, 1963, 1. Sammons and Cunningham, *Black Portsmouth* (Durham: University of New Hampshire Press, 2004), 188–191.

23. "For Civil Rights," *Portsmouth Herald*, February 19, 1964, 4; Louis Wyman to Barney Hill, February 12, 1964, and Barney Hill to Norris Cotton, January 30, 1964, both in Oversized Box 3, Folder 2, BBHP; "Portsmouth Man Cited for Service to State," *New Hampshire Sunday News*, September 26, 1965, 1; "Air Base Activities," *Portsmouth Herald*, December 1, 1964, 12; "NAACP Conducts Voter Drive," *Portsmouth Herald*, October 14, 1964, 2; Betty Hill to Walter Webb, October 20, 1964, BBHF; Marden and Friedman, *Captured*, 179–180; Betty Hill to George Fawcett, January 6, [1986?], BBHF.

24. Samuel Simmons, Director, Field Services Division of the US Commission on Civil Rights to Barney Hill, May 21, 1965, Oversized Box 3, Folder 2, BBHP; James Keenan to

Austin Quinney, July 9, 1965, Oversized Box 3, Folder 2, BBHP; "Several State Groups in Support of a Human Rights Commission," *Portsmouth Herald*, June 12, 1965, 14.

25. My discussions of OEO and particularly the Community Action Program are shaped by James Patterson, *America's Struggle with Poverty in the Twentieth Century* (Cambridge: Harvard University Press, 2000), 122–150, and William Clayson, *Freedom Is Not Enough: The War on Poverty and the Civil Rights Movement in Texas* (Austin: University of Texas Press, 2010), 25–40, 65–83.

26. "Maley to Speak at Two Meetings," *Portsmouth Herald*, January 26, 1966, 24.

27. "Epping Notes," *Portsmouth Herald*, July 12, 1967, 30; "Action Directors Meet Thursday," *Portsmouth Herald*, August 29, 1967, 3; "Officials Preparing for Head Start," *Portsmouth Herald*, February 15, 1966, 9; "Poverty War Seeks Television Enlistments," *Portsmouth Herald*, April 21, 1966, 8; "VISTA Volunteers Keep Busy," *Portsmouth Herald*, December 21, 1966, 28; "Action Program to Have Art Classes," *Portsmouth Herald*, June 17, 1967, 2; "Day Care Center Opens Fundraising Campaign," *Portsmouth Herald*, November 21, 1967, 11.

28. BBHHT, April 4, 1964, 3, 5.

29. Betty Hill to Walter Webb, August 23, 1965, BBHF.

CHAPTER 10. MONOGENESIS

1. Joseph Dinneen, "A Sad Week for Newsmen," *Boston Globe*, July 2, 1967, 12.

2. "John H. Luttrell," *Boston Herald*, September 15, 2011, 15; Betty Hill to Walter Webb, August 23, 1965, BBHF; Richard France to John LuTrelle [*sic*], September 1, 1965, Box 5, Folder 14, BBHP; John Luttrell, "Nothing to Fear, Said Man from Space Ship," *Boston Traveller*, October 27, 1965, 55, quotes from the hypnosis sessions. Marden and Friedman, *Captured*, 184–186. Later Fuller and Simon would speculate that the Hills wanted publicity. In the spring of 1966 Simon said, "they want a place in the sun" and expressed irritation that they "publicized this a lot more than they said." DSC, 48. The Hills' own words force us to at least qualify this judgment, at least until after Luttrell's story was published.

3. John Luttrell, "A UFO Chiller: Did THEY Seize Couple?," *Boston Traveller*, October 25, 1965, 1.

4. Edward U. Condon, *Final Report of the Scientific Study of Unidentified Flying Objects* (New York: E. P. Dutton, 1969), 591, 582, 583; see also Jacobs, *UFO Controversy in America*, 200–235 and Thurs, *Science Talk*, 123–130; Condon cited on 123.

5. Loretta Leone, "The Facts about Flying Saucers," *Boston Herald*, November 21, 1965, 1.

6. Lizabeth Cohen, *A Consumer's Republic: The Politics of Mass Consumption in the Postwar Era* (New York: Knopf, 2008), 292–345; Christina von Hodenberg, *Television's Moment: Sitcom Audiences and the Sixties Cultural Revolution* (New York: Berghahn Books, 2015), 1–4.

7. Phil Donahue to Betty and Barney Hill, April 12, 1968, Box 1, Folder 26, BBHP; "This and That," *Baltimore Sun*, April 5, 1967, 42; "Tele-Vues," *Long Beach Press-Telegram*, December 11, 1966, 116; "Flying Saucer Victims Report to TV Millions," *Norfolk New Journal*, December 3, 1966, 16.

8. Barry Palmer, "Portsmouth Couple Awes 600 Persons Here," *Nashua Telegraph*, December 1, 1965, 3.

9. "Documentaries Examine Arab Refugees, Air Pollution, and UFOs," *Philadelphia Inquirer,* August 30, 1967, 15.

10. "Space Creatures Stumped by Teeth," *San Francisco Examiner,* November 18, 1966, n.p.

11. John Barker, "Local Couple Tell of Meeting UFO," *Portsmouth Herald,* October 26, 1964, n.p., copy in Box 6, Folder 15, BBHP.

12. Poppy Cannon White, "Strange Visitors," *Amsterdam News,* December 17, 1966, 19.

13. John Luttrell, "Was This the Moment of Truth?," *Boston Traveller,* October 29, 1965, 5; John Luttrell, "Now Don't You Believe in Flying Saucers?," *Boston Traveller,* October 26, 1965, 24.

14. John G. Fuller, "Interrupted Journey," *Minneapolis Star,* October 22, 1966, 3; John G. Fuller, "Barney Fought Memory of His UFO Encounter," *Morning Call,* December 24, 1966, 5.

15. Bobbie Barbee, "Negro, White Wife Say They Were Kidnaped, Taken in Outer Space," *JET,* October 20, 1966, 21–22. Spelling original. On Johnson's publication strategies, Renee Romano, *Race Mixing: Black-White Marriage in Postwar America* (Cambridge: Harvard University Press, 2003), 58-60, 66–67 on the 1960 census Brenna Greer, *Represented: The Black Imagemakers Who Reimagined African American Citizenship* (Philadelphia: University of Pennsylvania Press, 2019), 144-146.

16. Myrdal, *American Dilemma,* 606.

17. Hannah Arendt, "Reflections on Little Rock," in *Responsibility and Judgment* (New York: Schocken Books, 2003), 203. Romano, *Race Mixing,* 155–157.

18. Romano, *Race Mixing,* 55–58; Randall Risdon, "A Study of Interracial Marriages Based on Data for Los Angeles County," *Sociology and Social Research* 39 (1945), 92–95; George Little, "Analytical Reflections on Mixed Marriages," *Psychoanalytic Review* 29 (January 1942), 22.

19. Romano, *Race Mixing,* 98–102; Susan Courtney, *Hollywood Fantasies of Miscegenation: Spectacular Narratives of Gender and Race* (Princeton: Princeton University Press, 2005), 277–294.

20. Benjamin Simon to Philip Klass, October 28, 1975, Collection of Robert Scheaffer; DSC, 2.

21. Daniel Patrick Moynihan, *The Negro Family: A Case for National Action* (Washington, DC: Office of Policy Planning and Research, United States Department of Labor, 1965), 46–47; O'Connor, *Poverty Knowledge,* 203–205; Daniel Geary, *Beyond Civil Rights: The Moynihan Report and Its Legacy* (Philadelphia: University of Pennsylvania Press, 2015), 48–67.

22. Benjamin Simon, notes on manuscript draft of Fuller, "The Interrupted Journey," Box 2, Folder 4, JGFC.

23. "A Fresh Look at Flying Saucers," *Time,* August 8, 1967, 73.

24. Daniel Tuttle, "Saucers," *Look,* November 29, 1966, 10.

25. Francyl Howard, "Strange Space Ship Lands in New Hampshire," *Greater Oregon,* January 9, 1970, 3.

26. Allen Spraggett, "Kidnapped by a UFO," *Fate,* January 1967, 40.

27. Albert Baller to Betty and Barney Hill, November 26, 1966, Box 2, Folder 1, BBHP; Benjamin Simon to Betty Hill, December 8, 1966, Box 2, Folder 1, BBHP.

28. Fuller, *Interrupted Journey*, 4, 8, 10. Jodi Dean, *Aliens in America: Conspiracy Cultures from Outerspace to Cyberspace* (Ithaca: Cornell University Press, 1998), 164–165.

29. Walter Webb to Betty and Barney Hill, January 19, 1967, Box 2, Folder 5, BBHP; Fuller, *Interrupted Journey*, 87, 127; compare to BBHHT, Hypnosis Session 2, February 28, 1964, 9, 14.

30. Tuttle, "Saucers," 10. For arguments that root the "grays," as these aliens are known, in the Hill case, see Brown, *They Know Us Better Than We Know Ourselves*, 91–92, Thomas E. Bullard, "Lost in the Myths," in David M. Jacobs, ed., *UFOs and Abductions: Challenging the Borders of Knowledge* (Lawrence: University Press of Kansas, 2008), 175.

31. Much scholarly literature on race and aliens makes this point; see, for instance, Christopher Roth, "Ufology as Anthropology: Race, Extraterrestrials and the Occult," in Debbora Battaglia, ed., *ET Culture: Anthropology in Outerspaces* (Durham: Duke University Press, 2006), especially 61–66; Luise White, "Alien Nation: The Hidden Obsession of UFO Literature," *Transition* 63 (1994), 24–33; for a counterpoint, see Jonathan Z. Smith, "Close Encounters of Diverse Kinds," in Susan Mizruchi, ed., *Religion and Cultural Studies* (Princeton: Princeton University Press, 2001), 3–21, which sees in alien bodies the compression of racial difference.

32. BSBS, 171.

33. Betty Hill to Donald Keyhoe, September 26, 1961, in BBHF; also transcribed in Webb1, 39; Howard Roy, "The Off-Beat," Box 5, Folder 14, BBHP.

34. Webb2, 5.

35. BBHHT, Hypnosis Session 1, February 22, 1964, 15, 16; Hypnosis Session 2, February 29, 1964, 7, 12.

36. BBHHT, Hypnosis Session 1, February 22, 1964, 15, 18.

37. Betty Hill, "Dreams or Recall?," 1–2, Box 4, Folder 2, BBHP.

38. Hill, "Dreams or Recall?," 2. David Drysdale, in "Alienated Histories, Alienating Futures: Raciology and Missing Time in *The Interrupted Journey*," *English Studies in Canada* 34:1 (March 2008), 103–123, notes the significance of the Hills' differing perceptions of their abduction, arguing that the story as Fuller tells it warns the Hills, and particularly Barney, of the potential elimination of his identity and story alike.

39. BBHHT, Session 8, March 28, 1964, 8–9.

40. Carleton Coon, *The Origin of Races* (New York: Knopf, 1962), 657.

41. Coon, *The Origin of Races*, 656. On Coon's work, the standard account is John P. Jackson, "In Ways Unacademical: The Reception of Carleton S. Coon's 'The Origin of Races,' " *Journal of the History of Biology* 34:2 (Summer 2001), 247–285; see also Michael Yudell, *Race Unmasked: Biology and Race in the Twentieth Century* (New York: Columbia University Press, 2001), 167–168. Roth, "Ufology as Anthropology," 66–67, and Drysdale, "Alienated Histories, Alienating Futures: Raciology and Missing Time in *The Interrupted Journey*," 112–113, have discussed Coon in relation to the Hills.

42. Cited in Jackson, "In Ways Unacademical," 280.

43. Jackson, "In Ways Unacademical," 250–259; on Boas and Coon's feud, John P. Jackson, *Science for Segregation: Race, Law, and the Case against Brown v. Board of Education* (New York: New York University Press, 2005), 19–43. On polygenesis and monogenesis, see Colin Kidd, *The Forging of Races: Race and Scripture in the Protestant Atlantic World, 1600–2000* (New York: Cambridge University Press, 2006), 27–30.

44. Fuller, *Interrupted Journey*, 262–263. In BSBS, 170, the transcripts of Fuller's interviews with the Hills, Betty gives the statements Fuller ascribes to Barney in the book.

45. Betty Hill to Walter Webb, October 20, 1964, Box 2, Folder 2, BBHP. Betty's description here is quite similar to her statements to Fuller and the passage Fuller attributes to Barney.

46. BSBS, 169–170. Spelling corrected.

47. BSBS, 170–171, 182. Spelling original.

48. Betty Hill to Marjorie Fish, July 12, 1989, Box 1, Folder 10, BBHP; Jack Mendelsohn, *Why I Am a Unitarian* (New York: Thomas Nelson and Sons, 1960), 79.

49. David Baker to Betty and Barney Hill, October 2, 1967; Betty Hill to David Baker, n.d., but clearly in response to Baker's letter, BBHF.

50. Transcript attached to Betty and Barney Hill to J. Allen Hynek, April 17, 1968, BHF.

51. Betty Hill to Walter Webb, March 3, 1968, BBHF. She makes the claim again in Betty Hill to J. Allen Hynek, April 17, 1968, BHF. In the latter letter she names the psychiatrist: Stephen Black, a noted British researcher into hypnosis and the paranormal.

52. Betty Hill, "The Aliens," undated, BBHF; Benjamin Simon to Betty Hill, March 8, 1965, Box 2, Folder 1, BBHP.

53. Betty Hill to Mark Rodeghier, May 17, 1994, BHF.

54. BSBS, 2, 184, 13.

55. Barney Hill to Norris Cotton, January 30, 1964, Oversized Box 3, Folder 2, BBHP.

56. "NAACP Argues Civil Rights with Wyman," *Portsmouth Herald*, April 4, 1964, 3.

57. Keesler Montgomery to Barney Hill, May 20, 1964; Barney Hill Statement, May 8, 1964; Anonymous to Barney Hill, March 23, 1965; Geraldine Grant to Thomas Cobbs, October 23, 1965; Casey Moher to Legal Office, Pease Air Force Base, June 4, 1964, all in Oversized Box 3, Folder 2, BBHP.

58. Barney quoted from Barney Hill, manuscript for a speech, undated, Oversized Box 3, Folder 3, BBHP. This manuscript is difficult to date. It appears to have been composed on two different typewriters and includes a page of handwritten material. Though it touches on similar themes and events throughout, it may not be a single piece of work. Dates mentioned in the text help to place it in time.

59. "70 Marchers Mourn Victims of Race Bomb," *Portsmouth Herald*, September 19, 1963, 1; "Slain Hub Clergyman Hailed at Portsmouth," *Portsmouth Herald*, March 17, 1965, 2; Jason Sokol, *All Eyes Are upon Us: Race and Politics from Boston to Brooklyn* (New York: Basic Books, 2014), 98–100; Hasan Kwame Jefferson, *Bloody Lowndes: Civil Rights and Black Power in Alabama's Black Belt* (New York: NYU Press, 2009), 81–83, 132; Gerald Horne, *Fire This Time: The Watts Uprising and the 1960s* (Charlottesville: University of Virginia Press, 2005). Barney Hill, manuscript for a speech, no date, Oversized Box 3, Folder 3, BBHP.

60. A. E. Prescott to Barney Hill, April 20, 1966, Oversized Box 3, Folder 3, BBHP.

61. Barney Hill, manuscript for a speech, no date, Oversized Box 3, Folder 3, BBHP.

62. John Papandrew, "Who Am I? What Can I Do?," *Register-Leader*, December 1962, 4.

63. Papandrew, "Who Am I? What Can I Do?," 5.

64. John Papandrew, "A Letter to My Congregation," November 17, 1963, Box 333, Folder 7, JPF.

65. Papandrew, "Who Am I? What Can I Do?," 6.

66. Papandrew, "A Letter to My Congregation."

67. Barney Hill, manuscript for a speech, undated, Oversized Box 3, Folder 3, BBHP. no date, Oversized Box 3, Folder 3, BBHP.

68. Barney Hill, notes on "Barbershop Report," Oversized Box 3, Folder 3, BBHP. Capitalization original.

69. Claude A. Clegg, *The Life and Times of Elijah Muhammad* (Chapel Hill: University of North Carolina Press, 2014), 33–36; Karl Evanzz, *The Messenger: The Rise and Fall of Elijah Muhammad* (New York: Knopf, 2011), 94–96.

70. Elijah Muhammad, *Message to the Blackman in America* (Chicago: Temple Number 2, 1965), 17–18, 291; Elijah Muhammad, *The Theology of Time* (Atlanta: Messenger Elijah Muhammad Propagation Society, 1997), 99–101.

71. Edward E. Curtis IV, "Science and Technology in Elijah Muhammad's Nation of Islam: Astrophysical Disaster, Genetic Engineering, UFOs, White Apocalypse and Black Resurrection," *Nova Religio* 20:1 (2016), 5–31; Brenda Denzler, *The Lure of the Edge: Scientific Passions, Religious Beliefs, and the Pursuit of UFOs* (Berkeley: University of California Press, 2010), 124–130; Michael Lieb, *Children of Ezekiel: Aliens, UFOs, The Crisis of Race, and the Advent of End Time* (Durham: Duke University Press, 1998), 155–178.

72. Elijah Muhammad, *The True History of Master Fard Muhammad* (Atlanta: Messenger Elijah Muhammad Propagation Society, 1996), 109, 115; Stephen C. Finley, "The Meaning of 'Mother' in Louis Farrakhan's 'Mother Wheel': Race, Gender, and Sexuality in the Cosmology of the Nation of Islam's UFO," *Journal of the American Academy of Religion* 80:2 (June 2012), 434–465.

CHAPTER 11. A NEW AGE

1. Charles Fort, *The Book of the Damned* (New York: Liveright, 1919), 248; on Fort's philosophy, Jeffrey Kripal, *Authors of the Impossible: The Paranormal and the Sacred* (Chicago: University of Chicago Press, 2010), 92–141.

2. All Vallée quotations to this point from Jacques Vallée, *Forbidden Science: Journals 1957–1969* (New York: Marlowe, 1996), 85, 75–76, 159, 55–56.

3. This summary of Valleé's mature thought relies on his *Passport to Magonia: From Folklore to Flying Saucers* (Chicago: Henry Regnery, 1969) and *The Invisible College: What a Group of Scientists Has Discovered about UFO Influences on the Human Race* (New York: E. P. Dutton, 1975), as well as Kripal, *Authors of the Impossible*, 142–197.

4. Webb1, 1.

5. Vallée, *Forbidden Science*, 55.

6. Daniel Rodgers, *Age of Fracture* (Cambridge: Harvard University Press, 2011); Casey Nelson Blake, Daniel Borus, and Howard Brick, *At the Center: American Thought and Culture in the Mid-Twentieth Century* (Lanham, MD: Rowman and Littlefield, 2019). I draw here also on the work of Jodi Dean, who has argued that the UFO narrative "is widespread enough to conflict with the concept of a unitary public reason." *Aliens in America: From Outerspace to Cyberspace* (Ithaca: Cornell University Press, 1998), 11.

7. Jack Mendelsohn, *Why I Am a Unitarian* (Boston: Beacon Press, 1960), 7; Charles Merrill, "Negro Pressure and White Liberals," *Register-Leader,* June 1967, 5.

8. Eric Alterman, *When Presidents Lie: A History of Official Deception and Its Consequences* (New York: Penguin Books, 2009), 222–238; David Schmitz, *Richard Nixon and the Vietnam War: The End of the American Century* (Lanham, MD: Rowman and Littlefield, 2014), 110–136; Scott Laderman, *The Silent Majority Speech: Richard Nixon, the Vietnam War, and the Origins of the New Right* (New York: Routledge, 2019).

9. The most prominent critic of the notion of a unified a "New Age movement" is Steven Sutcliffe, *Children of the New Age: A History of Spiritual Practices* (London: Routledge, 2003), 9–31; Steven Sutcliffe and Ingvild Saelid Gilhus, "All Mixed Up: Thinking about Religion in Relation to New Age Spiritualities," in Sutcliffe and Gilhus, eds., *New Age Spirituality* (London: Routledge, 2013), 1–16. For a defense of the term, George Chryssides, "Defining the New Age," in Darren Kemp and James R. Lewis, eds., *Handbook of the New Age* (Leiden: Brill, 2013), 5–25.

10. On seekers, Robert Wuthnow, *After Heaven: Spirituality in America since the 1950s* (Berkeley: University of California Press, 1998), 2–18; Wade Clark Roof, *Spiritual Marketplace: Baby Boomers and the Remaking of American Religion* (Princeton: Princeton University Press, 1999), 96–119. Roof applies the term primarily to baby boomers; Wuthnow sees it as a broader theme emerging in the 1960s.

11. Courtney Bender cautions us against assuming that "spirituality" or the "New Age" imply isolation on the part of practitioners; *The New Metaphysicals: Spirituality and the American Religious Imagination* (Chicago: University of Chicago Press, 2010), 65–66. On the notion of milieu, Wouter Hanegraaff, *New Age Religion and Western Culture: Esotericism in the Mirror of Secular Thought* (Leiden: Brill, 1996), 14–16; Michael Barkun, *A Culture of Conspiracy: Apocalyptic Visions in Contemporary America* (Berkeley: University of California Press, 2003), 24–26. Both cite Colin Campbell's seminal article, "The Cult, the Cultic Milieu, and Secularization," *Sociological Yearbook of Religion in Britain* (London: SCM Press, 1972), 5:119–136.

12. Wouter Hanegraaff emphasizes the occult heritage of the New Age movement in *New Age Religion and Western Culture*, especially 384–411, and distinguishes the "occult" as a post-Enlightenment manifestation of the "esoteric." The concept of bricolage as applied to the New Age is popular among scholars; see Sutcliffe, *Children of the New Age*, 4–5; Stef Aupers and Dick Houtman, "Beyond the Spiritual Supermarket: The Social and Public Significance of New Age Spirituality," in Sutcliffe and Gilhus, eds., *New Age Spirituality*, 174–176.

13. Joscelyn Godwin, *The Theosophical Enlightenment* (Albany: State University of New York Press, 1994), particularly 307–333; Bruce Campbell, *Ancient Wisdom Revived: A History of the Theosophical Movement* (Berkeley: University of California Press, 1980), 53–75, and Olav

Hammer, *Claiming Knowledge: Strategies of Epistemology from Theosophy to the New Age* (Leiden: Brill, 2004), 56–80.

14. Brenda Denzler has argued that "science" is the language by which UFO believers speak of traditionally religious ideas like human destiny and human nature. *The Lure of the Edge: Scientific Passions, Religious Beliefs and the Pursuit of UFOs* (Berkeley: University of California Press, 2001), 33–35; see also the work of Benjamin Zeller on the intersections between science and UFO religions in *Prophets and Protons: New Religious Movements and Science in Late Twentieth-Century America* (New York: New York University Press, 2010), 117–162, and "(Dis)enchanted Ufology: The Boundaries of Science and Religion in MUFON, The Mutual UFO Network," *Nova Religio* 25:2 (November 2021), 61–86.

15. David Hess, *Science in the New Age: The Paranormal, Its Defenders and Debunkers, and American Culture* (Madison: University of Wisconsin Press, 1993), 8–17; Egil Asprem, "Psychic Enchantments of the Educated Classes: The Paranormal and the Ambiguities of Disenchantment," in Asprem and Kennet Granholm, eds., *Contemporary Esotericism* (New York: Routledge, 2014), 330–350; R. Laurence Moore, *In Search of White Crows: Spiritualism, Parapsychology, and American Culture* (New York: Oxford University Press, 1977), 188–240. Hanegraaff, *New Age Religion and Western Culture*, 64, describes the New Age's version of science as *naturphilosophie*, the quest for a unified way of understanding the world in imitation of German idealist philosophy, even at the expense of more contemporary expectations of falsifiability or experimentation.

16. Jacques Vallée, *Messengers of Deception: UFO Contacts and Cults* (Brisvegas, Australia: Daily Grail Publishing, 2009), 13–14.

17. The draft letter is in Box 3, Folder 1, JGF; Sutcliffe, *Children of the New Age*, 45–55.

18. Betty's diary entries are reproduced in Marden and Friedman, *Captured*, 176–177. Frank Edwards, *Flying Saucers: Serious Business* (New York: Bantam, 1966), 48–50, records an interview with Wilbert Smith, the deceased UFO investigator, by C. W. Fitch (the NICAP member who pestered the Hills with calls and letters in the early 1960s) in which Smith discusses his relationship with Knowles. Betty recounts D'Allessandro's claim in Berthold Schwarz, "Talks with Betty Hill 1: The Aftermath of the Encounter," *Flying Saucer Review* 23:2 (August 1977), 21.

19. "Adm. Herbert Knowles, 81," *New York Times*, March 6, 1976, 23; "Admiral Buys East Eliot Home," *Portsmouth Herald*, February 17, 1949, 5; "Ladies Circle," *Portsmouth Herald*, April 11, 1956, 6; "Legion to Sponsor Lecture on ESP," *Portsmouth Herald*, March 9, 1971, 20; "OMS Wives Meet," *Portsmouth Herald*, April 10, 1971, 7.

20. Hess, *Science in the New Age*, 3–17.

21. "OMS Wives Meet," *Portsmouth Herald*, April 10, 1971, 7.

22. "Sunday," *Nashua Telegraph*, January 18, 1962, 7; "Speaker Hits UFO Secrecy," *Nashua Telegraph*, May 8, 1958, 6; "First Unitarian," *Nashua Telegraph*, March 22, 1954, 4. For similar events, see "Berwick Academy Senior," *Portsmouth Herald*, May 13, 1950, 2; "UFO Sighters to Take Part in Jaycees Forum," *Nashua Telegraph*, November 22, 1965, 32; "Liberty Topic of Universalist Church Speaker," *Nashua Telegraph*, February 24, 1954, 12.

CHAPTER 12. PSYCHOPHYSICS

1. Betty Hill to Robert Hohmann, July 15, 1965; Robert Hohmann to Walter Webb, April 1, 1965; Robert Hohmann to Betty Hill, August 4, 1965; Robert Hohmann to Betty Hill, August 24, 1965; Box 1, Folder 17, BBHP. On "stigmatized knowledge," Michael Barkun, *A Culture of Conspiracy: Apocalyptic Visions in Contemporary America* (Berkeley: University of California Press, 2003), 30–33.

2. Robert Hohmann to Betty Hill, October 29, 1965, Box 1, Folder 17, BBHP.

3. Robert Hohmann to Betty Hill, November 15, 1965, Box 1, Folder 17, BBHP. Hohmann does not specify the person present other than the Hills and himself.

4. Robert Hohmann to Betty Hill, March 2, 1966, Box 1, Folder 17, BBHP.

5. Robert Hohmann to Betty Hill, March 2, 1966; Robert Hohmann to Betty Hill, November 15, 1965, Box 1, Folder 17, BBHP.

6. Philip Jenkins, *Dream Catchers: How Mainstream America Discovered Native Spirituality* (New York: Oxford University Press, 2004), 154–175; Lisa Aldred, "Plastic Shamans and Astroturf Sun Dances: New Age Commercialization of Native American Spirituality," *American Indian Quarterly* 24:3 (Summer 2000), 329–352.

7. Robert Hohmann to Betty Hill, June 26, 1967; Robert Hohmann to Betty Hill, April 27, 1966, Box 1, Folder 17, BBHP.

8. Betty Hill to Robert Hohmann, January 14, 1966, Box 1, Folder 17, BBHP.

9. Betty Hill to Robert Hohmann, January 14, 1966; Betty Hill to Robert Hohmann, April 4, 1966, Box 1, Folder 17, BBHP. Spelling corrected.

10. Robert Hohmann to Betty Hill, January 23, 1966, Box 1, Folder 17, BBHP.

11. Betty Hill to Robert Hohmann, April 4, 1966, BBHP.

12. Betty Hill to Robert Hohmann, April 29, 1966; Betty Hill to Robert Hohmann, August 23, 1966, Box 1, Folder 17, BBHP. Robert Hohmann to Betty Hill, June 26, 1966, Box 1, Folder 17, BBHP, asks Betty and Barney if "there have been any new developments in your plans" for an organized event, but the Hills do not appear to have responded until August.

13. Robert Hohmann to Betty Hill, August 29, 1966; Robert Hohmann to Betty Hill, April 3, 1967, Box 1, Folder 17, BBHP. Valleé and Hohmann discuss the term "transducer" in *Forbidden Science*, 279; Hynek uses the term in the same sense in J. Allen Hynek and Jacques Vallée, *The Edge of Reality: A Progress Report on Unidentified Flying Objects* (Chicago: Henry Regnery, 1975), 262.

14. Frederick Kingdon and Nicolaas Prins, *Psychophysics: A Practical Introduction* (San Diego: Academic Press, 1997), 1–7; Erica Fretwell, *Sensory Experiments: Psychophysics, Race, and the Aesthetics of Feeling* (Durham: Duke University Press, 2020), 1–13.

15. Horatio Dresser, *The Power of Silence* (New York: Putnam, 1908), 133–134; for James and Dresser's relationship, see Robert Richardson, *William James: In the Maelstrom of American Modernism* (Boston: Houghton Mifflin, 2006), 275–276. On the New Age's roots in New Thought, see Sarah M. Pike, *New Age and Neopagan Religions in America* (New York:

Columbia University Press, 2004), 50–56; J. Gordon Melton, "New Thought and the New Age," in Melton and James Lewis, eds., *Perspectives on the New Age* (Albany: SUNY Press, 1992), 15–29.

16. Norman Vincent Peale, *The Power of Positive Thinking* (New York: Prentice Hall, 1987), 118; Jacob Needleman, *Gurdjieff: Essays and Reflections* (New York: Continuum Books, 1996), 70–86; Robert Masters and Joan Houston, *Mind Games: The Guide to Inner Space* (Wheaton, IL: Theosophical Publishing House, 1972), 10. Pike, *New Age and Neopagan Religions in America,* 70–72; Donald Meyer, *The Positive Thinkers: Religion as Pop Psychology* (New York: Pantheon Books, 1980), 120–130.

17. Robert Hohmann to Betty Hill, May 23, 1967, Box 1, Folder 17, BBHP.

18. J. Allen Hynek to Edward Condon, January 5, 1967, Hynek Correspondence File, Center for UFO Studies, Chicago; Vallée, *Forbidden Science,* 280.

19. Hynek and Vallée, *Edge of Reality,* 32, 1–72.

20. Robert Hohmann to Betty Hill, May 23, 1967, May 31, 1967, June 3, 1967, Box 1, Folder 17, BBHP.

21. Robert Hohmann to Betty Hill, June 6, 1967, Box 1, Folder 17, BBHP. Marden and Friedman discuss this plan in *Captured,* 219–220, claiming that Betty began this routine one week before the event.

22. Vallée, *Forbidden Science,* 277.

23. Jacques Vallée, *Passport to Magonia: From Folklore to Flying Saucers* (Chicago: Henry Regnery, 1969); Vallée, *Forbidden Science,* 380.

24. Vallée, *Forbidden Science,* 279, 280. Later the UFO investigator Raymond Fowler would tell Betty that several skywatchers saw UFOs several miles from the Hills' campsite. Betty Hill to Philip Klass, December 3, 1975, Collection of Robert Sheaffer; Raymond Fowler, "Telepathy and a UFO," *Official UFO,* January 1976, 14–15, 43–44. However, Fowler's sightings were reported for the night of July 20.

25. Vallée, *Forbidden Science.* 282. Jacques Vallée, *Dimensions: A Casebook of Alien Contact* (Chicago: Contemporary Books, 1988), 288–289.

26. Robert Hohmann to Betty and Barney Hill, September 14, 1967, Box 1, Folder 17, BBHP.

27. Robert Hohmann to Betty and Barney Hill, October 26, 1967, Box 1, Folder 17, BBHP. The September gathering is discussed in Robert Hohmann to Betty and Barney Hill, August 29, 1967, and Robert Hohmann to Betty and Barney Hill, September 14, 1967, Box 1, Folder 17, BBHP. Hohmann's response to the failure of the experiment—that is, to determine how the expectations of contact might remain true—is reminiscent of that of other contemporaneous UFO religions, which also faced such disappointment; the most famous case is documented in Leon Festinger, Henry Riecken, and Stanley Schachter, *When Prophecy Fails: A Social and Psychological Study of a Modern Group That Predicted the Destruction of the World* (New York: Harper, 1956).

28. Robert Hohmann to Betty and Barney Hill, January 20, 1969, Box 1, Folder 17, BBHP; see also Hohmann to the Betty and Barney Hill, January 2, 1968, and Hohmann to Betty and Barney Hill, June 13, 1968, Box 1, Folder 17, BBHP.

CHAPTER 13. MAPS

1. Betty Hill, "Barney's Death," Box 3, Folder 3, BBHP; UA1, [1]; J. Allen Hynek, "Notes on Conversation with Betty Hill, 4–9–72," BHF; "Barney Hill Dies in City at 46," *Portsmouth Herald*, February 26, 1969, 3.

2. Hill, "Barney's Death."

3. She asked for $550. "1964 Norton 750cc," *Portsmouth Herald*, June 26, 1969, 21.

4. Leo Sprinkle to Betty Hill, August 4, 1976, Box 2, Folder 2, BBHP; R. Leo Sprinkle, "Hypnotic and Psychic Aspects of UFO Research," Nancy Dornbos, ed., *Proceedings of the 1976 CUFOS Conference* (Chicago: Center for UFO Studies, 1976), 252–253.

5. Bob Schmidt to Betty Hill, April 1, 1976, Box 2, Folder 1, BBHP; Leo Sprinkle to Betty Hill, August 4, 1976, Box 2, Folder 2, BBHP.

6. Hill, "Barney's Death."

7. Marjorie Fish to Betty Hill, June 8, 1969, Box 1, Folder 10, BBHP; Betty Hill to Walter Webb, April 20, 1965, Box 2, Folder 5, BBHP.

8. Fish to Hill, June 8, 1969. A good review of Fish's process is Walter Webb, "An Analysis of the Fish Model," 2–4, BBHF.

9. Betty Hill to Marjorie Fish, July 12, 1969, Box 1, Folder 10, BBHP; Fish describes her visit in Marjorie Fish to Betty Hill, August 15, 1969, Box 1, Folder 10, BBHP.

10. Marjorie Fish to Betty Hill, September 1, 1969, BBHF; Marjorie Fish to Betty Hill, November 2, 1969, BBHF; Marjorie Fish to Betty Hill, November 9, 1969, BBHF; Marjorie Fish to Betty Hill, November 25, 1969, BBHF. "Junior" rests in Oversized Box 4, BBHP. Fish's successful Mensa test is now frequently cited by defenders of the map; see, for instance, Marden and Friedman, *Captured*, 234–235. The organization that had been so dismissive was the Aerial Phenomena Research Organization.

11. Betty Friedan, *The Feminine Mystique* (1963; New York: W. W. Norton, 1997), 525–526; Susan Oliver, *Betty Friedan: The Personal is Political* (New York: Pearson Longman, 2008), 105–106.

12. Webb, "An Analysis of the Fish Model," 2, 9–10; Marjorie Fish, "Betty Hill's Sky Map and Reality," 3, BHF; Marjorie Fish to Betty Hill, January 10, 1972, Marjorie Fish to Betty Hill, October 16, 1972, BBHF. Marden and Friedman, *Captured*, 236–237; David S. Stevenson, *Under a Crimson Sun: Prospects for Life in a Red Dwarf System* (New York: Springer, 2013), 27–38.

13. Webb, "Analysis of the Fish Model," 11; Fish, "Betty Hill's Sky Map and Reality," 4.

14. Stanton Friedman to Richard Stephens, National Science Foundation, May 18, 1973, Stanton Friedman File, 19–1, Center for UFO Studies, Chicago; Terrence Dickinson, "The Zeta Reticuli Incident," *Astronomy*, December 1974, 4–18; Marjorie Fish to Betty Hill, November 16, 1972, BBHF.

15. Walter Webb to Allen Hynek, August 18, 1974, Walter Webb File, 19–1, Center for UFO Studies, Chicago.

16. Stanton Friedman and B. Ann Slate, "UFO Star Bases Discovered," *Saga Magazine*, July 1973; Dave Eicher, "Thirty Years: Looking Back," *Astronomy* 31:9 (September 2003), 48–49.

17. Dickinson, "Zeta Reticuli Incident," 4–18.

—

18. *The Zeta Reticuli Incident* (Milwaukee: Astromedia Corporation, 1976), 24, 25, 29.

19. David Eicher, "The Zeta Reticuli, or Ridiculi, Incident," https://astronomy.com/bonus/zeta, accessed November 11, 2020.

20. Jacques Vallée, *Dimensions: A Casebook of Alien Contact* (Chicago: Contemporary Books, 1988, 262–266; Marjorie Fish to Betty Hill, November 8, 1969, BBHF.

21. Webb to Allen Hynek, August 18, 1974; Marjorie Fish to Betty Hill, December 9, 1972, BBHF; Stanton Friedman to J. Allen Hynek, January 27, 1975, Stanton Friedman File, 19–1, Center for UFO Studies, Chicago; J. Allen Hynek to Carl Sagan, October 28, 1975, Box 14, Folder 5, Seth McFarlane Collection of Carl Sagan and Ann Druyan Archive, Library of Congress.

22. Brenda Denzler describes this pivot in *The Lure of the Edge: Scientific Passions, Religious Belief and the Pursuit of UFOs* (Berkeley: University of California Press, 2001), 108–123.

23. Iosif Shklovskii and Carl Sagan, *Intelligent Life in the Universe* (San Francisco: Holden-Day, 1966), 455–456; Keay Davidson, *Carl Sagan: A Life* (New York: Wiley and Sons, 1999), 130–134, 147–150; Marjorie Fish to Betty Hill, July 16, 1969, Box 1, Folder 10, BBHP. For an example of academic critique of Sagan's speculation about Oannes, Herbert Malamud, "Is Anybody Out There?," *Physics Today* 20:6 (June 1967), 74.

24. Betty Hill to Marjorie Fish, July 12, 1969, Box 1, Folder 10, BBHP; Marjorie Fish to Betty Hill, August 15, 1969, Box 1, Folder 10, BBHP.

25. Marjorie Fish to Betty Hill, October 25, 1971, BBHF.

26. Marjorie Fish to Betty Hill, January 10, 1972, BBHF.

27. Marjorie Fish to Betty Hill, November 8, 1969, BBHF.

28. Erich von Däniken, *Chariots of the Gods: Unsolved Mysteries of the Past* (New York: Putnam, 1970), 55, 57.

29. Marjorie Fish to Betty Hill, August 22, 1972, BBHF.

30. Marjorie Fish to Betty Hill, September 4, 1969, BBHF.

31. Marjorie Fish to Betty Hill, November 25, 1969; July 21, 1972, BBHF. Charles Hapgood, *Maps of the Ancient Sea Kings: Evidence of Advanced Civilization in the Ice Age* (Philadelphia: Chilton Books, 1966), 193–207; von Däniken, *Chariots of the Gods*, 14–15.

32. Marjorie Fish to Betty Hill, December 30, 1971, BBHF. Charles Berlitz, *The Mystery of Atlantis* (1969; London: Granada Books, 1976), 132–133; Charles Berlitz, *The Bermuda Triangle* (New York: Avon Books, 1974), 126–142, 215–230.

33. Vera de Gill to Betty Hill, March 27, 1978, Box 1, Folder 2, BBHP.

34. Arguments to this end include Kathryn Olmsted, *Real Enemies: Conspiracy Theories and American Democracy, World War I to 9/11* (New York: Oxford University Press, 2011), 1–13; Peter Knight, *Conspiracy Culture: From the Kennedy Assassination to the X-Files* (New York: Routledge, 2002), 24–36; Stef Aupers, "'Trust No One': Modernization, Paranoia and Conspiracy Culture," *European Journal of Communication* 27:1 (2012), 22–34; Michael Barkun, *A Culture of Conspiracy: Apocalyptic Visions in Contemporary America* (Berkeley: University of California Press, 2003), 15–39; Michael Butter, *Plots, Designs, and Schemes: American Conspiracy Theories from the Puritans to the Present* (Boston: de Gruyter, 2014), 33–67.

35. Barkun, *Culture of Conspiracy*, 4–6.

36. Donald Keyhoe, *Aliens from Space* (New York: Doubleday, 1973), 202.

37. Frank Scully, *Behind the Flying Saucers* (New York: Henry Holt, 1950), xii; on the Second Red Scare, the standard histories are Ellen Schrecker, *Many Are the Crimes: McCarthyism in America* (Princeton: Princeton University Press, 1998), especially 266–309, and Stephen Whitfield, *The Culture of the Cold War* (Baltimore: Johns Hopkins University Press, 1996), 127–153; Knight, *Conspiracy Culture*, 5–11.

38. Scully, *Behind the Flying Saucers*, xii–xiii, 150.

39. Gray Barker, *They Knew Too Much about Flying Saucers* (New York: University Books, 1956), 129–130, 132.

40. Loch Johnson, *A Season of Inquiry: The Senate Intelligence Investigation* (Lexington: University Press of Kentucky, 1985), 48–53, 99–100.

41. Hal Lindsey, *The Late Great Planet Earth* (Grand Rapids: Zondervan, 1970); Gray Barker, *Men in Black: The Secret Terror among Us* (Jane Lew, WV: New Age Books, 1983), 37, 133. Paul Boyer, *When Time Shall Be No More: Prophecy Belief in Modern American Culture* (Cambridge: Harvard University Press, 1992), 126–128.

42. Fish to Hill, November 9, 1969, BBHF. Michael Barkun designates the 1970s and early 1980s as the era that birthed "UFO conspiracism," as UFO belief melded with conspiratorial theories about the New World Order and other conspiracies to dismantle democracy and human freedom. Barkun, *Culture of Conspiracy*, 82–91.

43. Fish to Hill, September 4, 1969, BBHF. William W. Turner, *Hoover's FBI: The Men and the Myth* (New York: Sherbourne Press, 1970).

44. Betty Hill, "Miracles," Box 4, Folder 5, BBHP. Betty routinely spelled "ufo" in lower case.

CHAPTER 14. OBSERVERS

1. Betty Hill, "My Life," Box 3, Folder 10, BBHP.

2. Betty Hill, "Observations of UFOs," Box 4, Folder 4, BBHP; Marden and Friedman, *Captured*, 269; Betty Hill to Ray Fowler, October 1, 1977, BHF; "UNH Professors Watch UFOs with Mrs. Hill," (Dover, NH) *Democrat*, October 6, 1977, 6; "Betty's Still Seeing Saucers," (Dover, NH) *Democrat*, October 5, 1977, 3; Betty Hill, "Miracles," 8, Box 4, Folder 5, BBHP.

3. Hill, "Miracles," 8–9; Hill to Fowler, October 1, 1977; Betty Hill to Philip Klass, November 13, 1975; and December 3, 1975, Collection of Robert Sheaffer; David Wysocki, "Reporters Given Chance to Visit UFO Landing Pad," *Nashua Telegraph*, October 10, 1977, 40.

4. Betty Hill, "Strange Events," 4, Box 3, Folder 11, BBHP.

5. Betty Hill, "I Am Not Psychic," Box 4, Folder 5, BBHP; on the proliferation of New Age courses and classes in things like psychic ability, see Pike, *New Age and Neopagan Religions in America*, 86–93.

6. Hill, "I Am Not Psychic."

7. Hans Holzer, *The UFOnauts* (Greenwich, CT: Fawcett Books, 1976), 142–143, 157.

8. P. M. H. Edwards to Betty Hill, March 10, 1982, Box 1, Folder 8, BBHP. Punctuation original.

9. David Webb and Ted Bloecher, "Catalogue of Humanoid Reports," 1952–05, Center for UFO Studies, Chicago; Brad Steiger, "Space Intelligences and Earth's New Species of Super-Kids," *UFO Reports* 3:5 (December 1976), 56–58.

10. Webb and Bloecher, "Catalogue of Humanoid Reports," 1952–05; Betty Hill, "Marianne: Diary of an Experiment," Box 4, Folder 5, BBHP; Berthold Schwarz, "Talks with Betty Hill 2: The Things That Happen Around Her," *Flying Saucer Review* 23:3 (October 1977), 11.

11. Webb and Bloecher, "Catalogue of Humanoid Reports," 1952–05.

12. Hill, "Marianne"; Schwarz, "Talks with Betty Hill 2," 11; David Webb and Ted Bloecher, "Catalogue of Humanoid Reports," 1952–05; Ted Bloecher to Betty Hill, March 17, 1977, Box 1 Folder 2, BBHP.

13. Hill, "Marianne."

14. Betty Hill, "Mystery Helicopters," Box 4, Folder 5, BBHP. Betty Hill, "Helicopter Investigation," Box 4, Folder 5, BBHP.

15. Betty Hill to Stuart Nixon, May 15, [1972], BHF; Betty Hill to Stuart Nixon, June 19, [1972], BHF. For Betty's opposition to the Vietnam War, see Thomas McIntyre to Betty Hill, September 1, 1970, Box 5, Folder 16, BBHP.

16. Betty Hill to Stuart Nixon, June 19, [1972].

17. Schwarz, "Talks with Betty Hill 2,"11; Schwarz, "Talks with Betty Hill 1," 19.

18. Schwarz, "Talks with Betty Hill 2," 12–13; Schwarz, "Talks with Betty Hill 1," 21–22.

19. Schwarz, "Talks with Betty Hill 1," 20. Segretti indeed used the pseudonym "Donald Simmons"; see "Dirty Tricks," *New York Times,* July 22, 1973, 206.

20. Stanton Friedman, *UFOs: Earth's Cosmic Watergate* (Houlton, ME: UFO Research Institute, 1981). Betty's mapping of the narratives of UFOs onto Watergate narratives of political corruption mirrors the "resonance" that Susan Lepselter identifies as key in the persistence of paranormal stories. *The Resonance of Unseen Things: Poetics, Power, Captivity and UFOs in the American Uncanny* (Ann Arbor: University of Michigan Press, 2016), 20–46.

21. Walter Webb to Betty Hill, January 19, 1967, BBHF. On Moseley, see Aaron Gulyas, *Extraterrestrials and the American Zeitgeist* (Jefferson, NC: McFarland, 2013), 45–48.

22. John Fuller to Betty Hill, January 8, 1979, copy to J. Allen Hynek with cover letter, BHF.

23. "National UFO Convention at Doral Inn," Box 5, Folder 5, BBHP; "Betty Hill Biography," Box 4, Folder 4, BBHP.

24. Betty Hill, *A Common Sense Approach to UFOs* (Greenland, NH: The Author, 1995), 43, 47, 51.

25. Hill, *Common Sense Approach to UFOs,* 57.

26. Hill, *Common Sense Approach to UFOs,* 47, 166, 129.

27. Hill, *Common Sense Approach to UFOs,* 170. Punctuation original.

28. Hill, *Common Sense Approach to UFOs,* 170. Punctuation original.

29. Hill, *Common Sense Approach to UFOs,* 171.

EPILOGUE

1. Percy Shain, "The UFO Incident Likely to Revive Controversy," *Boston Globe,* October 13, 1975, 71; Stuart Nixon to James Earl Jones, April 29, 1972, BHF; Betty Hill to Stuart Nixon, June 19, [1972], BHF.

2. Betty Hill to Stuart Nixon, May 15, [1972], BHF.

3. Hill to Nixon, June 19, [1972], BHF; Shain, "UFO Incident Likely to Revive Controversy."

4. Stuart Nixon to James Earl Jones, April 29, 1972, BHF; Stuart Nixon to James Earl Jones, April 18, 1973, BHF; Stuart Nixon to Betty Hill, June 5, 1972, BHF.

5. Dick Adler, "UFO: A Couple's Nightmare," *Los Angeles Times,* October 20, 1975, G1.

6. Percy Shain, "Unplaying Fenway Objects Replaced by a UFO Show," *Boston Globe,* October 21, 1975, 45.

7. Betty Hill to Walter Webb, April 23, 1976, BBHF. All quotations from the film in the previous paragraphs are from *The UFO Incident,* directed by Richard Colla (Universal Television, 1975).

8. Yervant Terzian and Elizabeth Bilson, *Carl Sagan's Universe* (New York: Cambridge University Press, 1997), xii.

9. *Cosmos,* "Encyclopaedia Galactica," episode 12. Directed by Adrian Malone. Written by Carl Sagan, Ann Druyan, and Steven Soter. PBS, December 14, 1980.

10. Betty Hill to John Fuller, March 24, 1981, Box 1, Folder 12, BBHP.

11. Stanton T. Friedman to William Young, December 16, 1980, Box 5, Folder 5, BBHP.

12. L. J. Lorenzen to Betty Hill, March 26, 1981, Box 1, Folder 1, BBHP.

13. John G. Fuller to William Lamb, January 10, 1982, Box 1, Folder 12, BBHP; Brenda Young to John Fuller, June 11, 1981, Box 1, Folder 12, BBHP.

14. Susan Lepselter's notion of the "resonance" of UFO stories is relevant here. *Resonance of Unseen Things,* 4–5.

15. Budd Hopkins, *Missing Time: A Documented Study of UFO Abductions* (New York: Richard Marek Publishers, 1981), 20–21, 22, 24; Budd Hopkins, "Hypnosis and the Investigation of UFO Abduction Accounts," in David Jacobs, ed., *UFOs and Abductions: Challenging the Borders of Knowledge* (Lawrence: University of Kansas Press, 2000), 217. Thomas Bullard has studied the abduction narrative as an emergent genre, comparable to other "supernatural kidnap narratives." "UFO Abduction Reports: The Supernatural Kidnap Narrative Returns in Technical Guise," *Journal of American Folklore* 102:404 (April 1989), 147–170; Thomas E. Bullard, *The Myth and Mystery of UFOs* (Lawrence: University of Kansas Press, 2010), 52–97.

16. Hill, *Common Sense Approach to UFOs,* 71.

17. Hill, *Common Sense Approach to UFOs,* 81, 85.

18. "Marjorie Eleanor Fish," *Port Clinton News Herald,* April 10, 2013, A2. BBHHT, Hypnosis Session 1, February 22, 1964, 15. Martin Kottmeyer, "Entirely Unpredisposed: The Cultural Background of UFO Abduction Reports," *Magonia* 35 (January 1990), 3–10; Martin Kottmeyer, "The Eyes That Spoke," *REALL News* 2:7 (July 1994), 2.

19. Marden and Friedman, *Captured,* 257–258; Jerome Clark to Betty Hill, June 29, 1995, Box 1, Folder 5, BBHP.

20. For such suggestions, see Robert Sheaffer. "The New Hampshire Abduction Explained." *Official UFO Magazine* (August 1976), 43, and Robert Sheaffer, "There Were No Extraterrestrials," in Peter Brookesmith and Karl Pflock, eds., *Encounters at Indian Head: The Betty and Barney Hill UFO Abduction Revisited* (San Antonio: Anomalist Books, 2007), 186–207; James D. McDonald, "What We Know and How We Know It," June 12, 2017, https://madhousemanor.com/2017/12/06/the-hill-case-part-1/, accessed January 30, 2021.

ACKNOWLEDGMENTS

Historians are used to traveling down odd roads in search of sources forgotten or long unseen, but this project took me down odder roads than most. My thanks to the guides along the way.

The great bulk of material for those interested in Betty and Barney Hill is in the collection of their papers at the Milne Special Collections and Archives, University of New Hampshire, donated as per Betty Hill's wishes by her family. My thanks to the staff there, who deal with a disproportionate number of Hill-related inquiries. Special thanks to Beth Scheckler, Nicole Colbath, Bill Ross, Rebecca Chasse, and Emeline Reynolds.

Thanks also to the staff of the Howard Gotlieb Research Center at Boston University, which holds the papers of John G. Fuller. This is the second most valuable collection to any Hill researcher, I would judge. Particular gratitude to Sarah Pratt (now at Simmons University) and also to Laura Russo, who put up graciously with more emails than she deserved.

The International UFO Museum and Research Center in Roswell, New Mexico, contains some Hill-related materials; of primary interest to me was Betty Hill's correspondence with Marjorie Fish. Thanks are due to the staff there.

ACKNOWLEDGMENTS

Kathleen Marden, the Hills' niece and best advocate, has graciously given of her time in conversations and correspondence.

Mark Rodeghier at the Center for UFO Studies in Chicago is doing heroic work. The Center preserves essential records, and Mark is generous with his time and his thoughts.

Robert Sheaffer, dean of the debunkers since Philip Klass's passing, has been accommodating with both his correspondence and his materials.

Thanks also to the friendly and accommodating staff of the Portsmouth Athenaeum, which hold the records of South Church, a collection quite relevant to a portion of the Hills' lives often overlooked.

Beyond these archivists, my gratitude must go to researchers. The talented genealogist Hazel Scullin tracked down the families of both Hills. Ryan Tobler spent time in the Unitarian Universalist Association Minister Files in Cambridge, chasing down the spotted career of John Papandrew. Seth Anderson filled in the gaps for me at the Gotlieb Center. Breanna Moore browsed through Philip Klass's papers at the American Philosophical Society archives in Philadelphia. Athena Angelos scanned the Library of Congress for images. Deep appreciations to all.

This book went through the wringer of two writing groups. Thanks to the careful reading of Angela Boswell, Suzanne Tartamella, Michael Taylor, and Travis Langley (the scourge of semicolons) at Henderson State University, and to Amanda Hendrix-Komoto, David Howlett, Melissa Inouye, Laurie Maffly-Kipp, Patrick Mason, and Jana Riess online.

Many others read bits and pieces, aided me on research trips, and generally offered encouragement. Thanks to Jessica Brown, Kristine Haglund, Cristy Meiners, Allison Pond, Joseph Stuart, and Kathy Wallace. Some read the entire draft, including J. Dennis Robinson, one of the world's great Hill experts, as well as John Turner, Greg Eghigian, Michael Kazin, and Audra Wolfe, whose keen eye for the history of science was of especially valuable help. Eliza Childs smoothed my prose and arguments. And thanks as well to my tireless agent, Giles Anderson, and my editor, Jennifer Banks, who fought for this project from the beginning and whose ideas helped clarify my own thinking.

And, finally, to family: my parents Maurice and Rosanne, Amy, John, Penny, Jack, Hazel and Henry. And Tamarra, who is better to me than I deserve.

INDEX

Photos and illustrations are indicated by italic page numbers.

INDEX